Great

in

Alabama

Football

This book starts with the first head football coach & goes to the Nick Saban era.

The book is written for those of us who love Alabama football.

It begins by telling the story about the university's first football game played by its first football team and its first season with E. B. Beaumont as the first head coach. The story goes on to describe how the Thin Red Line became the powerful Crimson Tide and it made Alabama football known to the world.

In 1892, the University's first football team assembled calling itself the "Thin Red Line." From a bit thin in the ranks, to later becoming the crushing "Crimson Tide," led by the nation's finest coaches, this book gets you there with many smiles. The progression leads to the Tide's many successful football seasons with some of the greatest immortal coaches that God ever created.

The first game in Alabama football history was played on November 11, 1892, against Birmingham High School and was won by the Cadets 56–0. Alabama then split a pair of games with the Birmingham Athletic Club, and closed out the first season with a 32–22 loss in the first Iron Bowl against Auburn on February 22, 1893. From then on, Alabama football, coached by the best there ever was, is a story of fulfilled dreams.

This book captures stories of the great coaches in Alabama Football. It tells the reader about all the great Alabama coaches within the 125 seasons worth of great games. It reflects on the coaches who created the great Alabama teams of the past – coaches such as Wallace Wade, Frank Thomas, Paul "Bear" Bryant, Gene Stallings, and of course Nick Saban. These coaches brought Alabama 16 championship, the most of any team ever. This book is about so many great coaches and great games that I can't wait to read it again.

You will not be able to put this book down

Brian Kelly

LETS GO! PUBLISH

Published by: LETS GO PUBLISH!
Editor in Chief Brian P. Kelly
Email: info@letsgopublish.com
Web site   www.letsgopublish.com

Library of Congress Copyright Information Pending
Book Cover Design by **Brian W. Kelly;**   Editor—**Brian P. Kelly**

ISBN Information: The International Standard Book Number (ISBN) is a unique machine-readable identification number, which marks any book unmistakably. The ISBN is the clear standard in the book industry. 159 countries and territories are officially ISBN members. The Official ISBN For this book is   **978-0-9986282-9-5**

The price for this work is: **$ 14.99 USD**

10   9   8   7   6   5   4   3   2   1

Release Date: March 2017

Alabama Season Records from 1892 through 2017

Year	Coach	Conference	Record	C-Record
1892	E. B. Beaumont #1	Independent	2-2-0	
1893	Eli Abbott #2	Independent	0-4-0	
1894	Eli Abbott	Independent	3-1-0	
1895	Eli Abbott	SIAA	0-4-0	0-4-0
1896	Otto Wagonhurst #3	SIAA	2-1-0	1-1-0
1897	Allen McCants #4	SIAA	1-0-0	0-0-0
1898	No Season—WW I			
1899	W. A. Martin #5	SIAA	3-1-0	1-0-0
1900	Malcolm Griffin #6	SIAA	2-3-0	1-3-0
1901	M. S. Harvey #7	SIAA	2-1-2	2-1-2
1902	Eli Abbott #8	SIAA	4-4-0	2-4-0
1903	W. B. Blount #9	SIAA	3-4-0	3.4-0
1904	W. B. Blount	SIAA	7-3-0	4-3-0
1905	Jack Leavenworth #10	SIAA	6-4-0	4-4-0
1906	J. W. H. Pollard #11	SIAA	5-1-0	3-1-0
1907	J. W. H. Pollard	SIAA	5-1-2	3-1-2
1908	J. W. H. Pollard	SIAA	6-1-1	1-1-1
1909	J. W. H. Pollard	SIAA	5-1-2	4-1-2
1910	Guy Lowman #12	SIAA	4-4-0	0-4-0
1911	D. V. Graves #13	SIAA	5-2-2	2-2-2
1912	D. V. Graves	SIAA	5-3-1	3-3-1
1913	D. V. Graves	SIAA	6-3-0	4-3-0
1914	D. V. Graves	SIAA	5-4-0	4-3-0
1915	Thomas Kelley #14	SIAA	6-2-0	5-0-0
1916	Thomas Kelley	SIAA	6-3-0	4-3-0
1917	Thomas Kelley	SIAA	5-2-1	3-1-1
1918	B. L. Noojin #15	SIAA	* WWI No games	
1919	Xen C. Scott #16	SIAA	8-1-1	6-1-0
1920	Xen C. Scott	SIAA	10-1-0	6-1-0
1921	Xen C. Scott	SIAA	5-4-2	2-4-2
1922	Xen C. Scott	SoCon	6-3-1	3-2-1
1923	Wallace Wade #17	SoCon	7-2-0	4-1-1
1924	Wallace Wade	SoCon	8-1-0	5-0-0
1925*	Wallace Wade	SoCon	10-0-0	7-0-0
1926*	Wallace Wade	SoCon	9-0-1	8-0-0
1927	Wallace Wade	SoCon	5-4-1	3-4-1
1928	Wallace Wade	SoCon	6-3-0	6-2-0
1929	Wallace Wade	SoCon	6-3-0	4-3-0
1930*	Wallace Wade	SoCon	10-0-0	8-0-0

1931	Frank Thomas #18	SoCon	9-1-0	7-1-0
1932	Frank Thomas	SoCon	8-2-0	5-2-0
1933	Frank Thomas	SEC	7-1-1	5-0-1
1934*	Frank Thomas	SEC	10-0-0	7-0-0
1935	Frank Thomas	SEC	6-2-1	4-2-0
1936	Frank Thomas	SEC	8-0-1	5-0-1
1937	Frank Thomas	SEC	9-1-0	6-0-0
1938	Frank Thomas	SEC	7-1-1	4-1-1
1939	Frank Thomas	SEC	5-3-1	2-3-1
1940	Frank Thomas	SEC	7-2-0	4-2-0
1941*	Frank Thomas	SEC	9-2-0	5-2-0
1942	Frank Thomas	SEC	8-3-0	4-2-0
1943	No games WW II			
1944	Frank Thomas	SEC	5-2-2	3-1-2
1945	Frank Thomas	SEC	10-0-0	6-0-0
1946	Frank Thomas	SEC	7-4-0	4-3-0
1947	Harold Drew # 19	SEC	8-3-0	5-2-0
1948	Harold Drew	SEC	6-4-1	4-4-1
1949	Harold Drew	SEC	6-3-1	4-3-1
1950	Harold Drew	SEC	9-2-0	6-2-0
1951	Harold Drew	SEC	5-6-0	3-5-0
1952	Harold Drew	SEC	10-2-0	4-2-0
1953	Harold Drew	SEC	6-3-3	4-0-3
1954	Harold Drew	SEC	4-5-2	3-3-2
1955	Jennings Whitworth #20	SEC	0-10-0	0-7-0
1956	Jennings Whitworth	SEC	2-7-1	2-5-0
1957	Jennings Whitworth	SEC	2-7-1	1-6-1
1958	Bear Bryant #21	SEC	5-4-1	3-4-1
1959	Bear Bryant	SEC	7-2-2	4-1-2
1960	Bear Bryant	SEC	8-1-2	5-1-1
1961*	Bear Bryant	SEC	11-0-0	7-0-0
1962	Bear Bryant	SEC	10-1-0	6-1-0
1963	Bear Bryant	SEC	9-2-0	6-2-0
1964*	Bear Bryant	SEC	10-1-0	8-0-0
1965*	Bear Bryant	SEC	9-1-1	6-1-1
1966	Bear Bryant	SEC	11-0-0	6-0-0
1967	Bear Bryant	SEC	8-2-1	5-1-0
1968	Bear Bryant	SEC	8-3-0	4-2-0
1969	Bear Bryant	SEC	6-5-0	2-4-0
1970	Bear Bryant	SEC	6-5-1	3-4-0
1971	Bear Bryant	SEC	11-1-0	7-0-0
1972	Bear Bryant	SEC	10-2-0	7-1-0

Year	Coach	Conference	Overall	Conference Record
1973*	Bear Bryant	SEC	11-1-0	8-0-0
1974	Bear Bryant	SEC	11-1-0	6-0-0
1975	Bear Bryant	SEC	11-1-0	6-0-0
1976	Bear Bryant	SEC	9-3-0	5-2-0
1977	Bear Bryant	SEC	11-1-0	7-0-0
1978*	Bear Bryant	SEC	11-1-0	6-0-0
1979*	Bear Bryant	SEC	12-0-0	6-0-0
1980	Bear Bryant	SEC	10-2-0	5-1-0
1981	Bear Bryant	SEC	9-2-1	6-0-0
1982	Bear Bryant	SEC	8-4-0	3-3-0
1983	Ray Perkins #22	SEC	8-4-0	4-2-0
1984	Ray Perkins	SEC	5-6-0	2-4-0
1985	Ray Perkins	SEC	9-2-1	4-1-1
1986	Ray Perkins	SEC	10-3-0	4-2-0
1987	Bill Curry # 23	SEC	7-5-0	4-3-0
1988	Bill Curry	SEC	9-3-0	4-3-0
1989	Bill Curry	SEC	10-2-0	6-1-0
1990	Gene Stallings #24	SEC	7-5-0	5-2-0
1991	Gene Stallings	SEC	11-1-0	6-1-1
1992*	Gene Stallings	SEC	13-0-0	8-0-0
1993	Gene Stallings	SEC	9-3-1 (1-0)	5-2-1 (0)
1994	Gene Stallings	SEC	12-1-0	8-0-0
1995	Gene Stallings	SEC	8-3-0	5-3-0
1996	Gene Stallings	SEC	10-3-0	6-2-0
1997	Mike DuBose #25	SEC	4-7-0	2-6-0
1998	Mike DuBose	SEC	7-5-0	4-4-0
1999	Mike DuBose	SEC	10-3-0	7-1-0
2000	Mike DuBose	SEC	3-8-0	3-5-0
2001	D. Franchione #26	SEC	7-5-0	4-4-0
2002	D. Franchione	SEC	10-3-0	6-2-0
2003	Mike Price #27	SEC	5 months --- No games	
2004	Mike Shula #28	SEC	4-9-0	2-6-0
2005	Mike Shula	SEC	6-6-0	3-5-0
2006	Mike Shula	SEC	10-2-0	6-2-0
2007	Shula Sanctions	SEC	0-2-0	0-2-0
2008	Mike Shula	SEC	6-7-0	2-6-0
2009	Joe Kines #29 Interim	SEC	0-1-0	0-0-0
2007	Nick Saban # 29	SEC	7-6-0	4-4-0
2008	Nick Saban	SEC	12-2-0	8-0-0
2009*	Nick Saban	SEC	14-0-0	8-0-0
2010	Nick Saban	SEC	10-3-0	5-3-0
2011*	Nick Saban	SEC	12-1-0	7-1-0

2012*	Nick Saban	SEC	13-1-0	7-1-0
2013	Nick Saban	SEC	11-2-0	7-1-0
2014	Nick Saban	SEC	12-2-0	7-1-0
2015*	Nick Saban	SEC	14-1-0	7-1-0
2016	Nick Saban	SEC	14-1-0	8-0-0

Total Wins   879
Total Losses 327
Total Ties   43   *** Prior to Overtime Rules**
Stats from   1892   *** Through December 2016**

Alabama Coaches Over the Years

Year	Coach	
1892	E. B. Beaumont	#1
1893	Eli Abbott	#2
1896	Otto Wagonhurst	#3
1897	Allen McCants	#4
1899	W. A. Martin	#5
1900	Malcolm Griffin	#6
1901	M. S. Harvey	#7
1902	Eli Abbott	#8 & #2
1903	W. B. Blount	#9
1905	Jack Leavenworth	#10
1906	J. W. H. Pollard	#11
1910	Guy Lowman	#12
1911	D. V. Graves	#13
1915	Thomas Kelley	#14
1918	B. L. Noojin	#15
1919	Xen C. Scott	#16
1923	Wallace Wade	#17
1931	Frank Thomas	#18
1947	Harold Drew	#19
1955	Jennings Whitworth	#20
1958	Paul "Bear" Bryant	#21
1982	Ray Perkins	#22
1983	Bill Curry	#23
1984	Gene Stallings	#24
1985	Mike DuBose	#25
1986	D. Franchione	#26
1987	Mike Price	#27
1988	Mike Shula	#28
1989	Joe Kines Interim	#29
2007	Nick Saban	#30

Those are the seasons and the numbers, folks!

Dedication

As a person with a big family on my side and on my wife's side. I am pleased to dedicate this book to my wonderful family.

Thank you to all of the Piotroski's— (Marty & Angel Cathy – Marty Jr., Erin, Scott & Lynn, Mackenzie, Merek, Myranda, & Mackiley) -- (Stan, Archie, Carol, Justin & Denise, Joseph & Lena) -- (Sue & Mitch. Matt, Alie)—for support in all of my publishing efforts.

Wily Ky Eyeley, my sage niece, offers most appreciated advice continually.

My entire family and friends make life easier for me in writing books and everything else. Thank you all— all the people I love the most in life for always being in my corner.

Thank you—for making me, me, God bless you all!

Acknowledgments:

I appreciate all the help that I received in putting this book together, along with the 107 other books from the past.

My printed acknowledgments were once so large that book readers needed to navigate too many pages to get to page one of the text. To permit me more flexibility, I put my acknowledgment list online at www.letsgopublish.com. The list of acknowledgments continues to grow. Believe it or not, it once cost about a dollar more to print each book.

Thank you all on the big list in the sky and God bless you all for your help.

Please check out www.letsgopublish.com to read the latest version of my heartfelt acknowledgments updated for this book. Thank you all!

References

I learned how to write creatively in Grade School at St. Boniface. I even enjoyed reading some of my own stuff.

At Meyers High School and King's College and Wilkes-University, I learned how to research, write bibliographies and footnote every non-original thought I might have had. I learned to hate ibid, and op. cit., and I hated assuring that I had all citations written down in the proper sequence. Having to pay attention to details took my desire to write creatively and diminished it with busy work.

I know it is necessary for the world to stop plagiarism so authors and publishers can get paid properly, but for an honest writer, it sure is annoying. I wrote many proposals while with IBM and whenever I needed to cite something, I cited it in place, because my readers, IT Managers, could care less about tracing the vagaries of citations. I always hated to use stilted footnotes, or produce a lengthy, perfectly formatted bibliography. I bet most bibliographies are flawed because even the experts on such drivel do not like the tedium.

I wrote 107 books before this book and several hundred articles published by many magazines and newspapers and I only cite when an idea is not mine or when I am quoting, and again, I choose to cite in place, and the reader does not have to trace strange numbers through strange footnotes and back to bibliography elements that may not be readily accessible or available.

Yet, I would be kidding you, if in a book about the great coaches in Alabama Football, I tried to bluff my way into trying to make you think that I knew everything before I began to write anything in this book. I spent as much time researching as writing. I might even call myself an expert of sorts now for all the facts that I have uncovered.

Without any pain on your part you can read this book from cover to cover to enjoy the stories about the many great coaches in Alabama Football.

It took me about two months to write this book. If I were to have made sure a thought that I had was not a thought somebody else ever had, this book never would have been completed or the citations pages would exceed the prose.

I used Alabama season summaries from whatever source I could to get the scores of all the games. I verified facts when possible. There are many web sites that have great information and facts. Ironically most Internet stories are the same exact stories. While I was writing the book, I wrote down a bunch of Internet references that I include within the paragraphs and sections and stories that I cite.

There are many great sources for information available for your perusal on many sources on the Internet—including the fine archives of the Crimson White Student Newspaper and of course the www.rolltide.com web site. Enjoy!

P.S. If the citations require additional information or if there is anything else which you think needs a specific citation, I would be pleased to change the text in a future printing.

.

Preface:

We all know that Paul 'Bear' Bryant was one of college football's most legendary coaches. As a head coach at Maryland, Kentucky, Texas A&M, and Alabama, Bryant impacted the lives of many and left a lasting legacy on the sport and the schools where he worked. He had a short life filled by leading the greatest football teams of all times. He always offered his thoughts about the notion of football and the strategies of many against whom he competed. The Bear took prisoners but he released them right after the games.

As a student and an athlete at Alabama, Bear Bryant represented all the great coaches who did not get his fame, such as Wallace Wade, and Frank Thomas, and Gene Stallings especially, He knew how to win in football and in life. Of course, current coach Nick Saban is rewriting Alabama records and national records every season. "If you want to walk the heavenly streets of gold, you gotta know the password, 'Roll, Tide, Roll' "—Bear Bryant.

There is a reason for everything in life.

"Crimson tide" is a term coined by an Alabama reporter to describe the University of Alabama football team's brilliant defense against rival Auburn during a 1907 football game played in a "sea of red mud." The term stuck and is, to this day, it is the nickname of the University of Alabama football team.

On October 8, 1930, sports writer Everett Strupper of the Atlanta Journal wrote a story of the Alabama-Mississippi game that he had witnessed in Tuscaloosa four days earlier. Strupper wrote:

"That Alabama team of 1930 is a typical Wade machine, powerful, big, tough, fast, aggressive, well-schooled in fundamentals, and the best blocking team for this early in the season that I have ever seen. When those big brutes hit you I mean you go down and stay down, often for an additional two minutes.

"Coach [Wallace] Wade started his second team that was plenty big and they went right to their knitting scoring a touchdown in the first quarter against one of the best fighting small lines that I have seen.

For Ole Miss was truly battling the big boys for every inch of ground.

"At the end of the quarter, the earth started to tremble, there was a distant rumble that continued to grow. Some excited fan in the stands bellowed, 'Hold your horses, the elephants are coming,' and out stamped this Alabama varsity.

Wade's way was to use the second team to soften the other team. The real elephants however, were only for show.

"It was the first time that I had seen it and the size of the entire eleven nearly knocked me cold, men that I had seen play last year looking like they had nearly doubled in size."

Strupper and other writers continued to refer to the Alabama linemen as "Red Elephants," the color referring to the crimson jerseys. Thus, today's elephant mascot for the Tide, is known as Big Al and Al is an elephant. But, Why?

Throughout the 1940s, for instance, the University kept a live elephant mascot named "Alamite" that was a regular sight on game days, and it would carry the year's Homecoming queen onto the field every year prior to kickoff at the Homecoming game.

In the early 1960s, Melford Espey, Jr., then a student, was the first to wear an elephant head costume to portray the Crimson Tide's unofficial mascot.

The mascot known as "Big Al" today was the brainchild of University of Alabama student Walt Tart in 1979 as he was working with Ann Paige on homecoming festivities.

Big Al appeared officially in the 1980 Sugar Bowl in which Alabama won handily 24-7. Big Al helped launch the 12-0 Crimson Tide as another of Bear Bryant's undefeated, untied, national champions.

Big Al celebrated his first year with Bear Bryant's 300th win against the Kentucky Wildcats and a victory against the Baylor Bears in the 1981 Cotton Bowl. Big Al has been part of the Alabama scene ever since.

Alabama built its first version of Bryant-Denny Stadium in the 1920's. It opened in 1929 and was originally named Denny Stadium in honor of George H. Denny. Today, for every home game, every Alabama player walks down the tunnel right before every home game. You will see in this book in the chapters about the most recent seasons, the coach shown in a photo with his football team right behind him waiting to take the field. It is the most exciting part of the pre-game—and then comes the action.

Before the festivities begin for the game, it is fun to visit a few spots on campus Of course all 101,821 Bryant-Denny Stadium fans cannot be in the same place at the same time before the game but they sure try. On the opposite side of Bryant-Denny Stadium from The QUAD is an area known as 'The Strip'.

This stretch of road consists of a few bars, restaurants, and retail shops. You can party on the patio of the Hound's-tooth Sports Bar, catch some live music at The Jupiter, purchase all the Crimson Tide apparel you'll need at the Alabama Bookstore and make sure to stop by Galette's and try their original drink, The Yellowhammer. One of the most popular pre-and post-game drinks in town!

On the way to the game, fans and players take on the Walk of Champions. The Walk of Champions begins approximately 2 hours and 15 minutes prior to kickoff. The team is dropped off in the team buses on the north side of the stadium at University Boulevard and proceeds through the Walk of Champions into the stadium. It is a grand experience.

Another major UA tradition is the Elephant Stomp. It is a great name for what Alabama likes to think of as an exciting Million Dollar Band pep rally! The fun of the Stomp begins on the steps of the Gorgas Library and it ends with a march to the stadium. The band begins one hour before kickoff but the drum line begins two hours prior to kickoff. It gets everybody in the spirit.

Today, the *Crimson Tide* as noted above are joined in the campus pre-game festivities to celebrate the goodness of football to the university. They join with members of the student body, faculty population, alumni, and fans to get the team into a mood for winning the day's game.

Fans are swept in by the stories, and the tradition, and the winning ways of the University of Alabama. This book reenacts many of the same emotions and will remind all the Alabama faithful about why they are the Alabama faithful.

Under its charter, the school is officially the University of Alabama and has been educating young minds since back in the 1820's. The football program began in 1892 and was very successful from the

"Cadets" first moment on the QUAD Field. It took a few years before the Crimson White became the Crimson Tide in 1907.

This new book by Brian Kelly, which highlights the <u>Great Coaches in Alabama Football</u> is one of the items that is available all 52 weeks and in fact all 365 days each year. It is now available to add to your Crimson Tide football experience. Once you get this book, it is yours forever unless, of course you give it away to one of the many who will be in awe.

Whether you get to the festivities and the great games on campus or not, this book about Alabama's great coaches brings the glory of Alabama football right to your bookshelf, your pocket, or right to your hands. Reading this book is like reliving the last game, the last football season, and / or all the seasons before last season without ever having to get on or off a plane.

The book examines more than just great coaches. Not all of Alabama's 30 football coaches for example, are named Bryant or Saban or Wade or Thomas. However, their teams were Alabama tough, nonetheless. That means they all fought hard for wins as the Crimson Tide. I hope you enjoy the contrast.

Opening its first story at the very beginning of Football as a sport in America, this book takes you all the way to Coach Nick Saban's last game.

It is written for those of us who love Alabama University (UA) Football. The book first tells the story about Alabama's first Football Game in 1892. It then advances through the years when coaches often lasted just a year, on to the great immortal University of Alabama Coaches of historical fame—Wade, Thomas, Stallings, and the inimitable Coach Bear Bryant through the present day with Coach Saban.

Predicting that another future immortal great is in our midst, the book takes us up to the current season with Coach Nick Saban, who is clearly on a path of excellence.

This book is all about the great coaches and the great teams in Alabama Football... It tells exhilarating stories about Alabama's 30 coaches and its 125 seasons worth of great games (900 wins, 326 losses, 43 ties = 1289 games).

I predict that you will not be able to put this book down

You are going to love this book because it is the perfect read for anybody who loves the University of Alabama and Alabama Football and wants to know more about one of the most revered athletic program of all time.

Few sports books are a must-read but Brian Kelly's <u>Great Moments in Alabama Football</u> will quickly appear at the top of America's most enjoyable must-read books about sports. Enjoy!

Who is Brian W. Kelly?

Brian W. Kelly is one of the leading authors in America with this, his 107th published book. Brian is an outspoken and eloquent expert on a variety of topics and he has also written several hundred articles on topics of deep interest to Americans.

Most of Brian's early works involved high technology. Later, he wrote a number of patriotic books and most recently, he has been writing human interest books such as <u>The Wine Diet</u> and <u>Thank you, IBM</u>. This is his ninth major sports book. Last year Brian actually wrote three children's books. He enjoyed writing the children's books almost as much as everybody enjoyed reading them. His books are always well received.

Brian Kelly's books are highlighted at www.letsgopublish.com. They are for sale at Amazon and Kindle, and most can be viewed by linking to amazon.com/author/brianwkelly.

The best!

Sincerely,

Brian P. Kelly, Editor in Chief
I am Brian Kelly's eldest son

Table of Contents

About the Author

Brian Kelly retired as an Assistant Professor in the Business Information Technology (BIT) Program at Marywood University, where he also served as the IBM i and Midrange Systems Technical Advisor to the IT Faculty. Kelly designed, developed, and taught many college and professional courses. He continues as a contributing technical editor to a number of technical industry magazines, including "The Four Hundred" and "Four Hundred Guru," published by IT Jungle.

Kelly is a former IBM Senior Systems Engineer. His specialty was problem solving for customers as well as implementing advanced operating systems and software on his client's machines. Brian is the author of 98 books and hundreds of magazine articles. He has been a frequent speaker at technical conferences throughout the United States.

Brian was a candidate for the US Congress from Pennsylvania in 2010 and he ran for Mayor in his home town in 2015. He loves Alabama Football and thoroughly enjoyed writing this book about Alabama football's great coaches.

Chapter 1 Introduction to the Book

Alabama celebrates its many national college football championships in its 125th football year.

Nick Saban, Immortal Alabama Coach "Post Bear" Leading the Crimson Tide

In 2017, Alabama celebrates its 125th year. As part of the celebration, the University would be pleased for you to visit its athletic website that honors all Crimson Tide Sports. Thank you for reading this book. I know you will love it as you love the Alabama Crimson Tide.

This book is proud through its coaches to celebrate Alabama University Football; its founding; its struggles; its greatness; and its long-lasting impact on American life. People like me, who love the greatness of Alabama University, will love this book.

The Birmingham News | al.com

We begin the rest of the Alabama Football Story in Chapter 2 with the founding of the football program and the first game. After looking at the many Alabama football venues from The QUAD to Bryant-Denny Stadium, we continue in subsequent chapters right through every coach in every season since 1892.

Nobody can write a full book about Alabama Football and its storied coaches that is all inclusive, because even if it can be written, it would be too big to ever be read. Read what you can in this book when you can. If you love Alabama football, it will surely be a fun experience.

I capture all the great coaches in this book, including the master of them all Coach Paul "Bear" Bryant.

After 30 great coaches and claims for sixteen legitimate national championships, the coaches of UA have been able to make Alabama the most respected program of its peers and it is also now the most feared and the most respected college football team of the modern era. If you don't believe that, then you are simply not paying attention.

Ask any coach in 2017, which team they would prefer not to play, and the answer would not be any team other than the University of Alabama. That is the reality of having a winning record and coaches who can win anywhere and almost all the time!

Who can deny Alabama is the greatest football team that ever endured. I bet Knute Rockne would give today's coach Nick Saban a fine "High Five."

Alabama has its own legacy as do many great college programs but an honest look says Alabama is so unusual, it is undeniably the greatest program ever in college football. It does not matter from which university you gained your alma mater. If you like football and you like honesty and you like winning, Alabama is the only good bet in town.

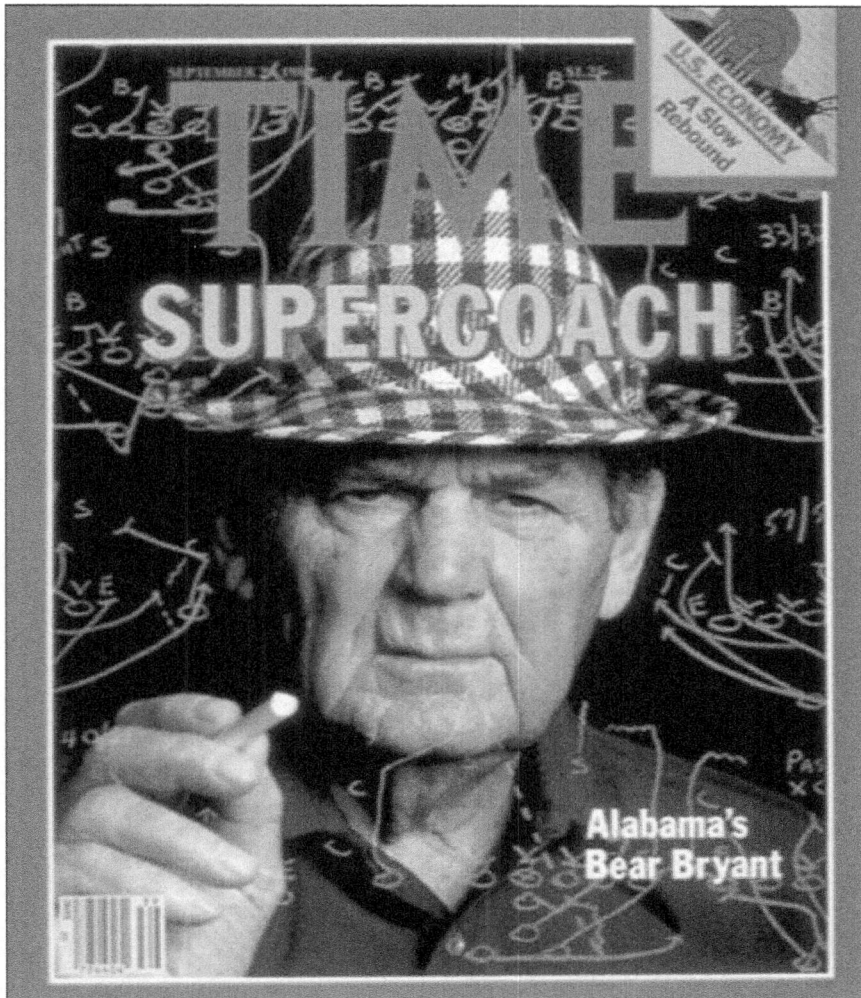

The secret in writing this book has been to know that there is always more. My job has been to show things that are known already in encyclopedias, and the vast resources of the Internet. I did not have to personally speak with Mr. Wade, Mr. Thomas, Mr. Bryant Mr. Stallings, or Mr. Saban to get the truth about what was happening in their lives or the football time-period in which they exceled. It shows in their records.

Alabama won lots of games with teams on offense and defense better than any others

My job in this book was to bring the story of all of the great Alabama coaches together, and to show enough to the reader to make the journey through the beginning of football through Coach Saban's last game much easier to make than otherwise it could have ever been. As I read and reread this book myself, I do believe I achieved that objective.

Instead of lots of research, the reader can just sit back and learn and enjoy the coaching stories about a football team and a university that we have come to love. Along the way, every now and then, all readers will probably fall asleep with a smile on theor faces. We'll be dreaming about a fine story starring "the Bear" "AJ McCarren," "Kenny Stabler, "Joe Namath", "Gene Stallings," Xen C. Scott, or Nick Saban himself!

How did I do it? How did I make this book inclusive and yet not exhaustive or exhausting?

I started right at the beginning of the Alabama football era, shortly after American football was being invented, and the rules were being formed by the greats of the day. Then, I began to write about things as they were happening back then with teams coached by dedicated Alabama professionals. I moved the book chapter by chapter to make sure that I got the essence of the program and that the tales were not boring.

After Wade Wallace and Frank Thomas, I eventually got to the Bear Bryant and Gene Stallings eras and I went through each and every one of the thirty University of Alabama football coaches in just enough measure so that we all would know their mission and their results. I made sure that we captured their best stories.

I thought you would like this print by Larry Pitts. Would you not like to have such a print in your rec room? This and other great Larry Pitts Alabama Prints are available at:

http://www.redelephants.com/acatalog/Alabama_Prints_By_Artist_Larry_Pitts_.html

From left to right, Gene Stallings, Nick Saban, Frank Thomas, Wallace Wade, Paul Bryant.   This is a Golden Flake Special Edition. Only 2001 prints available.

"BAMA HOLD 'EM"
Golden Flake Edition

The print on the prior page Larry Pitts mastered with all the National Champion coaches at Alabama, in a poker game. They are from left to right, Gene Stallings, Nick Saban, Frank Thomas, Wallace Wade, and of course, Bear Bryant.

Doug Shinholster Originals: Wallace Wade, Frank Thomas, Bear Bryant, Gene Stallings

http://www.thedowntowngallery.com/otherprints/shinholster_lead ersoflegacy_large.jpg

Eventually, as the flow took us through twenty-nine coaches by 2007, we began to examine the thirtieth coach. That's when Coach Nick Saban was hired by the University. Saban is missing from Shinholster's print above but the print itself is a classic nonetheless. So, when we hit 2007, we tell all about the Nick Saban era, through 2017 and the late season disappointments in the BCS Championship bowl. We're on our way back.

I have completed the University of Alabama coach's story and the Alabama football story within this book so that you can now fill your leisure time with smiles and wonderment. Don't you dare put this book down!

Coach Saban has extended the great Alabama coaching era right to today. Coach Nick Saban, not the least of the greats for sure, is also not the last. I see the current coach as he directs this team, to continue to become the best of the best. And the hallowed immortals will not be able to deny Coach Saban his immortality claim. Nor would they ever want to do so. Let Nick Saban live long and prosper!

In this book, we tell you the season, the coach, and we tell many game stories from the annals of Alabama football.

The University of Alabama is proud of its history and its founding by the state legislature and its first president Alva Woods. And, of course Alabama is very proud of its football program, and its legacy. The Crimson Tide was, is and will continue to be a great university first, and a great home for the greatest football teams that God has ever created or will create.

Thanks for choosing to take this fun ride with us through Alabama Football History accenting the accomplishments of Alabama's coaches and teams. The great coaches noted in this book are simply great!

Chapter 2 UA's Great Coaches & The First UA Football Team

Alabama

Alabama Cadets First Football Team – 1892

1892: Alabama launches its first football team

They say that Alabama football began with a game in Birmingham on a Friday afternoon in November of 1892. But, there was more to the story than just showing up for the game.

One of my favorite sayings in life is that "nothing worth having in life is easy." This saying applies even for something as simple as forming a football team at a premiere university that had little knowledge or inclination of the game. Sometimes, a little help from the outside is all that is needed to start a Tide rolling.

It happens that for the University of Alabama, all the historical logs suggest it was not the President or Board of Directors or an Athletic Director or a local sports club that got the Tide rolling for Alabama Football. No, it was none of those. It was a law student William G. Little of Livingston, Alabama.

He had learned how to play American football as it was evolving in the US, while he was attending prep school in Andover, Massachusetts. Little was smitten by the game and he soon began teaching the sport to fellow Alabama students in early 1892.

For full context, there was no football at Alabama in 1891. From then to now, it was a rarity when there was no football season for the University of Alabama. Only an event such as a poor administrative decision or a World War would stop Alabama's great football teams from playing.

Later that year (1892), thanks to Little and a dedicated crew of fellow football lovers, the school put together an official team of 19 players, Across the country, more and more colleges and universities were beginning to officially get on board with American football, so this was not exactly new but it sure was groundbreaking for the University.

It is said that when Little arrived, he was "carrying his uniform and a great bag of enthusiasm for the game in 1892." A number of students joined in with him when the season began in October after a lot of time spent on formative activities. There is an account in the Crimson White Student Paper from Nov. 25, 1926 that chronicles this trailblazing experience.

Little became the captain of the fledgling group and E. B. Beaumont was the first official head coach. The Collegiate newspaper remarked that Beaumont was fired at season end because he knew too little about the game.

The history for this time in football history is not perfect but it is known that among others on the team was William B. Bankhead, future U.S. Speaker of the House, and Bibb Graves, future governor of Alabama. This first team was referred to as the "Cadets", the "Crimson White", or simply as "the varsity. The guys on this team had one heck of a love for the game.

The 1892 Alabama Cadets football team represented the University of Alabama in the 1892 college football season. The Crimson Tide moniker had not yet been applied. The team was led by their head coach E. B. Beaumont and played their home games at Lakeview Park in Birmingham, Alabama.

Alabama's First Football Coach E. B. Beaumont

In what was the inaugural season of Alabama football, the team finished with a record of two wins and two losses (2–2). For this game scoring point values were different from those used in contemporary games. In 1892, for example, a touchdown was worth four points, a field goal was worth five points and an extra point was worth two points

Back to William Little of Livingston, Alabama. He is credited with being responsible for the introduction of football at the University. After playing the game in 1891 while in attendance at a northern prep school, he played a huge role in establishing the first team for the 1892 season.

The first game in Alabama football history was played on November 11, 1892, against Birmingham High School and was won by the Cadets 56–0. They then split a pair of games with the Birmingham Athletic Club, and closed out the season with a 32–22 loss in the first Iron Bowl against Auburn on February 22, 1893. After the season, Beaumont was fired as head coach and replaced by Eli Abbott for the 1893 season.

After Beaumont's departure, William G. Little continued the training of the team until Abbott was formally brought-in to serve as head coach for the 1893 season.

In early newspaper accounts of Alabama football, the team was often simply listed as the "varsity" or the "Crimson White" after the school colors.

The first nickname to become popular and used by headline writers was the "Thin Red Line." The nickname was used until 1906.

Folklore is sometimes lore but it sometimes is mixed with all the facts needed. The name "Crimson Tide" is supposed to have first been used by Hugh Roberts, former sports editor of the Birmingham Age-Herald. He used "Crimson Tide" to describe an Alabama-Auburn game played in Birmingham in 1907.

This ironically was the last football contest between the two schools until 1948 when the series was resumed. The 1907 game was played in a sea of mud and Auburn was a heavy favorite to win.

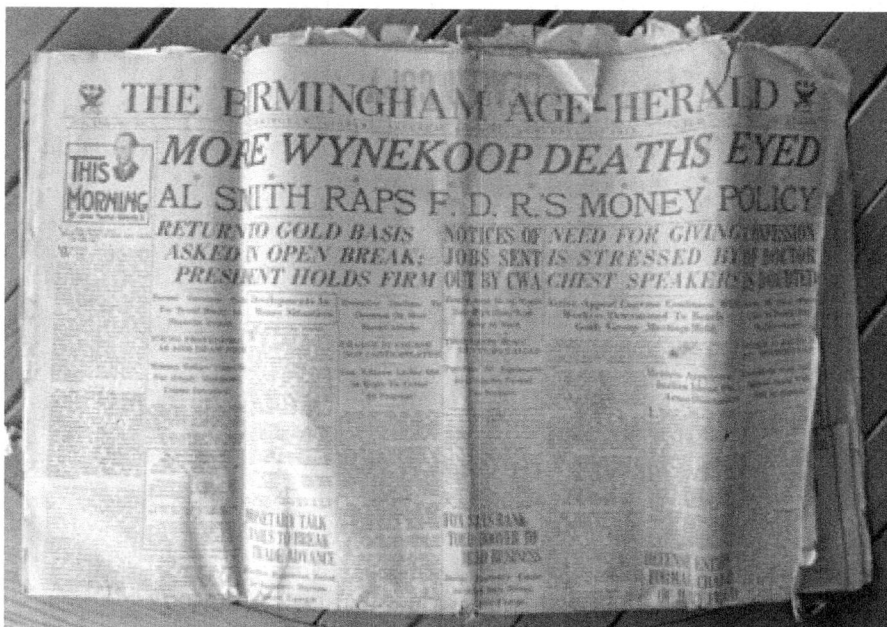

Birmingham Age Herald Front Page Circa 1933 (Last Edition in 1950)

But, evidently, the "Thin Red Line" played a great game in the red mud and held Auburn to a 6-6 tie, thus gaining the name "Crimson Tide." Zipp Newman, former sports editor of the Birmingham News, is credited with popularizing the name more than any other writer. Everything that is has a beginning and often beginnings recounted from times past are a little murky if not downright muddy.

In 1930, Everett Strupper of the Atlanta Journal described the team as 'elephants' when they stomped over Ole Miss, and the mascot stuck. This is a fitting sized animal to describe a program with a successful history of mammoth proportions.

The football team didn't garner national acclaim until a game in Philadelphia in 1922, where Alabama defeated the University of Pennsylvania 9-7. Wallace Wade became the coach the following season. The University of Pennsylvania was an early football powerhouse and had enjoyed prominence trouncing the better teams of the day, including Notre Dame.

Let me tell you all how much of a big win this was. Penn still was a tough team when Coach Wade took them on and won. Looking back, the Quakers have had 63 First Team All-Americans, and the college is the alma mater of John Heisman (the namesake of college football's most famous trophy). The team has won a share of 7 national championships (7th all-time) and competed in the "granddaddy of them all" (The Rose Bowl) as far back as in 1917. Penn's total of 837 wins puts them 11th all-time in college football (3rd in the FCS). Most would not know this.

http://bryantmuseum.com/page.asp?ID=19

The Bryant Web Site offers this account of the early goings:

"Alabama's first game was played in Birmingham on Friday afternoon, Nov. 11, 1892, at the old Lakeview Park. Opposition was furnished by a picked team from Professor Taylor's school and Birmingham high schools, with Alabama winning, 56-0. Early teams were a bit tougher than current squads, it seems, as the following afternoon Alabama played the Birmingham Athletic Club, losing 5-4 when Ross, of B.A.C., kicked a 65-yard field goal. Impossible though it may seem, this field goal was listed as a collegiate record at one time and Birmingham papers of the day featured its distance in writeups of the game.

"The gridiron sport rapidly caught the students' fancy and the game became a favorite with University athletes. In 1896 the University's board of trustees passed a rule forbidding athletic teams from traveling off the campus. The following season only one game was played and in 1898 football was abandoned at Alabama. Student opposition to the ruling was so strong that the trustees lifted the travel ban and football was resumed in 1899, to continue without interruption until the First World War forced cancellation of the 1918 games.

"Alabama first gained national recognition in 1922 when the University of Pennsylvania [a well-known major powerhouse at the time] was defeated, 9-7, in Philadelphia. The following season Wallace Wade became head coach and in 1925 led the Crimson Tide to its first undefeated and untied season and its first Rose Bowl invitation. On Jan. 1, 1926, an unheralded, underrated team from Tuscaloosa came from behind to upset Washington, 20-19, in the Rose Bowl and established a precedent of colorful play that Crimson Tide teams have continued to uphold."

Additional Crimson Tide information can be found at
https://en.wikipedia.org/wiki/Alabama_Crimson_Tide_football

Crimson Tide football through the years

The Alabama Crimson Tide football team represents the University
of Alabama (aka Alabama, UA, or 'Bama) in the sport of American
football. Alabama today competes in the Football Bowl
Subdivision (FBS) of the National Collegiate Athletic
Association (NCAA) and the Western Division of the Southeastern
Conference (SEC). Currently coached by Nick Saban, UA is one of
the most storied and decorated football programs in NCAA history.

Having begun play about 125 years ago in 1892, the program boasts
of 16 national championships. These have been coming for a long
time—over and over and over again...and they are still coming
today.

Ironically, as good as Alabama's program has been since its first
Championship in 1925, and despite numerous other national and
conference championships, it was not until 2009 that an Alabama
player received a Heisman Trophy. It was running back Mark
Ingram. He became the university's first winner. In 2015, Derrick
Henry became the university's second Heisman winner.

When the 2015 season was completed, Alabama had amassed 864
official victories in NCAA Division I and for those counting at
home folks, there were an additional 21 victories that were vacated
and another 8 victories and 1 tie were forfeited for various reasons
over the years.

The Crimson Tide today plays its home games at Bryant–Denny
Stadium, located on its campus in Tuscaloosa, Alabama. It is a huge
stadium. With a capacity of 101,821, Bryant-Denny Stadium is
the 8th largest non-racing stadium in the world and the seventh
largest stadium in the United States.

Head Football Coaches

Since 1892 when the program was formed and when the first game was played, Alabama has played 123 seasons with 30 head coaches. This includes a 1918 coach in a season in which no games were played and a temporary coach who coached one bowl game after his predecessor was fired.

Like all teams of the era save a few richer schools from the East, football, in the early years, was not such an easy college sport in which to form a competitive program.

Soon after the beginning of play and after a shutdown of the 1898 season due to a ban on away games. The "Crimson Tide" picked up its cherished nickname after the 1907 season. Overall, UA has played more than 1,200 games in their 125 seasons.

In that time, 12 coaches have led the Crimson Tide in postseason bowl games: Wallace Wade, Frank Thomas, Harold D. "Red" Drew, Bear Bryant, Ray Perkins, Bill Curry, Gene Stallings, Mike DuBose, Dennis Franchione, Mike Shula, Joe Kines, and Nick Saban. Eight of those coaches also won conference championships: Wade, Thomas, Drew, Bryant, Curry, Stallings, DuBose, and Saban. During their tenures, Wade, Thomas, Bryant, Stallings, and Saban all won national championships, totaling 16 with the Crimson Tide.

Of the 30 different head coaches who have led the Crimson Tide, Wade, Thomas, Bryant, and Stallings have been inducted into the College Football Hall of Fame. The current head coach is Nick Saban. Saban was hired in January 2007, and he fits the Alabama tradition like a glove. With the 2015 Championship season in the bag, and a 14-1 record in the 2016 season, Saban has amassed 120 victories which includes the great 2016 SEC Championship game and the 2016 Peach Bowl.

Alabama National Championships

Alabama is generally credited with 16 national championships though not all have been of the consensus variety. Most universities today give themselves the benefit of the doubt when there is doubt on a championship in a given year.

National Championships before the CFP bowls were hotly contested. National championships in NCAA FBS college football are debated but the NCAA does not officially award the championship. However, it does provide lists of championships awarded by organizations that it does recognize.

There is an official NCAA 2009 Division I Football Records Book, and this states that: "During the last 138 years, there have been more than 30 selectors of national champions using polls, historical research and mathematical rating systems. Beginning in 1936, the Associated Press (AP) began the best-known and most widely circulated poll of sportswriters and broadcasters. Before 1936, national champions were determined by historical research and retroactive ratings and polls.

The criteria for being included in this historical list of poll selectors is that the poll be national in scope, either through distribution in newspaper, television, radio and /or computer online.

Since World War II, Alabama only claims national championships awarded by the final AP Poll or the final Coaches' Poll. This policy is consistent with other FBS football programs with numerous national title claims, including Notre Dame, USC, and Oklahoma.

All national championships claimed by the University of Alabama were published in nationally syndicated newspapers and magazines, and each of the national championship selectors, and are cited in the Official 2010 NCAA FBS Record Book.

In addition to the championships claimed by the university, the NCAA has listed Alabama as receiving a championship for the 1945, 1966, 1975, and 1977 college football seasons.

In Alabama's own 1982 media guide, the last for Coach Bryant, 1934 is listed as the only national championship before Coach Bryant in a small footnote about the school's SEC history.

In the 1980s, Alabama's Sports Information Director Wayne Atcheson began to recognize five pre-Bryant national championship teams (1925, 1926, 1930, 1934, 1941). He added them to the University's Football Media Guide.

Atcheson said that he made the effort in the context of disputed titles being claimed by other schools, and "to make Alabama football look the best it could look" to compete with the other claimants. Atcheson believes that the titles are the school's rightful claims.

And, so the UA 2009 Official Football Media Guide states that Alabama had 12 national championships prior to winning the 2010 BCS National Championship Game. The 2009, 2011, 2012, and 2015 titles extend the total number of national championships claimed by Alabama to 16. Eleven of Alabama's national championships were awarded by the wire-services (AP, Coaches' Poll) or by winning the BCS National Championship Game.

In January 2013, CNN suggested that Alabama was college football's new dynasty, and in May 2013, Athlon Sports ranked Alabama's ongoing dynasty as the fourth-best since 1934, behind Oklahoma (1948–58), Miami (1986–92), and Nebraska (1993–97). Watch out to the top three for sure as Alabama is not done yet.

Conference Championships

Alabama has a winning tradition. A gambler can get rich betting on Alabama games. The teams over the years have won a total of 30 conference championships; this includes 4 Southern Conference and 26 SEC Championships.

UA captured its 4 Southern Conference titles in 1924, 1925, 1926, and 1930. Alabama captured the first SEC title in 1933 and the team has won a total of 26 SEC Championships (1933, 1934, 1937, 1945, 1953, 1961, 1964, 1965, 1966, 1971, 1972, 1973, 1974, 1975, 1977, 1978, 1979, 1981, 1989, 1992, 1999, 2009, 2012, 2014, 2015, 2016).

The school has won more SEC football titles than any other school, including seven since the conference split into separate divisions and added the Championship Game in 1992. Alabama is the only SEC school to win an SEC Championship in every decade since the conference was founded in 1933. Alabama is synonymous with winning. Bear Bryant fit the Alabama winning tradition 100%. Nick Saban looks like a Bear Disciple.

Divisional Championships

Since the 1992 season, the SEC has been split into two divisions. Alabama competes in the SEC West. Alabama has won or shared 12 division titles, and has posted a 7-4 record in the SEC Championship Game as of 2016.

Those of us who root always or often for Alabama are seldom disappointed. What a football tradition. Roll Tide.

Heisman Trophy

One can certainly make the case that with such a phenomenal record, Alabama is either fully team-oriented or consistently lacks individual talent. Many share my opinion that the University has been victimized by a biased voting system. Some may say UA is simply a victim of circumstance. I say the former. Can anybody believe that there were no Alabama Heisman Trophy Winners during Bear Bryant's storied career? It just does not seem right.

There is always irony in every story. Bear Bryant did coach one Heisman winner, John David Crow. However, Crow played for the Texas Aggies when the Bear coached there. Bryant then moved on to Alabama and the Crimson Tide are quite pleased that he did.

I have to admit, I scoured for sources that could explain the lack of Heisman Trophies at Alabama. If you are reading this and you know, let me know, and in a future update to this book, I will more than likely include your perspective. I cannot figure it out.

On December 12, 2009, the Heisman drought ended. Mark Ingram became Alabama's first Heisman Trophy winner. In the closest race, ever, he edged out Stanford running back Toby Gerhart by 28 points. The previous best finish for an Alabama player occurred in 1993, when David Palmer finished 3rd in the Heisman voting. AJ McCarron finished as runner-up for the 2013 season. Derrick Henry became Alabama's second Heisman trophy winner on December 12, 2015.

Alabama fans are typically very happy

Overall, those of us who root always and often for Alabama are seldom disappointed. What a football tradition. Roll Tide.

.

Chapter 3 Alabama's Football Fields & Stadiums

You need a good field in which to play

Few teams of which I am aware, consistently play home games at fields other than their one home field. Alabama has played its home games on many fields, and not just when one field is abandoned for the next expansion. Until recently when Bryant Denny Stadium was expanded to exceed 100,000 capacity, a team might play UA on one field on year and a different one the next.

Being so close to the state capital and its adopted field aka Legion Field and lots of other fields in Alabama, and being a state institution. Alabama played its home games wherever it wanted to play them in Alabama.

The QUAD

Although the Alabama campus is physically located in Tuscaloosa, through the history of the program, several stadiums located in

Tuscaloosa, Birmingham, Montgomery and Mobile have played host to the fine Alabama football teams during UA football's 125 seasons.

Before 1929, as you will see in the next chapter and some following that, the spot where many games were played on Campus at Tuscaloosa was called the QUAD. There really was no stadium per se, so they made a section of the campus into a field and they put the lines on it and the goal posts and whatever was necessary for the brand of football played at the turn of the prior century.

At the time the photo below was taken, the University of Alabama football team played its games on the QUAD. This would have been prior to 1916 when Denny Field was constructed behind Little and Moore Halls. Denny Field was used until 1929 when the football team moved to the present site of Bryant Denny Stadium.

Bryant-Denny Stadium

1929 The George Hutcheson Denny Stadium

That which today is known as Bryant–Denny Stadium has served as the on-campus home of the Crimson Tide since its opening on September 28, 1929. Originally this historic stadium was known as the George Hutchenson Denny Stadium or simply Denny Stadium after the university president of the same name,

Since Alabama is a state-run institution of higher learning, the state has some say in how the football team conducts the business of football as well as where it plays its games.

in 1975, for example, the Alabama state legislature renamed the stadium Bryant–Denny Stadium in honor of then coach Bear Bryant. Because the Bear was Bear and nobody else has ever been or could come close to BEAR, Alabama fans and supporters have a major affinity to Paul "Bear Bryant"

DENNY FIELD FROM THE TOP OF THE GYM

Image courtesy of the W.S. Hoole Special Collections Library, The University of Alabama | Reproduced with permission | www.lib.ua.edu/libraries/hoole

Denny Field

Denny Field served as the home stadium for the Crimson Tide football team from 1915 through the 1928 seasons, excluding 1918 when a team was not fielded due to World War I. Originally named

University Field, but renamed in 1920, during its tenure as the team's home field, Alabama amassed an overall home record of 43 wins to only 3 losses.

Originally, Denny Stadium only had seating for 12,000 fans. But, further expansions in 1950, 1961, and 1966 raised capacity to 25,000, 43,000, and 60,000, respectively. The first upper deck was added on the west side of the stadium in 1988, adding 10,000 more seats for a capacity of 70,123. 2nd pic below Denny Stadium 1966

The original Denny Stadium, completed in 1929.

On September 5, 1998, the stadium's eastern upper deck was opened, and raised its official seating capacity to 83,818 at a final cost of $35 million. The University moved all home games here from Legion Field in exchange for the funding given to the project by local municipalities.

1998 Expansion of Bryant-Denny

It did not end there. After the 2004 football season, the university spent another wad of money -- approximately $47 million on an expansion to the north end zone. This was completed days before the 2006 season opener against Hawaii. The expansion added a new upper deck to the North end zone area, complete with three different levels of skyboxes, which collectively are known as "The Zone."

There is so much revenue to be generated by the same game when a stadium is large, that more and more schools are spending money on expansions to accommodate fans and to assure future football program revenue.

This last expansion as discussed brought the number of skyboxes in the stadium to 123. Everybody one day in their lives should be able to watch a game from a skybox. This expansion brought Bryant-Denny capacity to 92,138 by the 2006 season.

Another expansion to the south end zone, completed during the Summer of 2010, increased its capacity to over 101,000 to make it the 8th largest stadium in the world by seating. All-time. There are times at Bryant Denny that there are no seats available. That is good of course but bad for fans who wish to attend games to support the Crimson Tide. Maybe still more seats are needed?

Bryant-Denny Stadium Today

Please tell me about Legion Field and its Role at Alabama

Legion Field

Well into the 1980s, Alabama played most of its important games, as well as the Iron Bowl, at Legion Field—to the point that most of Alabama's "home" football history from the 1920s to the 1980s took place in Birmingham and not on the campus field in Tuscaloosa.

Birmingham's Legion Field stadium hosted its first game on Nov. 19, 1927, when Howard College met Birmingham-Southern in a cross-town rivalry.

Here are some of the important dates and events in the 87-year-old stadium's history:

1927 -Legion Field stadium opened with 21,000 seats; Howard College (now Samford University) meets Birmingham-Southern in the first game.

1946 -The annual Alabama State-Alabama A&M game, later known as the Magic City Classic, was played at Legion Field for the first time.

1947 - Legion Field doubled its capacity to about 42,000, including the addition of the south end zone "horseshoe."

1948 - After not playing each other for 41years, Alabama and Auburn renew their intrastate rivalry at Legion Field in the Iron Bowl.

1961 - An upper deck was added to Legion Field's east side, increasing capacity to about 54,600.

1964 - A stadium bond issue funded an additional 14,000 seats in the north end zone; The Birmingham News and Birmingham Post-Herald donated $10,000 for two new scoreboards.

1965 -- A new press box was built, with elevators from the ground level to the top of the stadium.

1970 - An artificial surface, Poly-Turf, replaced the natural grass. Five years later, Astroturf replaced the Poly-Turf.

1977 - Another 7,000 seats were added by closing in the south end zone to create an enclosed bowl; Legion Field hosted the first Hall of Fame Classic bowl game.

1981 - Paul "Bear" Bryant won his 315[th]game to become college football's all-time winningest coach.

1988 - For the last time, Alabama and Auburn met in an Iron Bowl in which the tickets were split 50-50; Auburn moved its home games to its campus the next year.

1991 - The stadium expands for the final time, bringing seating capacity to slightly more than 83,000.

1992 - Legion Field hosts the first SEC Championship Game between Alabama and Florida; the game moves to Atlanta's Georgia Dome two years later.

2003 - Alabama plays its final home game at Legion Field against the University of South Florida.

2005 - In need of serious repairs, the east-side upper deck is removed, reducing the stadium's capacity to its current level of about 71,000.

Because of structural problems that were too costly to repair, the Legion Field upper deck was torn down in 2005. (Joe Songer/jsonger@al.com)

2008 - Legion Field hosts the Alabama High School Athletic Association's "Super 6" state football championships for the final time.

2014 - The UAB Blazers play their final game at Legion Field; UAB President Ray Watts shuts down the football program 10 days later.

Other UA Football Field / Stadium Venues

Rickwood Field provided for the fifth location of Alabama home games in Birmingham, and is located at the corner of 2nd Avenue West and 12th Street West in the West End. Alabama would play home games at Rickwood between the 1912 and 1927 seasons, with an all-time record at Rickwood Field of 23 wins, 12 losses and 5 ties.

The Birmingham Fairgrounds provided for the fourth location of Alabama home games in Birmingham, and is located in western Birmingham at the location of Birmingham International Raceway. Alabama would play home games at the fairgrounds between the 1905 and 1911 seasons, with an all-time record at the Birmingham Fairgrounds of 12 wins, 6 losses and 2 ties.

West End Park, also known as "Slag Pile Field", and also the home of the Birmingham Barons before Rickwood Field was constructed, was the third location of Alabama home games in Birmingham. The Crimsons would play home games at West End Park between the 1901 and 1904 seasons, with an all -time record at West End Park of 3 wins, 5 losses and 1 tie

Lakeview Park is Located at the present-day intersection of Highland and Clairmont Avenues, Lakeview Park has the distinction of being the first home of Alabama football. On November 11, 1892, Alabama would win its first all-time game against Birmingham High School 56–0 and lose the first Iron Bowl against Auburn 22–32 on February 22, 1893 at Lakeview. Alabama would play home games at Lakeview between the 1892 and 1894 seasons, with an all-time record at Lakeview Park of 2 wins and 5 losses.

The Cramton Bowl provided for the fourth and final location of Alabama home games in the capital city. The Tide played home games at the Cramton Bowl in the 1922 through 1932 seasons, in 1934, between the 1944 through 1946 seasons and again between the 1951 through 1954 seasons. Alabama's all-time record at the Cramton Bowl was 17 wins and 3 losses.

Highland Park provided for the second location of Alabama home games in the capital city. The Crimsons would play home games at Highland in the 1901, 1903, and the 1907 seasons. Alabama's all-time record at Riverside was 1 win, 0 losses and 2 ties.

Ladd Peebles Stadium--opening for Crimson Tide football on October 2, 1948, Ladd Peebles Stadium played host to Alabama through the 1948 and the 1959 seasons, the 1961 and the 1963 through the 1968 seasons. The Crimson Tide posted an all-time record at Ladd-Peebles Stadium of 10 wins, 7 losses and 2 ties.

Here are two more places on the next page. It is simply amazing the variety of stadiums and fields UA has used over the years.

Mobile

Ladd Peebles Stadium in 2003

Murphy Stadium

Murphy Stadium played host to Alabama for the 1944 season. The Crimson Tide posted an all-time record at Murphy Stadium of 2 wins, 0 losses and 0 ties. 1940—Alabama 26, Spring Hill 0 (Sept. 27, 1940, Mobile)In the first night game in Alabama football history, the Crimson Tide beat Spring Hill College, 26-0, in front of 7,500 fans at Murphy High School in Mobile.

Monroe Park

Records of the 1907 season indicate that Alabama played LSU at Monroe Park in Mobile on November 23, 1907, and defeated the Tigers 6–4. Penn State was mentored by is 11th coach at the time, J.H. W. Pollard.

Chapter 4 Football Coaches – First Ten Years 1892-1901

Year	Coach	Conference	Record	Conference
1892	E. B. Beaumont #1	Independent	2-2-0	
1893	Eli Abbott#2	Independent	0-4-0	
1894	Eli Abbott	Independent	3-1-0	
1895	Eli Abbott	SIAA	0-4-0	0-4-0
1896	Otto Wagonhurst #3	SIAA	2-1-0	1-1-0
1897	Allen McCants #4	SIAA	1-0-0	0-0-0
1898	No Season			
1899	W. A. Martin #5	SIAA	3-1-0	1-0-0
1900	Malcolm Griffin #6	SIAA	2-3-0	1-3-0
1901	M. S. Harvey #7	SIAA	2-1-2	2-1-2

1892 Alabama's 1st Football Season Coach E.B Beaumont # 1

The Alabama Cadets football program began its 1892 football season on November 11 with a game against Birmingham High

School. The Cadets won the game 56-0. The story of this season and Coach E. B. Beaumont is told in Chapter 2.

In 1892, football as we know, it was not completely defined. Association football, rugby, and even soccer was having a major influence at the time on the college football rules and game play. Unlike other startup teams its early years, UA was blessed with a coach. There were teams competing at the college level at the time that had no coach other than some players who stepped up to the plate.

1893 Coach Eli Abbot # 2

Eli Abbott was the head coach of the University of Alabama football program for four years over two stints in Tuscaloosa. He coached the Crimson Tide for three seasons from 1893-1895, going just 3-9 in that time.

He led the Tide to two winless 0-4 seasons in 1893 and 1895, but went 3-1 in 1894. He returned as Alabama's head coach in 1902, posting a 4-4 record. He also coached Alabama's baseball team in 1896. Abbott passed away in 1943 at the age of 73.

The 1893 Alabama Crimson White football team represented the University of Alabama in the 1893 college football season. The team changed its name after the 1892 season. It was called the "Crimson White" from 1893 to 1906, when their name changed to the currently used "Crimson Tide.

The team was led by first year head coach Eli Abbott and played their home games at Lakeview Park in Birmingham and The QUAD in Tuscaloosa, Alabama. It was not such a good second year as the

Crimson White finished with a record of zero wins and four losses (0–4).

They had finished their 1992 inaugural year with a .500 record, and afterwards, head coach E. B. Beaumont was fired and replaced with Abbott prior to the start of the season. The 1893 squad opened the season with a pair of losses against the Birmingham Athletic Club, first in Tuscaloosa and then again, a month later at Birmingham.

The Crimson White was then shutout by Sewanee in their first game against an out-of-state opponent, and then closed the season with a 40–16 loss in the Iron Bowl against Auburn at Montgomery. The winless season was the first of only three in the program's entire history.

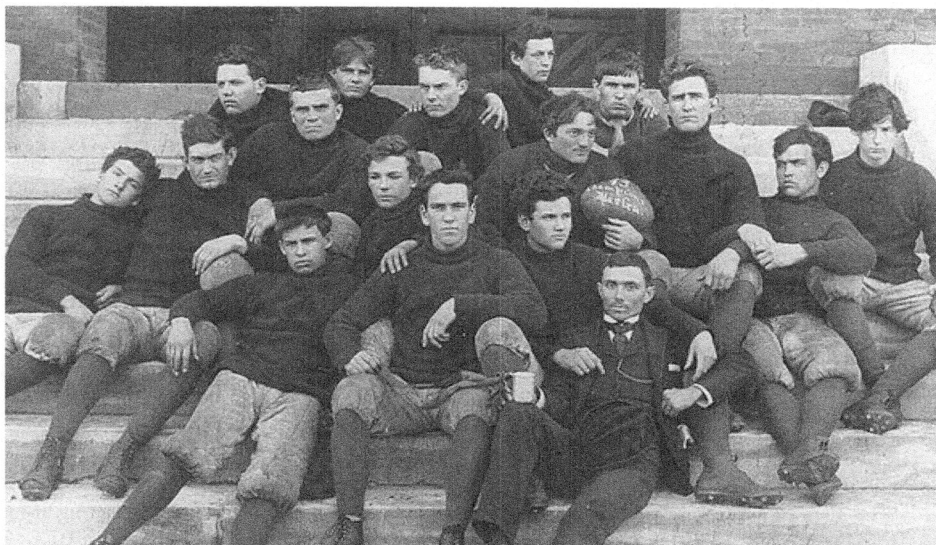

1893 Alabama Crimson White Football Team Eli Abbott Coach

1894 Coach Eli Abbot # 2

The 1894 Alabama Crimson White football team, (aka "Alabama", "UA" or "Bama") played a much better third season than in 1893. The team was led by second-year head coach Eli Abbott. The team finished with a record of three wins and one loss (3–1).

After a winless season in 1893, Abbott returned as a player-coach and led the 1894 squad. The Crimson White opened the season with a loss against Ole Miss in what was their first game ever played outside the state of Alabama. UA then won their final three games.

After a victory over Tulane at New Orleans, Alabama returned to Birmingham where they defeated Sewanee in their only home game of the season. They then closed the year with their first all-time win over Auburn at Montgomery in the Iron Bowl.

1895 Coach Eli Abbot # 2

In a repeat performance of the 1893 season, UA never got started and finished with another 0-4-0 record. The 1895 the Alabama Crimson White football team was again led by head coach Eli Abbott, in his third season.

The 1895 squad also was the first to compete in a conference, the Southern Intercollegiate Athletic Association (SIAA). After a one-loss season in 1894, Abbott returned as head coach and led the 1895 squad. Alabama opened the season with a loss at Columbus against the Georgia Bulldogs L (6-30).

The Crimson White next lost a pair of games L (0-32), and L (6-12) in Louisiana over a span of just three days. After a loss to Tulane at New Orleans, Alabama was defeated by LSU in the first all-time game between the schools. They then closed the year with a L (0-48) to Auburn in the first Iron Bowl ever played at Tuscaloosa. UA would go winless just one more time in its football history

1896 Coach Otto Wagonhurst # 3

The 1896 Alabama Crimson White football team was led by head coach Otto Wagonhurst (left) in his first season. Eli Abbot had graduated. They played their home games at The QUAD in Tuscaloosa, Alabama in what was the fifth season of Alabama football. UA finished with a record of two wins and one loss (2–1, 1–1 in the SIAA).

In spring 1895, the University Board of Trustees passed a rule that prohibited athletic teams from competing off-campus for athletic events. As such, all games scheduled for the 1896 season were played on campus at *The QUAD*. In their first game, Alabama shutout the Birmingham Athletic Club before they lost their only game of the season against Sewanee. The Crimson White then closed the season with their second shutout victory of the year against Mississippi A&M. It was tough to schedule teams when they knew that Alabama would never be the visiting team.

1897 Coach Allen McCants #4

The 1897 Alabama Crimson White football team was coached by Allen McCants in his first season. They played home games at The QUAD in Tuscaloosa, Alabama. This was the sixth season of Alabama football. The team was suffering from some restrictions on away games imposed by the Administration and had a tough time fielding a squad. Their record was one win and zero losses (1–0, 0–0 SIAA). There would be no Alabama football under any coach the following year.

As noted, in the spring of 1895, the University Board of Trustees passed a rule that prohibited athletic teams from competing off-campus for athletic events, and as such only one game was scheduled for the season. In their only game, the Crimson White shutout the Tuscaloosa Athletic Club W (6-0) on The QUAD. SIAA teams were not interested in playing only away games and thus no conference games were scheduled. The following year UA found no teams willing to play.

1897 Football Team Coach Allen McCants

1898: No season.

In the spring of 1895, the University Board of Trustees passed a rule that prohibited athletic teams from competing off-campus for athletic events. As such the 1898 season was canceled; however, the board subsequently rescinded this rule and the squad returned to the field for the 1899 season.

1899 Coach W. A. Martin # 5

The 1899 Alabama Crimson White football team was led by first year head coach W. A. Martin. They played their home games at The QUAD in Tuscaloosa, Alabama. Since there was no seventh season in 1898, this was the seventh season of play for Alabama football.

The team finished with a record of three wins and one loss (3–1, 1–0 SIAA).

UA 1899 Football Team

Coach W A Martin left…

On October 21, UA played Tuscaloosa Athletic Club at the QUAD in Tuscaloosa, for a win W (16–5). On November 11, the Montgomery Athletic Club came to The QUAD for another win W 16–0. On November 24, the Crimson White traveled to Mississippi Driving Park in Jackson, MS (and won another W (7–5)). With an undefeated season on the line, the next day on November 25 the New Orleans Athletic Club in the Athletic Park in New Orleans, LA, the Crimson White suffered its only defeat of the season, in a very close match L (0–2). It was tough finding other colleges with which UA could engage.

1900 Coach Malcolm Griffin # 6

The 1900 Alabama Crimson White football was led by head coach Malcolm Griffin in his first season. They played their home games at The QUAD in Tuscaloosa and one game at North Birmingham Park in Birmingham, Alabama.

In what was the eighth season of Alabama football, the team finished with a record of two wins and three losses (2–3, 1–3 SIAA).

<<< Malcolm Griffin Left.

The Crimson White opened the season with three consecutive games at the QUAD. After a shutout victory over the Taylor School W (35-0), Alabama opened SIAA play with a W (12–5) victory over Ole Miss.

However, the Crimson White did proceed to lose their final three games en route to a 2–3 record. After a L (0-6) loss to Tulane, Alabama traveled to Montgomery where they were defeated L (5-53) by Auburn and they closed the season with a L (0-35) loss to Clemson at Birmingham.

1901 Coach M. S. Harvey #7

The 1901 Alabama Crimson White football team was led by head coach M. S. Harvey, in his first season. The team played its home games at The QUAD in Tuscaloosa and one game each at Highland Park in Montgomery and at West End Park in Birmingham, Alabama.

It was the ninth season for Alabama football, the team finished with a record of two wins, one loss and two ties (2–1–2, 2–1–2 SIAA).
<<< Coach M S Harvey Left

On October 26 at home v Ole Miss, Alabama triumphed W (41-0). This was followed by a zero-zero tie on November 9 at Georgia in Montgomery Alabama T (0-0). In the Iron Bowl on November 15, Auburn played well and defeated the Crimson White L (0-17). Mississippi A&M then came to town and lost to the Crimson White in a blowout W (45-0) The next game was November 28 v Tennessee at West End Park T (6-6)

Chapter 5 Football Coaches – Next Thirteen Years 1902-1914

Seven coaches in thirteen years

Year	Coach	Conference	Record	C-Record
1902	Eli Abbott #8	SIAA	4-4-0	2-4-0
1903	W. B. Blount #9	SIAA	3-4-0	3.4-0
1904	W. B. Blount	SIAA	7-3-0	4-3-0
1905	Jack Leavenworth #10	SIAA	6-4-0	4-4-0
1906	J. W. H. Pollard #11	SIAA	5-1-0	3-1-0
1907	J. W. H. Pollard	SIAA	5-1-2	3-1-2
1908	J. W. H. Pollard	SIAA	6-1-1	1-1-1
1909	J. W. H. Pollard	SIAA	5-1-2	4-1-2
1910	Guy Lowman #12	SIAA	4-4-0	0-4-0
1911	D. V. Graves #13	SIAA	5-2-2	2-2-2
1912	D. V. Graves	SIAA	5-3-1	3-3-1
1913	D. V. Graves	SIAA	6-3-0	4-3-0
1914	D. V. Graves	SIAA	5-4-0	4-3-0

1892 Alabama's Thin Red Line

1902 Coach Eli Abbott #2 & # 8

Eli Abbott was one of the many good guys in Alabama football history (April 1, 1869 – February 13, 1943). He was very athletic. He played and coached football and baseball at the University of Alabama and the University of Pennsylvania, which according to the selectors was the best team in the country at the turn of the century. Abbott had previously coached the Alabama Crimson Tide football team from 1893 to 1895 and again in 1902. His picture shown in the prior write-up.

The 1902 Alabama Crimson White football team retained Coach Eli Abbott for just one additional season. It was thus his only season of his second stint (fourth season overall). The team played home games at The QUAD on campus in Tuscaloosa and at West End Park in Birmingham, Alabama.

James O. Heyworth served as a co-head coach with Abbott for this particular season. In what was the tenth season of Alabama football, the team finished with a record of four wins and four losses (4–4; 2–3 in the SIAA).

At this time, in the evolution of American football as played at colleges and universities, teams, especially those in conferences, were becoming able to schedule more games each season.

In 1902, the UA season opened on October 10 at home against a tough but undermanned Birmingham High School team at The QUAD in Tuscaloosa, AL. UA prevailed W (57–0). Teams would do whatever they had to get games—some played up and some played down. The huge victory margin brought Alabama's all-time record against Birmingham High School to 2–0.

On October 13, the Marion Military Institute came into the QUAD • in Tuscaloosa, AL. UA had no problem putting them away W (81–0) but nobody ever gave up. On October 18, Auburn, always a tough contest in the Iron Bowl arrived at West End Park in Birmingham, AL (Iron Bowl), and they prevailed L 0–23. On November 1, Georgia's Bulldogs were ready for a match and they slipped by with a slight win v Alabama L (0–5).

On November 8, Mississippi A&M visited the QUAD and were pushed way back throughout the game in a rivalry match. W (27–0). On November 11, Texas then played at the QUAD and the Crimson White lost L (0–10). It was the first all-time meeting against the University of Texas.

It was a game dominated by both defenses early, Texas scored their first touchdown with only 0:13 remaining in the first half on a ten-yard John A. Jackson run. He then scored the only other touchdown in the second half for the 10–0 Longhorn victory.

With two more games left, Abbot was toughening up his team. On November 27, Georgia Tech were well beaten up at West End Park • Birmingham, AL W 26–0. The one-game win streak ended on November 29 against LSU at the QUAD in Tuscaloosa L (0-11)

1903 Coach W. B. Blount # 9

The 1903 Alabama Crimson White football team was led by head coach W. B. Blount, in his first season. As teams before them, they played their home games at The QUAD in Tuscaloosa as well as the West End Park in Birmingham, Alabama.

<<< left W. A. Blount was the head football coach at the University of Alabama for two seasons in 1903 and 1904, leading the Crimson Tide to a 10-7 record during that time. After finishing just 3-4 in 1903, Blount led the Tide to a 7-3 season in 1904. He also coached at Howard College, which is now known as Samford University. Blount passed away in 1918 at the young age of 39.

This was the eleventh season of Alabama football. This team finished with a record of three wins and four losses (3–4, 3–4 SIAA). In 1903, the UA administration did not know this exactly, but there was a secret formula for football at Alabama that kept Crimson White; later the Crimson Tide, from never having another losing season until 1951. And, my friends, that is about as long as long is.

On October 10, 1903, UA played Vanderbilt at Dudley Field in Nashville, TN. The game went into the wrong column L 0–30. This was Alabama's 1903 season opener with a 0-30 loss against Vanderbilt University right out of the chute. It was the first all-time meeting between the schools at Dudley Field.

Vanderbilt took a 12–0 halftime lead after first half touchdowns were scored first by Ed Hamilton and followed by John J. Tigert. The Commodores then closed the game with three touchdowns in the second half scored by Hamilton, Dan Blake and Bob Blake for the 30–0 victory. The Vandies converted all five PAT's in their victory. Frank Kyle starred for the Commodores in the contest with runs of 30, 35, 48 and 50-yards against the Crimson White.

On October 16 at Mississippi A&M at the Columbus Fairgrounds in Columbus, MS, a soon-to-be rivalry, the Crimson White suffered another loss L (0–11). Shaking off the loser dust, UA proudly went to the Iron Bowl on October 23 vs. Auburn at Riverside Park in Montgomery, and the White brought home a nice win W (18–6). It was a welcome win after being shut out for their first two games.

Alabama upset the Alabama Polytechnic Institute (now known as Auburn University) 18–6 before 1,200 fans at Riverside Park in Montgomery. J. V. Boyles scored a touchdown for Alabama to cap a 19-play, 79-yard drive on their opening possession and with the extra point took a 6–0 lead.

In the second half, Alabama extended their lead to 12–0 after Truman Smith scored on a 45-yard touchdown run. After Auburn cut the lead to 12–6 with a W. G. Boyd touchdown run, Alabama scored the final points of the game on a 25-yard Smith run for the 18–6 victory. The victory brought Alabama's all-time record against Auburn to 2–6. Things would get better over time.

Sewanee was always tough and they were again tough on November 2 as UA went down L 0–23. LSU came to The QUAD in Tuscaloosa on November 9 and UA prevailed W 18–0.

This was Alabama's first victory over LSU with its 18–0 win at Tuscaloosa. Both John Roberts Peavy and W. S. Sherrill scored first half touchdowns for Alabama, and Truman Smith scored on a fake punt returned 65-yards to secure the 18–0 victory. This brought UA's all-time record against LSU to 1–2. These were the beginning years of a great program.

On November 14 v Cumberland at The QUAD, UA bit the dust L (0–44). Then, on November 26 v Tennessee at West End Park UA prevailed W (24-0). Coach Blount was beginning to get the hang of winning for Alabama.

1904 Coach W. B. Blount # 10

The Head Coach of the 1904 Alabama Crimson White football team was W. B. Blount, in his second season. They played their home games at The QUAD in Tuscaloosa and at West End Park in Birmingham, Alabama. This was the twelfth season of Alabama

1904 Team

football, the team finished with a record of seven wins and three losses (7–3, 4–3 SIAA).

Prior to the 1897 season a touchdown was worth four points. Beginning in 1897, a touchdown was worth five points, a field goal was worth four points and a conversion (PAT) was worth one point.

On October 3, UA took on the University of Florida at The QUAD W 29–0. On October 8 in West End Park, Clemson beat the Crimson White L 0–18. On October 15, it was Mississippi A&M at Columbus Fairgrounds, Columbus, MS (Rivalry) W (10–5). On October 24, Nashville came to The QUAD W (17–0).

On November 5, Georgia came to the QUAD and were defeated W (16–5). You can see four touchdowns scored and just one extra point. On November 12, the Iron Bowl was played at West End Park in Birmingham, AL. UA were beaten by Auburn L (5–29). Auburn used a delayed buck effectively. On this play, blockers swept around end, faking the ball. The ball carrier then drove through the line for substantial gains. Teams were quickly learning tricks to gain the advantage in college football games. Alabama was no exception.

On November 24, November 24 UA played Tennessee at West End Park L (0-5) On December 2. The Crimson White traveled to State Field in Baton Rouge to play LSU W (11-0).

Three games were played on successive days in Louisiana and Pensacola. On December 3 at Tulane in New Orleans, LA, UA won again, W (6–0). Then on December 4 at Pensacola Athletic Club in Pensacola, FL, The Crimson White won again W (10–6).

1905 Coach Jack Leavenworth # 10

In 1905 the Alabama Crimson White football team was coached by Jack Leavenworth in his first and only season as head coach and as history suggests, he did not move on to coach any other college sport at that time or any other time.

It was Alabama's 13th overall and 10th season as a member of the Southern Intercollegiate Athletic Association (SIAA). The team finished the season with a record of six wins and four losses (6–4 overall, 4–4 in the SIAA).

1905 Alabama v Georgia

On October 3, Alabama kicked off the season with a W (17-0) at The QUAD against Maryville. Four days later, on October 7, Vanderbilt defeated the Crimson White (0-34) at Dudley Field in Nashville. The following week on October 14, Mississippi A&M played at the QUAD and were defeated W (34-0).

In a close game on October 21at Georgia Tech in Brisbane Park • Atlanta, GA, UA almost pulled it through but were defeated in a close match L (5–12). Clemson was next on October 25 at the South Carolina State Fairgrounds. The Tigers won L (0-25)

<<<Coach Leavenworth -- left

On November 4, UA beat the Georgia Bulldogs at the Birmingham Fairgrounds W (36-0). On November 9, Centre came into town at The QUAD and were defeated by UA W (21-0). UA was at peak form against a scrappy Auburn team at Birmingham Fairgrounds on November 18 for the Iron Bowl W (30-0). Then, a tough Sewanee team beat UA on November 23 at the Birmingham

Fairgrounds L (6-42). In the season ender, Tennessee played hard at the Birmingham Fairgrounds but were defeated W (29-0).

1906 Coach J. W. H. Pollard # 11

The 1906 Alabama Crimson White football team was in its 14th season overall and its 11th season as a member of the Southern Intercollegiate Athletic Association (SIAA). The team was led by head

<<< Coach **J. W. H. Pollard (Left)**.

This was Pollard's first year, he serving as UA's eleventh football coach in just fourteen seasons.

Alabama finished this season with a record of five wins and one loss (5–1 overall, 3–1 in the SIAA).

Of particular note during this season was Alabama's embarrassing 78–0 loss to Vanderbilt. This loss was so bad that it still stands as the record for most points ever allowed by Alabama in a game and the most lopsided Alabama loss.

In this game, the Commodores led 57–0 at the half, and Alabama attempted to cancel this game after seven of their regular players were sidelined by injury but Vanderbilt refused.

It was the only loss of the year for the Alabama Crimson Tide (New name this year). It was its biggest ever loss to Vanderbilt, 78–0. Seven of Alabama's regular players were out with injuries. Vanderbilt executed several onside kicks from scrimmage. Owsley Manier scored five touchdowns as: "the back field frequently went twenty-five or thirty yards over the line". Alabama was held to just a single first down. Due to its injuries, Alabama had not wished to play, and: "the comparatively few who came to see them play were scarcely rewarded by seeing touchdowns made every two minutes." It was not a good day for Alabama and it was a much better day for Vanderbilt than it should have been.

Against Auburn in the Iron Bowl, Coach Pollard unveiled a "military shift" never before seen in the south. This was executed as star running back Auxford Burks scored all of the game's points in a W (10–0) victory. Auburn contended that Alabama player T. S. Sims was an illegal player but nothing came of this.

J. W. H. Pollard was a college football coach for seven seasons, four of which he spent coaching the Alabama Crimson Tide from 1906 through 1909. Pollard was a great coach for Alabama going 21-4-5 as coach, losing exactly one game in each of his four years in Tuscaloosa. He also coached baseball at UA 1907-1910. He passed away in 1957 at the age of 85—a great man and a great teacher of great athletes.

On November 17, at the Birmingham Fairgrounds • Birmingham, AL in the Iron Bowl, UA beat Auburn W (10-0). In the season finale at home in Birmingham, UA beat Tennessee W (51-0).

1907 Coach J. W. H. Pollard # 11

The 1907 Alabama Crimson Tide football team played their 15th overall and 12th season as a member of the Southern Intercollegiate Athletic Association (SIAA). The team was led by head coach J. W. H. Pollard, in his second year. They finished the season with a record of five wins, one loss and two ties (5–1–2 overall, 3–1–2 in the SIAA).

This Alabama team played several games of note during the season. Their 54–4 loss to an always tough Sewanee is the last time Alabama allowed an opponent to score 50 points in a regulation game. Admittedly, the 2003 team lost 51–43 to Tennessee in a game that went five overtimes). The victory over LSU at Monroe Park on Nov. 23 W (6-4) marked the first ever Alabama home game played in Mobile.

The Iron Bowl was again exciting on November 16 at the Fairgrounds T (6-6).

This year's 6–6 tie with Auburn was both the only tie in the history of the Iron Bowl and the last meeting between the two teams for forty years. Auburn was a 3 to 1 favorite going into the game, due to their earlier victory over Georgia and the fact that they had lost to Sewanee by only 6 points while Alabama lost to Sewanee by 50. Alabama missed a chance to win when a 15-yard field goal attempt failed.

Speculation as to why the Alabama–Auburn series was discontinued was originally thought to have been done as a safety precaution due violence both on the field and amongst the fans in the 1907 game. Instead, the game was canceled due to a disagreement between the schools on how much per diem to allow players for the trip to Birmingham, how many players each school should bring and where to find officials, and by the time all these matters were resolved, it was too late to play in 1908.

For forty years, the two teams failed to play each other, even though they were in the same state and members of the same conferences. Finally, pressure from the state legislature resulted in the renewal of the rivalry in 1948. Sometimes government does have a positive role.

UA ended the season on November 28 against Tennessee at the Birmingham Fairgrounds W (5–0).

This game is often referred to as *The Third Saturday in October*. It is an American college football rivalry game played annually by the University of Alabama Crimson Tide and the University of Tennessee Volunteers. The respective campuses are located approximately 310 miles (500 km) apart. It is known as the Third Saturday in October because the game was traditionally played then. Even when it is not played then, the rTennessee ivalry still carries the name.

1908 Coach J. W. H. Pollard; # 11

The 1908 Alabama Crimson Tide football team played its 16th overall and 13th season as a member of the Southern Intercollegiate Athletic Association (SIAA). The team was led by head coach J. W. H. Pollard, in his third year. They finished the season with a record of six wins, one loss and one tie (6–1–1 overall, 1–1–1 in the SIAA). In this section, we have opted to detail the season, taking more time to explain and showcase games so that we can all get a better feel for the state of Alabama football in its seventeenth year.

After opening the 1908 season with three consecutive shutouts, Alabama lost their only game of the season 6–11 at Georgia Tech. After a victory over Chattanooga and a tie against Georgia, Alabama played the Haskell Institute. Against Haskell, Alabama scored a touchdown on a 65-yard interception return, Haskell missed a field goal, and another Haskell drive ended with an interception deep in Alabama territory. In the season finale against Tennessee, Alabama back Derrill Pratt attempted eight field goals and made only one for a 4–0 Alabama victory.

On Oct. 3., Alabama won easily against the Wetumpka Agricultural School on the campus by the score of W (26-0). In the first half, Gresham scored on a tackle over tackle play and Henry Burks scored twice on line plunges. In the second half, Hurd scored on a pass. Another pass, Peebles to Hurd, carried the ball to the Wetumpka 5-yard line and Reidy went over for the touchdown.

On Oct. 10, UA defeated Howard in Birmingham by the score of W (17 to 0). In the second half, Pratt circled end for 35 yards and a touchdown from the "military formation." Later, with the ball on Howard's 30-yard line, Pratt was hurt. Mudd, substituting for him, broke through the line and ran 30 yards for a touchdown. Burks kicked the goal after.

On Oct. 17, Alabama met a heavier University of Cincinnati team at the Fairgrounds in Birmingham and won despite the weight disadvantage, W (16-0).

On Oct. 24, Georgia Tech resorted to some new trick plays to defeat Alabama L (6-11) in Atlanta.
On Oct. 31, UA defeated Chattanooga on the campus by the score W (23-6). The visitors scored in the first half when an Alabama punt was blocked and the ball was caught in the air by Ross, halfback of Chattanooga, who ran for a score. Burks, Reidy, D. Pratt and G. W. Pratt did not play because of "faculty trouble." Thus, the play was slow and marked by many fumbles. Austill scored on a line play ending a drive of 60 yards. Joe Mudd, halfback, Alabama's star

of the day, made three touchdowns on line plays and a delayed pass. Peebles kicked three goals after touchdowns.

On Nov. 14., Alabama played Georgia in Birmingham in one of the most spectacular and interesting games ever played between the two schools. The issue was unsettled until the final whistle. The score was tied T (6-6).

The Game

There was plenty of excitement from the beginning. Georgia kicked to Alabama's 10. A pass was attempted, a fumble resulted and Georgia recovered. Burks intercepted a Georgia pass and ran the ball out of danger. Alabama fumbled and Georgia recovered. A forward pass from a place kick formation was completed on Alabama's 5-yard line. Alabama stopped Franklin and Bostwick for a one yard gain before Newsome went over by inches. Hodgson kicked the goal.

Alabama fumbled the kickoff and Georgia recovered on Alabama's 30-yard line. After two plays failed, Alabama blocked a place kick by Hodgson, recovered the ball but was soon forced to punt. Georgia soon tried another place kick which Alabama again blocked but Woodruff of Georgia recovered. Hodgson later made a third attempt at goal from placement which failed, Greene of Alabama recovered the ball. He was tackled from behind by Woodruff and a touchdown prevented.

Reidy and Pratt circled ends for 10 yards each. Burks and Gresham gained 20. After two plays failed, quarterback Peebles called the signal for the "military formation." No one thought that Alabama would punt from this formation. And certainly no one expected an "onside" kick. Peebles gave them both in one dose. Pratt kicked to the Georgia 5, the ball bounded over the goal and Arant, right guard, fell on the ball for a touchdown. Reidy kicked the goal and the score was tied.

Georgia was completely fooled by the play. An additional element of surprise was in the fact that a guard and not an end or halfback was standing away from the team and behind the kicker to be eligible to recover the free ball.

Starting the second half, Alabama marched to the Georgia 30-yard line. Pratt circled end for 25 yards, Woodruff nailing him and preventing a touchdown. Alabama fumbled, Georgia recovered and promptly punted. Alabama then drove to Georgia's 30-yard line where the prettiest play of the game occurred.

Pratt and Reidy got into position for a place kick with Reidy piling up the dirt and kneeling to receive the ball from center. Instead, the ball was snapped to Pratt, who rushed forward faking a kick and throwing his headgear into the air. He slipped the ball to Reidy, who tore out around right end for a 25-yard gain. But Georgia tightened, got the ball on downs and punted to safety. Pratt later tried a placement which failed.

Both sides punted frequently for the rest of the game. Alabama gained on the exchanges as Pratt out kicked Derrick and Hodgson. This advantage, however, was offset by Alabama fumbles and brilliant returns by Woodruff. It was Georgia's ball on the Alabama 15-yard line as the game ended. The star of the game was Woodruff, a fine field general, a very fast open field runner and a deadly tackier.

On Nov. 20., in the writer's viewpoint, Alabama played the most spectacular game ever on the University campus. UA accomplished the seemingly impossible by defeating the Haskell Indians by the score of 9 to 8 W (9-8). The Crimsons were outweighed 25 pounds to the man, but fought determinedly against their more experienced opponents, who presented a fast, daring and resourceful team.

Time after time, the Indians drove from one end of the field to the other only to surrender the ball to a lion-hearted Alabama team who put up a stone wall defense when a touchdown appeared certain.

Haskell Indian Nations University opened in 1884

Alabama scored first when Derrill Pratt kicked a placement from the 35-yard line at a difficult angle for four points. A few plays later, the Indians made two points when an Alabama man was tackled behind the goal.

Final score: Alabama 9, Haskell Indians 8.

1909 Coach J. W. H. Pollard # 11

In 1909 Alabama Crimson Tide football team played its 17th overall and 14th season as a member of the Southern Intercollegiate Athletic Association (SIAA). The team was led by head coach J. W. H. Pollard, in his fourth and final year. They their home games at the University of Alabama QUAD in Tuscaloosa and the Birmingham Fairgrounds in Birmingham, Alabama. They finished the season with a record of five wins, one loss and two ties (5–1–2 overall, 4–1–2 in the SIAA).

Defensively, Alabama had six consecutive shutouts to go 5–0–1 before they surrendered their first touchdown against Tulane in their 5–5 tie. Alabama completed their season with a 12–5 loss to LSU at Birmingham to finish 5–1–2.

1910 Coach Guy Lowman; # 12

The 1910 Alabama Crimson Tide football team played its 18th overall and 15th season as a member of the Southern Intercollegiate Athletic Association (SIAA).

The team was led by head coach Guy Lowman in his first and last year. Few coaches were around more than a year and that affected the Tide's record for sure.

UA played home games at the University of Alabama QUAD in Tuscaloosa and the Birmingham Fairgrounds in Birmingham, Alabama. They finished the season with a record of four wins and four losses (4–4 overall, 0–4 in the SIAA).

Coach Guy Lowman (left)

After the team opened the season with shutouts over both Birmingham College and the Marion Military Institute, the Crimsons were feeling pretty good. But, then they lost four consecutive games to SIAA opponents by a margin of 104–0. That made it a tough season. The squad did rebound with non-conference victories over Tulane at New Orleans L (5-3) and Washington & Lee W (9–0) to finish the season with an overall record of 4–4.

In March 1910, J. W. H. Pollard announced his resignation as head football coach and athletic director. He was offered and accepted the same positions at Washington and Lee University. After several months of searching for a replacement, in August the University's Committee on Athletics hired Guy Lowman from the University of Missouri to serve as both head football coach and athletic director.

With his hiring, many expected him to successfully guide the football team through what was viewed as its toughest schedule in school history. The team reported for its first practice on September 10, and at that time six players returned with at least one season of experience with the Crimson and White. At the start of practice, coach Lowman identified as the team's weakest positions being the linemen and backs. Things did not look too great.

On October 1 at the QUAD, Alabama opened the season with a 25–0 victory over Birmingham College W (25-0) On October 8, again at home, the Crimson Tide won its second straight game W (26-0) — this one against the Marion Military Institute at Tuscaloosa. In the game, Robert Bumgardner scored three touchdowns with Adrian Van de Graff scoring the fourth on a 70-yard run in the victory.

On October 15, at the Birmingham Fairgrounds against the Georgia Bulldogs, Alabama lost its first game of the season L (0-22) before 12,000 fans at Birmingham. On October 22, at the QUAD, it was more punishment against the Georgia Tech Yellow Jackets L (0-36). On November 5, in Greenville, Mississippi, the Ole Miss Rebels added to the UA losing streak L (0-16). Finally, on November 12 at the Birmingham Fairgrounds • Birmingham, Alabama, UA lost to the always-tough Sewanee Tigers L (0-30). This was the fourth consecutive loss and all shutouts. The loss brought Alabama's all-time record against Sewanee to 1–6.

On November 19 at "First" Tulane Stadium in New Orleans, UA ended its losing streak with a W (5-3) victory over the Tulane Green Wave. The Crimson Tide led 2–0 at halftime with their only points coming on a first quarter safety, which occurred after a Tulane player tried to return a missed Alabama field goal. After Tulane took a 3–2 lead in the third, Farley Moody kicked a 20-yard, game-winning field goal for Alabama. The victory brought Alabama's all-time record against Tulane to 3–2–1 On November 24, at Birmingham Fairgrounds, UA defeated the Washington and Lee Generals W (9-0).

The victory also marked the return of former Alabama head coach J. W. H. Pollard, who resigned his position with the Crimson Tide to take the head coaching position with the Generals in the spring of 1910. The victory is Alabama's only all-time matchup against Washington and Lee.

1911 Coach D. V. Graves; # 13

The 1911 Alabama Crimson Tide football team played its 19th overall and 16th season as a member of the Southern Intercollegiate Athletic Association (SIAA).

D.V. GRAVES

The team was led by head coach << D. V. Graves (left), in his first year. UA finished the season with a record of five wins, two losses and two ties (5–2–2 overall, 2–2–2 in the SIAA).

The Crimson Tide opened the season well, with a shutout victory W (24-0) over Howard (now Samford University) followed with another win v Birmingham W (47-5). Both games were at the QUAD. Then, UA lost at the Fairgrounds to Georgia L (3-11). The Crimson Tide dug out from the Georgia loss with two ties on the road. One was against Mississippi A&M T (6-6) (now Mississippi State University) and the other against Georgia Tech T (0-0). The Georgia Tech game ended in a scoreless tie after time expired as Alabama drove to the Tech three-yard line.

Alabama then finished the season with victories over the Marion Military Institute Nov. 4 away-- W (35-0), Tulane (Nov 11) @ The QUAD, W (22-0). Against the tough Sewanee team (Nov 14), the opponents kicked a field goal with two minutes left to defeat the Tide L (3-0). UA finished Nov. 30 against Davidson @ Birmingham Fairgrounds (W (16-0).

1912 Coach —D. V. Graves; # 13

The 1912 Alabama Crimson Tide football team played its 20th overall and 17th season as a member of the Southern Intercollegiate

Athletic Association (SIAA). The team was led by head coach D. V. Graves, in his second year. They finished the season with a record of five wins, three losses, and one tie (5–3–1 overall, 3–3–1 in the SIAA).

Alabama opened the season with victories over the Marion Military Sept 28--W (QUAD 52-0), and Oct 5 Birmingham College --now Birmingham–Southern College— (QUAD W 62-0). They followed this with three consecutive SIAA losses to Oct 12 Georgia Tech L (3-20), Oct 18 Mississippi A&M (now Mississippi State University) L (0-7), and Oct 26 Georgia.

In the Georgia game, the Bulldogs ran a trick play in which they threw the ball to a receiver who was dressed as a waterboy, on the field, carrying a bucket. The play did not prove decisive, as Georgia fumbled the ball away soon after, but the Bulldogs won the game after they recovered a botched Alabama field goal and scored in the final minutes.

Alabama then finished the season with victories v Tulane Nov. 2 W 7-0), Ole Miss Nov. 9. (Bama beat Ole Miss 10–9 after the Rebels missed an extra point and two late field goals,) and Tennessee Nov. 28 W (6-0) Before the Tennessee game, UA tied Sewanee on Nov. 9 in what was the first Alabama football game played at Rickwood Field.

1913 Coach —D. V. Graves   # 13

The 1913 Alabama Crimson Tide football team played the Crimson Tide's 21st overall and 18th season as a member of the Southern Intercollegiate Athletic Association (SIAA). The team was led by head coach D. V. Graves, in his third year They finished the season with a record of six wins and three losses (6–3 overall, 4–3 in the SIAA).

Alabama began the season exceptionally strong, with three consecutive shutout victories over Howard (Sept 27) (now Samford University) W (27-0); on Oct 4, Birmingham College (now Birmingham–Southern College) W (81-0) and Oct 11 Clemson W (20-0). All three games were at the QUAD. The 81 points against Birmingham set a new school record.

Bama lost its first game of the season Oct 18, against Georgia L (0-20). After a pair of road victories against Oct 25 Tulane W (26-0) and Nov 1 Mississippi College W (21-3), Alabama finished its season with a win on Nov 14 at The QUAD against Tennessee W (6-0) and losses against Nov 9 Sewanee (L 7-10). and Nov. 27 Mississippi A&M (now Mississippi State University) L (0-7)

1914 Coach D. V. Graves   # 13

The 1914 Alabama Crimson Tide football team played the Crimson Tide's 22nd overall and 19th season as a member of the Southern Intercollegiate Athletic Association (SIAA). The team was led by head coach D. V. Graves, in his fourth and final year. Alabama always had tough and resilient teams right from its inception as a football power.

However, even with the fine four years that D. V. Graves put in at Alabama, they had yet to have a coach last more than four years, and unfortunately, Graves would not be the exception. Alabama from 1910 was a great football institution looking for a champion coach to move it forward deeper into the win column. The team finished the season with a record of five wins and four losses (5–4 overall, 4–3 in the SIAA).

Chapter 6 Football Coaches – Next Eight Years 1915-1922

Kelley & Scott were both well acclaimed coaches. Noojin was a place holder.

Year	Coach	Conference	Record	C-Record
1915	Thomas Kelley #14	SIAA	6-2-0	5-0-0
1916	Thomas Kelley	SIAA	6-3-0	4-3-0
1917	Thomas Kelley	SIAA	5-2-1	3-1-1
1918	B. L. Noojin	SIAA	* WWI No games played	
1919	Xen C. Scott #15	SIAA	8-1-1	6-1-0
1920	Xen C. Scott	SIAA	10-1-0	6-1-0
1921	Xen C. Scott	SIAA	5-4-2	2-4-2
1922	Xen C. Scott	SoCon	6-3-1	3-2-1

1915 Coach Thomas Kelley # 14

Alabama V Texas 1915

The 1915 Alabama Crimson Tide football team was becoming noticed. Newt Rockne was already playing college ball. Alabama as an institution wanted to make its mark in academics and also athletics. This was the Crimson Tide's 23rd overall and 20th season as a member of the Southern Intercollegiate Athletic Association (SIAA). The team was led by brand new head coach Thomas Kelley, *next page*, in his first year. Kelley was a get-it-done guy.

<<< Thomas Kelley
It was in 1915 that Alabama moved its on campus home games from the QUAD, where all on-campus home games had been played since 1892, to a new location, University Field (later renamed Denny Field in honor of school president George Denny in 1920).

To accommodate "excessive" fans, home games were also played at close-by Rickwood Field in Birmingham, Alabama. The Crimson Tide finished the first Kelley season with a 6-2 record. They were 5-0 in their own conference the SIAA. It was their best year ever in the conference. Maybe Kelley would be the magic.

William T. "Bully" Van de Graaff (left) was an all-everything player at UA. He punted, kicked, and played tackle. For his valiant and alert play, he was named Alabama's first All-American in 1915, when he was selected second-team All-America by Walter Camp. Walter Camp, as noted in this book was continuing to refine the rules of American Football while the game was being played across the US.

Alabama opened the season 5-0 with four shutout victories W (44-0; 67-0; 40-0; 16-0, and a 23-10 win over Sewanee, an unusual event for sure. The lineup for the losses had never lined up before: Howard, Birmingham, Mississippi,

Tulane, and Sewanee. What a rip for Alabama in 195. What a beginning to any season. Was Kelley a Rockne – to – be?

Against Mississippi College Van de Graaff kicked four field goals and missed a fifth from 54 yards out when the ball hit the upright.

The victory over Sewanee was the first for Alabama in that series since 1894. Alabama led the Tigers 10–0 at the half and continued to lead by that score after Sewanee marched inside the Alabama 20 four times in the third but came away with no points.

The Tigers finally scored a touchdown on the first play of the fourth quarter, then blocked a punt and kicked a field goal to tie the game 10–10. However, Van de Graff knocked the ball out of a Sewanee player's hand and ran it back 65 yards for a touchdown, then tacked on two more field goals as the Tide beat the Tigers for only the second time in 12 meetings.

Like most teams, Alabama had dreaded playing Sewanee, now they had beaten them in unquestionable terms/

Coach Kelley was hospitalized with typhoid fever two days prior to the Tulane game, and as a result, he missed the last five games of the season. Athletic director B. L. Noojin (the 1918 non-coach) and former quarterback Farley Moody then served as co-head coaches for the remainder of the season. They helped for sure to bring a good season in "good."

The Crimson ties lost in this period on Nov 6 to Georgia Teach away (L (7-21). They then lost to Texas on Nov 13, at Texas L (0-20). Finally, they regrouped and bet the tar out of Ole Miss at home W (53-0)

1916 Coach —Thomas Kelley; # 14

The 1916 Alabama Crimson Tide football team played in the 24th overall and 21st season as a member of the Southern Intercollegiate Athletic Association (SIAA). The team was led by head coach Thomas Kelly, in his second year, and played their home games at University Field in Tuscaloosa and at Rickwood Field in

Birmingham, Alabama. They finished the season with a record of six wins and three losses (6–3 overall, 4–3 in the SIAA).

Three brothers, Dexter, Walter, and Jack Hovater, were starters for the 1916 Tide. Alabama began its season with six consecutive victories Sept 30 Birmingham College W (13-0) at University Field, and Oct 7 Southern College (now combined as Birmingham–Southern College) W (80-0), Oct 14 Mississippi College W (13-7), Oct 21 away at Florida W (16-0), Oct 28 Ole Miss W (27-0) and Nov 4 Sewanee @ Rickwood Field W (7-6).

In those first six games, Alabama outscored their opponents by a margin of 156 to 13. Sewanee almost beat Alabama after making two interceptions and stopping the crimson Tide on 4th and goal at the 1, but Alabama scored late and kicked the extra point. Sewanee's kick had failed. UA got the victory over a really tough squad.

The defeat of Ole Miss was thanks to a late rally. However, the Crimson Tide were shut out in the final three games with losses on November 30 at Georgia Tech L 0-13), Nov 18 at Tulane L (0-33), and home in Rickwood Nov. 30 against Georgia L (0-3) to finish with an overall record of 6–3. Georgia Tech held Alabama to just two first downs and 60 yards of offense.

1917 Coach --Thomas Kelley; # 14

The 1917 Alabama Crimson Tide football team played its 25th overall and 22nd season as a member of the Southern Intercollegiate Athletic Association (SIAA). The team was led by head coach Thomas Kelly, in his third and final year. It played home games at University Field in Tuscaloosa, as well as Rickwood Field in Birmingham and also at Soldiers' Field in Montgomery, Alabama. It depended on the size of the anticipated crowd. They finished the season with a record of five wins, two losses and one tie (5–2–1 overall, 3–1–1 in the SIAA).

Alabama opened its season with an Oct. 3 opener against the "Second Ambulance Company of Ohio." It was played at Soldiers Field in Montgomery and was the only game the Crimson Tide ever played at that location. The 2nd Amb. Co., part of the 37th Division training in Montgomery, only got two first downs in the whole game.

Alabama had another great season start with four consecutive, shutout victories over the Second Ambulance Company W (7-0), Oct 12 at home -- Marion Military Institute W (13-0), Oct 20, at home, Mississippi College W 46-0), and Oct. 26 Ole Miss W (64-0). In those four games, Alabama outscored their opponents by a margin of 130 to 0.

After a Nov 3 tie against Sewanee T (3-3), and a loss on Nov 10 to Vanderbilt L (2-7) at Rickwood Field, Alabama won their only road game on Nov. 17 at Kentucky W (27-0).

In the season finale, Camp Gordon, the second military opponent Alabama faced as the country mobilized for World War I, beat the Tide L (19–6). Camp Gordon had several players with college experience, including Adrian Van de Graaff, formerly of Alabama.

Joe Sewell, who went on to a Hall of Fame baseball career with the Cleveland Indians and New York Yankees, lettered in football for Alabama in 1917, 1918 and 1919.

1918 Coach —B. L. Noojin; #15 No Season

The 1918 Alabama Crimson Tide football team (variously "Alabama", "UA" or "Bama") was prepared to represent the University of Alabama in the 1918 college football season. However, the season was canceled due to the effects of World War I.

B. L. Noojin had been expected to serve as head coach for the season. Because he was named, even though he never coached he is listed as coach # 15. University officials canceled the season as a result of multiple opponents canceling their contests against Alabama and a military policy that only allowed for the team to practice for less than one hour per week. World War I was the biggest thing on anybody's mind at the time.

Alabama also did not field a team in 1898 due to campus rules prohibiting athletic teams from traveling off campus to compete and in 1943 due to the effects of World War II.

In December 1917, Alabama had already released its tentative schedule for the 1918 season. At that time, the Crimson Tide were scheduled to open the season against Kentucky in Tuscaloosa and play Vanderbilt at Dudley Field. In the February that followed, the official schedule was released that featured four games in Tuscaloosa, two in Birmingham and one on the road.

Date	Opponent	Site
October 5	Birmingham	University Field
October 11	Marion Military	University Field
October 26	Howard	University Field
November 2	Sewanee	Rickwood Field
November 9	Vanderbilt	Rickwood Field
November 16	LSU	State Field • Baton Rouge, LA
November 28	Mississippi A&M	University Field

1919 Coach —Xen C. Scott; #16

The 1919 Alabama Crimson Tide football team played its 26th overall and 23rd season as a member of the Southern Intercollegiate Athletic Association (SIAA). The team was led by head coach Xen C. Scott, in his first year. They continued to play home games at University Field in Tuscaloosa and at Rickwood Field in Birmingham, Alabama.

They finished the season with a great record of eight wins and one loss (8–1 overall, 6–1 in the SIAA). UA won eight games in a season for the very first time, and was awarded a share of the SIAA title by a number of groups.

This was the year after not fielding a team for the 1918 season because of World War I. In May 1919 Xen C. Scott was hired to serve as head coach of the Head Coach of The Crimson Tide.

Coach Xen C. Scott

Alabama then opened the season with four consecutive shutout victories at University Field in Tuscaloosa. After Scott defeated Birmingham–Southern on October 4 in his debut as Crimson Tide head coach (17-0), the next week on October 11, he defeated Ole Miss W (49-0) for his first SIAA victory.

Scott may over time be inserted in the history books as one of Alabama's immortals. His life ended too soon.

After a pair of blowout victories over both Howard on October 18 and the Marion Military Institute on October 24, on November 1, Alabama defeated Sewanee 40–0 in what was the most anticipated game of the season at Rickwood Field.

After the Sewanee win, Alabama traveled to Nashville on Nov. 8, where they lost their only game of the season against Vanderbilt L (12-16). After the loss, the Crimson Tide rebounded with wins on at Nov. 15 at LSU W (23-0) and Georgia on Nov. 22 W (6-0), and at Birmingham over Mississippi A&M on Nov. 27 (Thanksgiving) to close the season W (14-6).

After the departure of Thomas Kelley as head coach of the Crimson Tide following their 1917 season, then athletic director B. L. Noojin was chosen as his successor. However, as previously noted, Noojin never led the team as head coach since the 1918 season was canceled due to the effects of World War I.

When football was brought back for the next season, Xen C. Scott was hired to serve as head coach in May 1919. Scott was not a newbie and he had coaching experience as head coach of the Cleveland Naval Reserve team that had upset the national champion Pittsburgh Panthers to close their 1918 season. There were great expectations for Scott.

Scott had also previously served as head coach for both Western Reserve University (1910) and the Case Institute of Technology (1911–1913) in Cleveland. He opened his first fall practice on September 1. Ten players from previous Alabama squads returned including stalwarts T. L. Brown, Jack Hovater, Walter E. Hovater, Ralph Lee Jones, E. B. Lenoir, Emmet Noland, J. T. O'Connor, Isaac Rogers, Tram Sessions and Riggs Stephenson.

After two weeks of practice, Scott divided the players into four teams to determine starting line-ups. At his time, Scott, also did not utilize a quarterback, but instead would simply snap the ball directly to the runner.

Before game preparation began for their game against Birmingham–Southern, Isaac Rogers was selected as team captain for the season by the returning lettermen on September 25. Rogers was previously elected to serve as team captain for the 1918 season that was cancelled. It was expected to be a great season and it was—despite no football at all the prior year.

A look at a few of the games

Alabama opened the 1919 season against Birmingham–Southern and shutout the Panthers in the first all-time game between the schools. The opening kickoff was at 1:30 and was played in a newly expanded University Field (capacity 2000) with seating for 800 spectators. Charles Bartlett scored the final points of the game with his fourth quarter touchdown that made the final score 27–0.

In their second game, Alabama shutout their SIAA rival, the Ole Miss Rebels 49–0 at Tuscaloosa. After being held scoreless for the first ten minutes, Alabama scored their first touchdown on Mullie Lenoir run late in the quarter. A pair of second quarter touchdown runs from first Riggs Stephenson and then by Charles Bartlett that made the halftime score 18–0. The victory improved Alabama's all-time record against Ole Miss to 9–2–

In what was the most anticipated game of the season, the entire University population and educators traveled to Birmingham for their game against Sewanee. In the game, Alabama defeated the Tigers 40–0 at Rickwood Field, in the largest margin of victory ever for Alabama over Sewanee to date. UA took an early 7–0 lead in the first quarter on a 15-yard Riggs Stephenson touchdown run and then extended it to 14–0 at halftime on a 45-yard Walter E. Hovater touchdown run in the second. The Crimson Tide then closed the game with four Mullie Lenoir touchdown runs, two in the third and two in the fourth quarter. The victory improved Alabama's all-time record against Sewanee to 3–9–2. Sewanee always came ready to play.

In its final game of the season, Alabama defeated the Mississippi A&M (now known as Mississippi State University) Aggies 14–6 on Thanksgiving at Rickwood Field. After a scoreless first half, H. S. Little scored the Aggies' only points of the game with his 80-yard kickoff return that opened the third quarter. Alabama then took the lead later in the third on a short Riggs Stephenson touchdown run.

They then made the final score 14–6 in the fourth after T. L. Brown blocked an A&M punt that was recovered by Isaac Rogers in the end zone for a touchdown. The victory improved Alabama's record against Mississippi A&M to 7–4–1. It was a great season for Alabama. First-year coach Scott had surely proven his worth to the Crimson Tide.

1920 Coach Xen C. Scott; #16

The 1920 Alabama Crimson Tide football team played its 27th overall and 24th season as a member of the Southern Intercollegiate Athletic Association (SIAA). The team was led by head coach Xen C. Scott, in his second year, and played their home games at University/Denny Field in Tuscaloosa and at Rickwood Field in Birmingham, Alabama. They finished the season with a phenomenal record of ten wins and one loss (10–1 overall, 6–1 in the SIAA).

This was the first ten-win season in the history of Alabama football. Starting with Coach Scott, the 16th Alabama coach every Alabama coach has won ten games in a season at least once, except for Jennings B. Whitworth, the 20th coach.

Alabama opened the season tough with six consecutive shutout victories. On Sept 25, it was the Southern Military Academy W (59-0), On Oct. 2, Marion Military W (49-0), On Oct. 9, Birmingham–Southern W (45-0), On Oct 16, Mississippi College W (57-0), On Oct. 23, Howard W (33-0), and Oct 30, Sewanee W (21-0). All six games were played at home.

In their seventh game against Vanderbilt on November 6, Alabama allowed its first touchdown of the season, but still won 14–7 after the Commodores threw an interception on a fourth and goal from the three-yard line in the fourth quarter.

After their shutout victory on Nov. 11, over LSU on what was the first homecoming game played at Alabama, the Crimson Tide lost their only game of the season on November 20 at Atlanta against Georgia L (14-21) in a nail biter. The Bulldogs did not score on offense but won 21–14 after touchdowns were scored on a fumble return, a blocked punt return and a blocked field goal return.

The loss snapped Alabama's then school-record 11-game winning streak. Alabama won tits final two games Nov. 25 against Mississippi A&M (24-7) and November 27 in Cleveland at Case W (40-0). UA finished a great season 10–1.

After a well-done 8–1 campaign in Scott's first season as head coach at Alabama, the Crimson Tide were viewed as a potential championship team by the media as they entered the 1920 season.

During the week of September 12, Alabama held its first scrimmages of the season. Scott thought his team was much "heavier" than in the previous year. As he did the first year, he again divided the squad into initial first and second teams.

His "A" squad was coached by Scott and the "B" squad was coached by athletic director Charles A. Bernier. Prior to their opening game against the Southern Military Academy on September 23, Scott announced his starting lineup for the 1920 season. Additionally, at that time, right guard Sidney Johnston was selected as season captain by his teammates.

Southern Military

The opening game was a 59–0 shutout over the Southern Military Academy (SMA). It was the only all-time game between the schools at Tuscaloosa. After a slow start that saw Alabama only up by a touchdown after the first quarter, the Crimson Tide scored an additional eight touchdowns and won the game going away.

Mullie Lenoir scored five and both Luke Sewell and Riggs Stephenson scored a pair of touchdowns in the victory. Defensively, the Crimson Tide did not allow SMA a single first down in the game.

Sewanee

In what was the most anticipated game of the season to that point, Alabama defeated the always-tough Sewanee Tigers 21–0 at Rickwood Field. In the first quarter, Alabama stopped a Sewanee scoring opportunity when J. T. O'Connor intercepted a Tigers' pass in the end zone. With the game, scoreless, the Crimson Tide then took a 7–0 lead in the second quarter after Riggs Stephenson scored on a 12-yard run.

In the third, Luke Sewell threw a long touchdown pass of 45-yards to Mullie Lenoir that extended their lead to 14–0 In the final period, Stephenson had a 60-yard interception return for a touchdown called back on a penalty, but then made the final score 21–0 with a long touchdown run on the drive that ensued.

In the game, Stephenson gained 286 and Lenoir gained 212 total yards. Alabama was also heavily penalized throughout the game that resulted in touchdown runs of 65 and 35-yards by Lenoir being nullified. The victory improved Alabama's all-time record against Sewanee to 4–9–2.

Vanderbilt:

As they entered their game against Alabama, Vanderbilt had played seven consecutive undefeated teams. The game was played at Birmingham. The University called a holiday and the entire school made the trip to Rickwood and saw Alabama defeat the Commodores 14–7 for their first victory over Vanderbilt in school history. Scott was a great coach for sure.

After a scoreless first, Alabama took a 14–0 second quarter lead on touchdown runs of four-yards by Riggs Stephenson and one-yard by Mullie Lenoir. Vanderbilt then responded with a short Oliver Kuhn touchdown pass to Jess Neely that made the final score 14–7. The victory improved Alabama's all-time record against Vanderbilt to 1–5.

1921 Coach Xen C. Scott #16

The 1921 Alabama Crimson Tide football team played the 28th overall and 25th season as a member of the Southern Intercollegiate Athletic Association (SIAA). The team was led by head coach Xen C. Scott, in his third year, and played their home games at Denny Field in Tuscaloosa and at Rickwood Field in Birmingham, Alabama. They finished the season with a record of five wins, four losses and two ties (5–4–2 overall, 2–4–2 in the SIAA).

In the opener on Sept. 24, Alabama spotted Howard a 14–0 first-quarter lead before they rallied and won, W (34–14). After a victory over Spring Hill on Oct. 1 in their second game W (27-7), the Crimson Tide outscored Marion Military Institute on Oct. 8, W (55-0) and Bryson College on Oct. 12 W (95-0) by a combined 150–0.

It was another great start 4–0 to open the season. The fast start did not translate to winning much more for the remainder of the season as UA lost four of its next five games.

In their first Rickwood Field game of the season on Oct 22, the Crimson Tide was shut out by Sewanee L (0-17) and they followed this loss with a tie-on Oct. 29 against LSU T (7-7) in their first road game of the season at New Orleans. Alabama returned to Rickwood on Nov. 5 for its next game, in which they were shut out by Vanderbilt L (0-14), followed by a loss on November 11 to Florida L (2-9) at Denny Field in Tuscaloosa and then on Nov 19 to Georgia L (0-22) at Atlanta.

After this team finally came close to another win on Nov. 24 but it was not to be. Instead, they tied Mississippi A&M T (7-7) in their final home game of the year. The Crimson Tide did all it could on December 3 at Tulane claiming an upset W (14-7). This prevented their first losing season since 1903.

As they had lost several starters from the previous season, Alabama had the normal season-startup concerns but they got off nonetheless to a spectacular start but could not sustain it for the full season.

After their October loss to Sewanee, Alabama scrimmaged both Cullman High School and Tuscaloosa High School as part of their preparation for their first road game of the season. At Heinemann Park in New Orleans, the best they could do was tie LSU T (7–7), when the Tigers scored a late touchdown in the fourth quarter.

On homecoming in Tuscaloosa, the Florida Gators upset the Crimson Tide 9–2 at Denny Field. Florida took a 6–0 lead on a 12-yard Ark Newton run in the first quarter. After a scoreless second, Alabama scored their only points in the third after L. O. Wesley blocked a Newton punt that was recovered by Newton for a safety.

The Gators then made the final score 9–2 on a 20-yard Newton field goal in the fourth quarter. The loss brought Alabama's all-time record against Florida to 1–1.

1922 Coach Xen C. Scott; #16

The 1922 Alabama Crimson Tide football team played its 29th overall and 1st season as a member of the Southern Conference (SoCon). No more SIAA for Alabama.

For the fourth and his final head coaching year, the team was led by Xen C. Scott. UA played home games at Denny Field in Tuscaloosa, Rickwood Field in Birmingham and the Cramton Bowl in Montgomery, Alabama. They finished the season with a record of six wins, three losses and one tie (6–3–1 overall, 3–2–1 in the SoCon).

So, the 1922 season marked the first for the Crimson Tide as a member of the SoCon, as Alabama was one of the twenty members of the Southern Intercollegiate Athletic Association that left the Association to form the SoCon following the 1921 season.

On September 30, Alabama opened its season with a whopping W (110–0) victory over an out-classed Marion Military Institute. This still stands as the school record for largest margin of victory and as the Crimson Tide's only 100-point game. After a victory over Oglethorpe on Oct 7 W (41-0), Alabama went winless for the next three games. The team lost on October 14 to Georgia Tech L (7-33) and on Oct. 28 at Texas L (10-9). These two games were interspersed with an Oct. 21 tie against Sewanee T (7-7). Anything other than a loss at Sewanee for years was considered a victory.

With a record of 2–2–1, the Crimson Tide played undefeated Penn, an Eastern Powerhouse for years. On November 4. UA came into the game clear underdogs but they must have liked the air in Philadelphia's Franklin Field as they chewed up a few nails before the game for iron-like strength and they bullied the Quakers, sort of, for four quarters by a few nails W (9-7). This was their first encounter with the always tough Penn Quakers.

The following game has been determined by the pundits to be one of the most significand football games in Crimson Tide History.

We're wrapping up the great coach Xen Scott's career here so let's talk about this fine game by UA. Scott was one heck of a great coach.

UA V The Penn Quakers – A Great Game!

OK Let's look a bit deeper into one of the greatest UA games of all time. 1922—Alabama v Pennsylvania – After the game the crowds were saying "These Southern Boys Really Can Play!" What a treat to the ears of those rooting for Alabama Football.

After starting the 1922 season 2-2-1, the Crimson Tide traveled to Philadelphia, Pennsylvania on November 4 to take on the Penn Quakers. In the 1920s, the Ivy League was considered the best college football in the country.

Penn, along with Harvard, Princeton, and Yale, were the class of the game. Southern football was not respected, but Xen Scott and the Tide were looking to change that impression.

Alabama v Penn 1922

Alabama was a big underdog going into the game, having gone 0-2-1 in their last three games. Penn was coming off a big win over Navy. Legendary sportswriter Grantland Rice famously predicted that Penn would easily beat the Tide, 21-0. Rice and the rest of the country were wrong, as Alabama used a late sack to secure a 9-7 victory over coach John Heisman's Quakers. Yes, that's Heisman as in the Heisman "trophy!" What a game!

Alabama's quarterback Charles Bartlett led the drive that resulted in the only touchdown for the Tide and would later receive an All-American honorable mention. After defeating the Quakers, Alabama would return home the following week and cruise to a 47-3 win over the LSU Tigers. The Crimson Tide finished the 1922 season with a 6-3-1 record. They had beaten the best of the best.

This game, three seasons before the famed Rose Bowl victory over Washington, was an early claim to the legitimacy of Southern football teams.

A year earlier it hadn't seemed possible that a team that finished in the middle of the Southern Conference could beat one of the great old Ivy League teams, but that's exactly what the Tide had done.

The Crimson Tide then completed its season as previously noted with a homecoming win W (47-3) on November 10 over LSU; a loss L (0-6) at Kentucky on November 18, and a win (10-6) over Georgia in Alabama's first game at the Cramton Bowl in Montgomery AL. UA garnered another win on November 30 over Mississippi A&M W (59-0) to close a fine season for Coach Scott.

Coach Scott deserves a few medals

Xen Scott was a great coach. He had a very tough personal year in 1922. He coached the 1922 season while dying of oral cancer. Today's cures were unavailable. He spent the whole season suffering from the effects of his illness, losing weight, barely able to speak, coaching against the advice of a doctor who had told him to quit immediately.

He loved the team and the game of football. He was bedridden except when attending practices and games. After the Oglethorpe game, Scott tendered his resignation, effective at the end of the season. Scott died in April 1924 at age 41. He was clearly one of the good ones in football and in life. With today's modern medicine, we all know that he would have been with us for many more years.

Chapter 7 Coach Wallace Wade 1923-1930

Wallace Wade was a highly competitive Rockne Era coach

Year	Coach	Conference	Record	SoCon
1923	Wallace Wade #17	SoCon	7-2-0	4-1-1
1924	Wallace Wade	SoCon	8-1-0	5-0-0
1925	Wallace Wade*	SoCon	10-0-0	7-0-0
1926	Wallace Wade*	SoCon	9-0-1	8-0-0
1927	Wallace Wade	SoCon	5-4-1	3-4-1
1928	Wallace Wade	SoCon	6-3-0	6-2-0
1929	Wallace Wade	SoCon	6-3-0	4-3-0
1930	Wallace Wade*	SoCon	10-0-0	8-0-0

* National Championship

Tide Legend Coach Wallace Wade

Wallace Wade Did not know he was immortal!

As we discussed in the 30 years of UA football before this chapter on Wallace Wade, in the formative years of college football, there were no Wallace Wades' who would do well and stay for Alabama! It actually took Alabama tracking down and finding the one and only Wallace Wade. Could UA have gotten a sniff of future greatness from the future?

It was tough to get a coach to take a team for much more than a year in the 1920's and before. Looking back, guys like you and me know intrinsically that continuity adds so much to the game that despite its great coaches before 1924, and its great players, Alabama, like all great football teams, needed a sense of continuity to begin continued greatness. Of course, greatness must first be established before greatness can flow through the years.

Alabama as an institution and its supporters before expectations ran rampant, also needed a modicum of trust so that once a good coach came along, the fan arrows would not kill him before he could ever become great for everybody as well as the institution.

Thankfully, now that we are moving to Wade Wallace and a number of great coaching years, the moon must have come into the seventh house and perhaps Jupiter had just aligned with Mars, and this happening had become the dawning of Wallace Wade as a regular guy thinking better than regular things—a guy who could begin a trek beyond the stars

The people of 1922 needed to demand to know how to get a coach at Alabama who could deliver the goods to the institution, the players, and the fans. I think that UA brought the right guy in to fill the bill.

Writings About Wallace Wade

Author Lewis Bolling wrote a wonderful book about Alabama Coach Wallace Wade in 2006. He titled it: Championship Years at Alabama and Duke.

If you like great historical sports book, especially about Alabama, this is recognized as a great read. When I examined the book, it was selling for $25.00 and readily available. One thing about a point in time history books, such as Wallace Wade up to 2006, the history rarely changes so this book is as current today as when it was written. Let's learn a bit of Wallace Wade from this book:

Great UA Coach Wallace Wade is without question one of the greatest college football coaches in the history of the game. He won three national championships at Alabama and took Duke to two Rose Bowls. His Alabama team won what is considered to be the most important victory in the history of southern football, when they defeated Washington in the 1926 Rose Bowl.

He is the man who established the tradition of outstanding football at Alabama, and he is also credited with bringing big-time college football to the state of North Carolina with his powerhouse Duke teams of the 1930s and 1940s. The Wade biography chronicles the life of Wallace Wade's life in football, and also his participation in two world wars and his time as commissioner of the Southern Conference.

"Wallace Wade, Alabama's first 'Bear' three decades before Bear Bryant, is one of the most important and least known figures in the history of college football. Lewis Bowling's biography brings him out of the shadows for the first time and puts clothes on a ghost. This book should have enormous appeal to the fans of Duke, Alabama, and every other school where college football is a tradition."

— Allen Barra, author of The Last Coach—A Life of Paul "Bear" Bryant

"The narrative is enlivened with numerous quotes from Wade and contemporary sources. Wade's decision to leave a championship program at Alabama for the challenge of building the football program at Duke is particularly well documented and fascinating... Summing up: Recommended." — CHOICE Magazine

1923 Coach Wallace Wade #17

The 1923 Alabama Crimson Tide football team played its 30th overall and 2nd season as a member of the Southern Conference (SoCon). The team was led by head coach Wallace Wade, in his first year. Home games were played at Denny Field in Tuscaloosa; at Rickwood Field in Birmingham; and at the Cramton Bowl in Montgomery, Alabama. They finished the season with a record of seven wins, two losses and one tie (7–2–1 overall, 4–1–1 in the SoCon).

Alabama opened its 1923 season September 29 v Union University at Denny Field, and defeated the Bulldogs W (12–0) in what was Wallace Wade's first game as head coach of the Crimson Tide. In a game dominated by both defenses, Alabama did not score any points until the fourth quarter. Pooley Hubert scored first on a one-yard run and was followed by a six-yard Allen Graham MacCartee touchdown pass to Ben Hudson with only 00:15 left in the game. The victory brought Alabama's all-time record against Union to 2–0.

<<< Coach Wade -- Left

Alabama opened conference play against Ole Miss on Oct 6, and defeated the Rebels 56–0 at Denny Field. The Crimson Tide scored eight touchdowns in the contest.

1923 marked the first season for new head coach Wallace Wade, a former assistant at Vanderbilt. One year after Alabama's triumphal trip to Penn, the Tide went on another northeast road trip with a different outcome, losing to Syracuse on Oct 13 L (0-13).

The Sewanee game played on Oct 20, was scoreless until the last two minutes, when Johnny Mack Brown intercepted a pass, giving the ball to Alabama at the Tiger 48. Pooley Hubert scored with seconds left and Sewanee had time to run only two plays before the game ended W (7-0).

On October 27, UA beat Spring Hill at Monroe Park in Mobile, AL W (59–0). Against Georgia Tech on Nov 3, Alabama was very lucky to escape with a T (0–0) tie. Tech had 18 first downs to none for Alabama, and the Tide never advanced the ball beyond its own 27-yard line. A driving rain and sixteen punts from Grant Gillis helped Bama to hold Tech scoreless. Tech drives stalled on the Alabama 2, 8, and 11-yard lines.

On Nov. 10   UA, defeated Kentucky in a close match at Denny Field W (16–8). On November 16, in the Cramton Bowl at home, UA defeated LSU W (30–3). Then, on November 24 against Georgia, UA prevailed W 36–0.

A season-ending l (6-16) upset loss on Nov. 29 to coach James Van Fleet's Florida Gators cost coach Wade and the Tide the Southern Conference championship.

1924 Coach Wallace Wade #17

1924 Alabama Crimson Tide football team played its 31st overall and 3rd season as a member of the Southern Conference (SoCon). The team was led by head coach Wallace Wade, in his second year, and played their home games at Denny Field in Tuscaloosa, at Rickwood Field in Birmingham and at the Cramton Bowl in Montgomery, Alabama. They finished the season with a record of eight wins and one loss (8–1 overall, 5–0 in the SoCon) and as Southern Conference champions.

The season opener was on September 27 against Union (TN), played at Denny Field in Tuscaloosa, AL. UA gained a nice win W (55–0). On October 4 at Furman played in Manly Field, Greenville, SC. UA again prevailed W (20–0). Already having a great season, on October 11, Mississippi College came to Denny Field and were soundly defeated W (51–0). Sewanee, always tough from the first game played against them, were tough again on October 18 at

Rickwood Field in Birmingham, AL. UA played a fine game for a victory W (14–0).

The 1924 Alabama Crimson Tide football team

On October 25, UA traveled to Grant Field in Atlanta to win a nice game against Georgia Tech W (14–0). It appeared Wade Wallace's team was unstoppable. At the Crampton Bowl in Montgomery, UA defeated Ole Miss on Nov.1 W 61–0. On Nov. 8, Kentucky took a licking from the Crimson Tide at Denny Field in Tuscaloosa W (42–7). A tough Centre team played Alabama on November 15 at Rickwood Field in Birmingham and defeated the Crimson Tide L (0-17). It was the Tide's only loss of the season.

In the Season Finale on November 27, Georgia's Bulldogs were no match for UA as the Crimson Tide gained its eighth victory of the year W (33-0).

Some 1924 Game Highlights

The Crimson Tide started its with season with seven consecutive victories, and was only really challenged once—in the Georgia Tech game. In the 14-0 victory over Georgia Tech, Tech drove the ball to the Alabama 6 in the third with a chance to tie the game up but was stopped on 4th and 1. Another Tide TD in the fourth clinched the victory.

Alabama lost their only game of the season to Centre at Rickwood Field. Alabama would not lose another game until the 1927 season. Centre quarterback Herb Covington overwhelmed all opponents that year and was named to the 1924 College Football All-America Team.

After its season finale victory over Georgia a week after its loss to Centre, Alabama secured its first SoCon championship. "Two TD passes by Hubert, two field goals by Compton and a 65-yard interception return for a TD by Brown sewed up the contest for UA.

1925 Coach Wallace Wade #17

The 1925 Alabama Crimson Tide football team played its 32nd overall and 4th season as a member of the Southern Conference (SoCon).

1925 National Champions—Alabama Crimson Tide

The team was led by head coach Wallace Wade, in his third year. Home games were played at Denny Field in Tuscaloosa; at Rickwood Field in Birmingham; and at the Cramton Bowl in

Montgomery, Alabama. The Crimson Tide finished this season with its first ever perfect record (10–0 overall, 7–0 in the SoCon), as Southern Conference champions and as national champions after they defeated Washington in the Rose Bowl. This was Alabama's first national championship claimed of 16 total. Four are unclaimed.

1925 was right in the middle of the Knute Rockne era. Rockne had led ND to its first championship with the infamous Four Horsemen in 1924 and so it was a great honor for Wallace Wade to win the National Championship in the Rockne Era. College Football was really taking off and Wallace Wade was ready to lead the Crimson Tide to victory after victory. He sure did.

The Crimson Tide entered the 1925 season as the defending Southern Conference champions after finishing the 1924 season with an 8–1 record. Alabama would then go on and shutout all but one of their regular season opponents while gaining a second consecutive Southern Conference championship.

UA then accepted an invitation to participate as the first Southern team in the annual Rose Bowl Game. In this game, UA defeated Washington 20–19. This was a huge victory in Crimson Tide history. It subsequently has been recognized as one of the most important games not just for Alabama but for Southern football history. It was deemed "the game that changed the South."

Alabama as an institution was ready to win all the time. Xen Scott had gotten UA moving in that direction. Wallace Wade was the perfect coach to continue the UA winning tradition. He remembered that in the prior year, the Tide had been upset by Centre. The University did not want something like that to happen again. So, Former center and alumnus Shorty Propst was hired to the coaching staff to help the team perform even better.

There was no summer practice other than unofficial. The regular season began on September 26 against Union University from Tennessee at Denny Field W (53–0). On Oct. 2, Birmingham–Southern played at Denny Field. UA prevailed W (50–7). On Oct. 10, The Tide traveled to LSU at Tiger Stadium in Baton Rouge, LA for the traditional rivalry W (42–0). Then, on Oct. 17, UA picked off a tough Sewanee Team at Rickwood Field W (27–0)

UA traveled to Georgia Tech in Atlanta on Oct 24 and won a nail biter W 7-0). On October 31, it was Mississippi A&M at Denny Field in another one too close for the faint of heart in the middle of an undefeated season, W (6-0) On November 7, Kentucky played UA at Rickwood Field in Birmingham, and were shut out W (31–0). Next was Florida   in on Nov 14 in the Cramton Bowl W (34–0). On Nov. 26, The Georgia Bulldogs came to Rickwood Field in the UA season finale W (27-0).

The season topper was played in Pasadena California as UA engaged in its first Rose Bowl on January 1, 1926 for the National Championship. UA toughed it out and beat Washington in a nail-biter (20-19). UA completed a 10-0 season and won the National Championship before 55,000

January 1, 1926 Rose Bowl

The UA season was extended when Alabama received an invitation to play in the Rose Bowl. It was the school's first bowl game ever and the first time any southern team had ever been invited to play in what then was college football's only bowl game... the granddaddy of them all. The Washington Huskies were heavy favorites.

As the game progressed it did not look good for the Crimson Tide but the team kept battling. Washington's star halfback George Wilson intercepted a pass in the first quarter and then led his team 63 yards for a touchdown and a 6–0 lead. In the second quarter Wilson ran for 36 yards and then threw a 22-yard touchdown pass, and Washington went up 12–0. Both extra point tries failed.

At the half, coach Wade changed his game style. Pooley Hubert would now run more often. In the third quarter Alabama struck finally scored. A short punt set up them up on Huskies' 42 and Alabama quickly capitalized, Hubert scored on a 1-yard run to make the score 12–7. The Huskies couldn't move the ball without Wilson, who had injured his ribs in the first half.

Shortly thereafter Hubert hit Brown on a 59-yard touchdown pass and suddenly Alabama led 14–12. Washington fumbled in their next possession and the Crimson Tide recovered at the Husky 30.

Hubert found Brown for another touchdown pass on the very next play. The extra point failed, but Alabama still led 20–12. The Tide scored three touchdowns in seven minutes of clock time. Wilson was able to return to the Huskies lineup in the fourth quarter and he threw a late touchdown pass, but the two missed extra points in the first half proved decisive, and Alabama won this exciting match 20–19.

It was Alabama's first real perfect season in school history. (The school was undefeated in 1897 when the Tide played and won its only game.) Johnny Mack Brown and Pooley Hube The NCAA retroactively deemed Alabama to be the consensus "national champion" for 1925 due to its selection by a majority of authorities. who were later inducted into the College Football Hall of Fame. Brown capitalized on his Rose Bowl exposure in southern California by signing a motion picture contract with MGM and beginning a 40-year career in the movies.

Brown played mostly in Westerns. He was very handsome and his athleticism gave him a powerful physique. He was once the athlete portrayed on Wheaties cereal boxes. Soon after he began his movie career, in1927 in Hollywood, he played a role as silent film star Mary Pickford's love interest in her first talkie Coquette (1929, for which Pickford won an Oscar.

1926 Rose Bowl "The Game That Changed the South"

This is recognized as one of greatest games ever played by Alabama

The 1926 Rose Bowl is called "the game that changed the South" because it was the first bowl game appearance of the Alabama Crimson Tide. Alabama's opponents in their very first Rose Bowl appearance were the Washington Huskies. Alabama won the game 20 – 19 and earned its very first national championship.

1926 Coach Wallace Wade #17

The 1926 Alabama Crimson Tide football team played its 33rd overall and 5th season as a member of the Southern Conference (SoCon). The team was led by highly successful head coach Wallace Wade, in his fourth year. The team played its home games at Denny Field in Tuscaloosa, at Rickwood Field in Birmingham and at the Cramton Bowl in Montgomery, Alabama.

Alabama finished the season with a record of nine wins, zero losses and one tie (9–0–1 overall, 8–0 in the SoCon), as Southern Conference champions.

It was another great season—the second in a row. They tied undefeated Stanford in the Rose Bowl. The 1926 Alabama team was retroactively named as the 1926 national champion by Berryman QPRS, Billingsley Report, College Football Researchers Association, and Poling System, and as a co-national champion by the Helms Athletic Foundation and National Championship Foundation. Back then, a consensus of various sources determined National Championships.

In 1925, the team lost many fine starters from graduation. They had just ten lettermen to start the season. Key players such as Pooley Hubert, Johnny Mack Brown, Bill Buckler and other stars from the 1925 team were not part of the 1926 squad. Yet, with Alabama Pride, and Coach Wallace Ward's expert coaching, the mostly new squad gained what was necessary to carry on Alabama's winning tradition.

1927 Coach Wallace Wade #17

The 1927 Alabama Crimson Tide football team (played its 34th overall and 6th season as a member of the Southern Conference (SoCon). The team was led by head coach Wallace Wade, in his fifth year, The Tide played their home games at Denny Field in Tuscaloosa, at Rickwood Field and Legion Field in Birmingham and at the Cramton Bowl in Montgomery, Alabama. In what one would call a rebuilding year after two national championship titles in a row, they finished the season with a record of five wins, four losses and one tie (5–4–1 overall, 3–4–1 in the SoCon).

1927 TEAM—Top Row: Patton, Holm, McDonald, Bowdoin, Brosfield, Pickhard, Payne, Hurt, Garrett, E. Smith, Partlow, Manager.   Third Row: Spetz., Skidmore, Douglas, M. Smith, Pearce, Dye, Eberdt, Black, Starling, Robinson.   Second Row: Rogers, Dobbs, Hogler, Dismukes, Griffin, Sailor, McClintock, Brown, (Red) Hamner. Bottom Row: Fowler, Newton, Hicks, B. Brown, Wallace Wade, Jr., Ellis, Holder, Tuck, Bowman.

1927 Alabama Football Team

1928 Coach Wallace Wade #17

The 1928 Alabama Crimson Tide football team played its 35th overall and 7th season as a member of the Southern Conference (SoCon). The team was led by head coach Wallace Wade, in his sixth year. It played its home games at Denny Field in Tuscaloosa, at Legion Field in Birmingham and at the Cramton Bowl in Montgomery, Alabama. They finished the season with a record of six wins and three losses (6–3 overall, 6–2 in the SoCon).

1929 Coach Wallace Wade #17

The 1929 Alabama Crimson Tide football team played its 36th overall and 8th season as a member of the Southern Conference (SoCon). The team was led by head coach Wallace Wade, in his seventh year. It played its home games at Denny Stadium in Tuscaloosa, at Legion Field in Birmingham and at the Cramton Bowl in Montgomery, Alabama. The team finished the season with a record of six wins and three losses (6–3 overall, 4–3 in the SoCon).

1930 Coach Wallace Wade #17

The 1930 Alabama Crimson Tide football team played in its 37th overall and 9th season as a member of the Southern Conference (SoCon). The team was led by head coach Wallace Wade, in his eighth and final year. They played home games at Denny Stadium in Tuscaloosa, at Legion Field in Birmingham, and at the Cramton Bowl in Montgomery, Alabama. They finished the season with a perfect record (10–0 overall, 8–0 in the SoCon), as Southern Conference champions and as national champions after they defeated Washington State in the Rose Bowl. This was Coach Wade's third national championship

National Champion 1930 Alabama Crimson Tide Coach Wallace Wade

Wade resignation

After eight seasons as Alabama's head coach, on April 1, 1930, Wallace Wade announced he would resign his position at the conclusion of the 1930 season to take the same position with Duke. When he made his announcement, Wade did not give a reason for his departure other than that his contract was set to expire on September 1, 1931.

The rumors were that Wade himself, friends and former players attributed his resignation to criticism he received during the 1927, 1928, and 1929 seasons, as well as his desire to return to a private university. Wallace Wade completed his Alabama tenure with a 61–13–3 record (.812). He was an outstanding coach as wee many in Alabama history. He won four conference titles, and three national championships. He also coached several star players as well. Wade followed up his success at Alabama with a longer and almost as successful run at Duke. He was later inducted into the College Football Hall of Fame.

1931 Rose Bowl

Immediately after their victory over Georgia in the season finale, University president George Denny accepted an invitation to play in the 1931 Rose Bowl against the Washington State Cougars. The Crimson Tide overwhelmed the Cougars with their 24–0 victory before 60,000 fans at Pasadena.

The game went like this: After a scoreless first, Alabama scored three second-quarter touchdowns in a six-minute blitz to take a commanding 21–0 lead. The first score came on a 61-yard Jimmy Moore touchdown pass to John Henry Suther with the other two coming on touchdown runs of one and 43-yards by John Campbell.

Jennings B. Whitworth scored the final points of the game with his 30-yard field goal to give Alabama the 24–0 victory.

The starting lineup was: Dobbs (left end), Clement (left tackle), Sanford (left guard), Sharpe (center), Whitworth (right guard), Godfree (right tackle), Elmore (right end), Tucker (quarterback), Long (left halfback), Holley (right halfback), and Boykin (fullback).

About the "consensus" National championships

The NCAA recognizes consensus national champions as the teams that have captured a championship by way of one of the major polls since the 1950 college football season. Prior to 1950, such as in 1930, national championships were chosen by a variety of selectors.

Over fifty years after the season—in the 1980s, Alabama finally claimed the 1930 championship as one of its claimed/recognized national championships. As such, Alabama claims a share of the 1930 national championship, with Notre Dame, due to each school being selected national champion by various major selectors.

Specifically, Alabama was selected national champion by Football Research, Parke Davis, and Sagarin and Sagarin (ELO-Chess). I would suspect that Notre Dame and Knute Rockne prior to his death in a plane crash in 1930, were pleased to share such honors with such a fine team as the Alabama Crimson Tide with a coach as tuned into winning as Knute Rockne himself.

This 1931 Rose Bowl game has been determined by the pundits to be one of the most significand football games in Crimson Tide History. An expanded narrative of the game is provided below from bamahammer:

Chapter 8 Coach Frank Thomas 1931-1945

Frank Thomas was one of the best college football coaches of all time.

Year	Coach	Conference	Record	SoCon/SEC
1931	Frank Thomas #18	SoCon	9-1-0	7-1-0
1932	Frank Thomas	SoCon	8-2-0	5-2-0
1933	Frank Thomas	SEC	7-1-1	5-0-1
1934*	Frank Thomas	SEC	10-0-0	7-0-0
1935	Frank Thomas	SEC	6-2-1	4-2-0
1936	Frank Thomas	SEC	8-0-1	5-0-1
1937	Frank Thomas	SEC	9-1-0	6-0-0
1938	Frank Thomas	SEC	7-1-1	4-1-1
1939	Frank Thomas	SEC	5-3-1	2-3-1
1940	Frank Thomas	SEC	7-2-0	4-2-0
1941*	Frank Thomas	SEC	9-2-0	5-2-0
1942	Frank Thomas	SEC	8-3-0	4-2-0
1943	WWII No Alabama games played this year			
1944	Frank Thomas	SEC	5-2-2	3-1-2
1945	Frank Thomas	SEC	10-0-0	6-0-0
1946	Frank Thomas	SEC	7-4-0	4-3-0

* National Championship

1931 Alabama Football Team Frank Thomas Coach

1931 Coach Frank Thomas #18

The 1931 Alabama Crimson Tide football team played its 38th overall and 10th season as a member of the Southern Conference (SoCon). The team was led by head coach Frank Thomas, in his first year. It played its home games at Denny Stadium in Tuscaloosa, at Legion Field in Birmingham and at the Cramton Bowl in Montgomery, Alabama. The team finished the season with a record of nine wins and one loss (9–1 overall, 7–1 in the SoCon).

The Crimson Tide's 1930 team had won the Southern Conference championship, the 1931 Rose Bowl and a share of the national championship in Wallace Wade's final year at Alabama. The Crimson Tide lost each and every one of its starters from their 10–0 1930 team except for Johnny Cain, but the team still played almost as well. It was unexpected.

Frank Thomas was a very capable coach. He was hired Wade Wallace's successor, and you could have fooled the fans. It was as if the highly competent Wallace was still coaching.

Alabama won its first three games of the 1931 season against Howard, Ole Miss and Mississippi A&M before they suffered their only loss of the season against Tennessee. The Crimson Tide responded from the loss to win their final five regular season games against Sewanee, Kentucky, Florida, Clemson and Vanderbilt.

Alabama then competed in a pair of charity games scheduled in early November to follow the regular season finale against Vanderbilt. In these two games, the Crimson Tide defeated Chattanooga and then three separate Washington, D.C. schools in an exhibition that featured an all-star collection of former Crimson Tide players. Even after the season, the team was enjoying football along with its new coach.

Although Alabama did have considerable success on the field, tragedy did strike the team on November 17 when freshman center James Richard Nichols died from complications due to a spinal injury he suffered during a football practice.

His death was the first major accident associated with the Alabama football program in its history. It was a sad day, indeed.

Prior to the start of the 1930 season, as previously discussed, head coach Wallace Wade announced his resignation in order to become the head coach at Duke. On July 26, 1930, former Chattanooga head and then Georgia assistant coach Frank Thomas was announced as Wade's successor by the University Athletic Committee. Thomas was signed to a three-year contract,

Frank Thomas would take over as head coach on January 1, 1931, with the 1931 season being his first as head coach. For the 1931 season, coach Thomas retired Wade's single-wing offense and installed the Notre Dame Box formation that he learned as both a player and assistant coach at Notre Dame under Knute Rockne.

On September 26 at Denny Stadium, UA defeated Howard W (42-6. The team followed this up the next week at Denny with another win on October 3 against Ole Miss W (55-6). The Tide traveled to Greer Memorial Field in Meridian, MS for a rivalry match on October 10 at Mississippi A&M W (53–0). Following this, on Oct 17, at Tennessee's Shields–Watkins Field in Knoxville, in the (Third Saturday in October) game, UA suffered its only loss of the season, L 0–25 with 23,000 in attendance.

Sewanee never came back to peak form like the olden days and were beaten by UA on October 24 at Legion Field in Birmingham W (33–0). Kentucky was beaten by UA on Oct 31 in a very close game at Denny Stadium W (9-7). UA then had its way with Florida on Oct 31 at Legion Field W (41-0). On November 14, Clemson had not yet to begin to play UA caliber ball and were defeated in a blowout W (74-7). On November 26, at Dudley Field in Nashville v Vanderbilt, UA prevailed W (14-6). In its last game of the season at Chattanooga's Chamberlain Field, The Crimson Tide won its season finale W (39-0)

1932 Coach Frank Thomas #18

The 1932 Alabama Crimson Tide football team played its 39th overall and 11th and final season as a member of the Southern

Conference (SoCon). The team was led by head coach Frank Thomas, in his second year. The team played its home games at Denny Stadium in Tuscaloosa, at Legion Field in Birmingham and at the Cramton Bowl in Montgomery, Alabama. They finished the season with a record of eight wins and two losses (8–2 overall, 5–2 in the SoCon).

1933 Coach Frank Thomas #18

The 1933 Alabama Crimson Tide football team played its 40th overall and 1st season as a member of the Southeastern Conference (SEC). The team was led by head coach Frank Thomas, in his third year, and played its home games at Denny Stadium in Tuscaloosa and Legion Field in Birmingham, Alabama. They finished a fine season with a record of seven wins, one loss and one tie (7–1–1 overall, 5–0–1 in the SEC), and as the first SEC champions. Today the SEC is recognized in the US by all the pundits as the powerhouse conference—even more powerful than the Big Ten.

1934 Coach Frank Thomas #18

The 1934 Alabama Crimson Tide football team played its 41st overall season and 2nd as a member of the Southeastern Conference (SEC). The team was led by head coach Frank Thomas, in his fourth year. It played its home games at Denny Stadium in Tuscaloosa, Legion Field in Birmingham and the Cramton Bowl in Montgomery, Alabama. The team finished this season with a perfect record (10–0 overall, 7–0 in the SEC), as Southeastern Conference champions for the second consecutive season. At the end of the season, they knocked out Stanford in the Rose Bowl on January 1, 1935. Frank Thomas knew how to win.

Five of the 13 selectors recognized as official by the NCAA (Berryman, Dunkel, Houlgate, Poling, and Williamson) recognize the 1934 Minnesota team as the national champion. Sportswriter Morgan Blake called it the best football team he ever saw. The 1934 Alabama team had a right to contest their opinion.

1935 Rose Bowl – Now We Can Call It a Tradition

When Alabama performed so well in the 1935 Rose Bowl, it was no longer a fluke that a fine Southern School could beat the big guys from the North and West.

In the 1935 Rose Bowl and Alabama is once again headed out west to teach the Pacific Coast Conference a lesson. This time the Crimson Tide would face off against the Cardinal of Stanford. And this time the Tide would be led by their new head coach Frank Thomas, who was about as good a coach as there could be.

Stanford took the lead in the first quarter on a 1-yard run by Bobby Grayson. The Tide came roaring back in the second half, scoring three touchdowns and kicking a field goal.

Alabama won the 1935 Rose Bowl over Stanford by a score of 35-19.

End Don Hutson's 54 yard catch for a touchdown might have been the highlight of the game, but halfback Dixie Howell was the MVP of the game. Howell would of course go on to coach Furman's baseball AND football team.

The other end besides Hutson was a young man named Paul "Bear" Bryant. Can you imagine the humility of this man? The 1934 national championship was the first Alabama national championship involving the Crimson Tide's future head coach

This was the third Rose Bowl win for the Crimson Tide, and their third national championship. After three it's safe to move the needle up from trend to tradition. From 1935 on Alabama would be the favorite, the great, Alabama Crimson Tide.

1935 Rose Bowl Champion Alabama coming home to a huge crowd

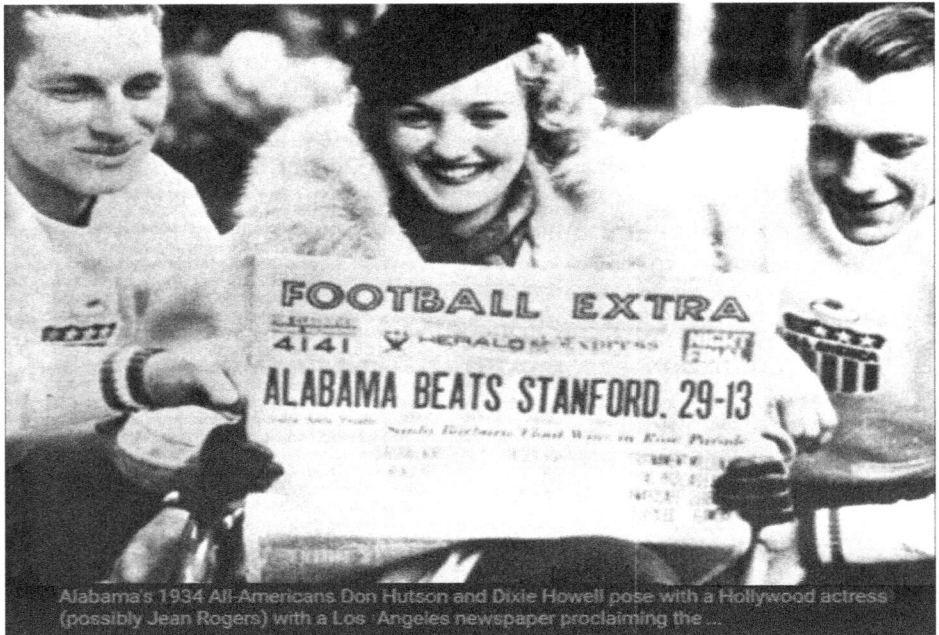

Celebrating the Rose Bowl Win Over Stanford

1935 Coach Frank Thomas #18

The 1935 Alabama Crimson Tide football team played its 42nd overall and 3rd season as a member of the Southeastern Conference (SEC). The team was led by head coach Frank Thomas, in his fifth year, and played their home games at Denny Stadium in Tuscaloosa and Legion Field in Birmingham, Alabama. They finished the season with a record of six wins, two losses and one tie (6–2–1 overall, 4–2–0 in the SEC).

1936 Coach Frank Thomas #18

The 1936 Alabama Crimson Tide football team played its 43rd overall and 4th season as a member of the Southeastern Conference (SEC). The team was led by head coach Frank Thomas, in his sixth year, and played their home games at Denny Stadium in Tuscaloosa and Legion Field in Birmingham, Alabama. They finished the season with a record of eight wins, zero losses and one tie (8–0–1 overall, 5–0–1 in the SEC).

1937 Coach Frank Thomas #18

The 1937 Alabama Crimson Tide football team played its 44th overall and 5th season as a member of the Southeastern Conference (SEC). The team was led by head coach Frank Thomas, in his seventh year, and played their home games at Denny Stadium in Tuscaloosa and Legion Field in Birmingham, Alabama. They finished the season with a record of nine wins and one loss (9–1 overall, 6–0 in the SEC), as SEC champions and with a loss against California in the 1938 Rose Bowl.

With this well-played undefeated and untied regular season, Alabama accepted an invitation to play in the 1938 Rose Bowl on January 1, 1938. They lost this game L (0-13) to California before 87,000.

After the 1936 season, the first expansion of Denny Stadium was undertaken. The stadium originally opened for the 1929 season, and the concrete stands had a seating capacity of 12,000.

Alabama's 1937 coaching staff: Tilden Campbell, Henry Crisp, Head Coach Frank Thomas, Harold Drew, Paul Burnham, **Paul W. Bryant**

The 1937 expansion included the construction of a 6,000-seat eastern addition that was utilized primarily by students. Its construction was financed with a combination of funding from both the university ($140,000) and a grant from the Public Works Administration ($90,000).

Designed after the Yale Bowl, at the time of this expansion the school envisioned an eventual build-out of Denny Stadium at a much larger capacity. As you will see in this book, this vision became a reality.

The Rose Bowl – one blemish in an otherwise perfect season

On November 30, Alabama accepted an invitation to play in the 1938 Rose Bowl against the California Golden Bears. In the game, the Crimson Tide were defeated in their only game of the season with a 13–0 shutout loss before 87,000 fans at Pasadena.

Vic Bottari scored both touchdowns for the Golden Bears on runs of four-yards in the second and five-yards in the third. UA simply could not hold onto the ball. In the loss, the Crimson Tide turned the ball over eight times, on four fumbles and four interceptions. Alabama had two scoring opportunities end within the California ten-yard line, one was lost on a fumble at the one-yard line and the other at the six-yard line. The loss was also Alabama's first in the Rose Bowl Game. Close game but no cigar.

After the season, UA's Leroy Monsky was a consensus selection and both Joe Kilgrow and James Ryba were selected to various 1937 College Football All-America Teams.

1938 Coach Frank Thomas #18

The 1938 Alabama Crimson Tide football team played its 45th season overall and 6th season as a member of the Southeastern Conference (SEC). The team was led by head coach Frank Thomas, in his eighth year. UA played home games at Denny Stadium in Tuscaloosa and Legion Field in Birmingham, Alabama. They finished the season with a record of seven wins, one loss and one tie (7–1–1 overall, 4–1–1 in the SEC).

Prior to the season, on December 5, 1937, Frank Thomas announced the 1938 schedule. The intersectional game against USC was announced in August 1937 and was the first between the two football powers. The remaining schedule included road games at Kentucky and Georgia Tech with the remaining three games split evenly between Denny Stadium and Legion Field.

The Crimson Tide opened the season on Sept 24 with a W (19–7) victory in an intersectional contest against USC at Los Angeles. They then followed up the win with consecutive shutouts, all home victories over non-conference opponents Howard Oct 1 W (34-0); NC State Oct 8 W (14-0) on homecoming.

However, Alabama on Oct 15 was shut out L (0-13) by Tennessee. It was the Bama's first loss against the Volunteers since 1932. The Crimson Tide then rebounded with a victory on Oct 22 against Sewanee W (32-0) at Denny; Oct 29 at Kentucky W (26-6) and

Tulane at Legion Field on Nov 5 W (3-0). After a T (14–14) tie at Georgia Tech on November 12, Alabama defeated Vanderbilt W (7-0) at Legion Field on November 24 in their season finale.

USC Trojans

In August 1937, university officials announced Alabama would open the 1938 season in Los Angeles against the University of Southern California (USC). Looking for some level of "revenge" after their January loss in the Rose Bowl, the Crimson Tide defeated the Trojans 19–7 at the Los Angeles Memorial Coliseum.

The first quarter was scoreless. Then, Alabama scored two touchdowns in the second quarter to take a 13–0 halftime lead. The scores came on a pair of Herschel Mosley touchdown passes, the first on a seven-yard pass to Billy Slemons and the second on an 18-yard pass to Gene Blackwell.

The Trojans came right back after the first Alabama touchdown with their deepest drive into UA territory of the game. On the drive, Robert Peoples connected with Grenny Lansdell for a 36-yard gain to the Alabama 22. However, the stingy Alabama defense held, and USC failed to score after they turned the ball over on downs at the Alabama 13-yard line.

UA held its 13–0 lead through the third quarter, Hal Hughes intercepted an Oliver Day pass and returned it 25-yards for an Alabama touchdown to make the score 19–0. Vic Bradford missed his second extra point of the game.

Later in the fourth quarter, the Trojans scored their only points of the game. The one-yard Day touchdown run was set up after Al Krueger recovered a Charley Boswell fumbled punt at the Alabama one-yard line. The victory was their first all-time against USC.

Six thousand happy and excited Crimson Tide fans greeted the team at the Alabama Great Southern Railroad station in downtown Tuscaloosa upon their arrival the following Tuesday to celebrate their victory. It was a fine celebration indeed, but then the season had just begun. Howard had to be defeated the following Saturday.

Some Season Notes:

After all of the regular season games were completed, the final AP Poll was released in early December. In the final poll, Alabama held the No. 13 position. UA was also recognized by the Associated Press for having the best record (40–4–3) and highest winning percentage (.909) of any major, college team for the five-year period between 1934 and 1938. Statistically, the 1938 defense was one of the best in school history. The 1938 squad still holds numerous defensive records. Frank Thomas was a great coach.

1939 Coach Frank Thomas #18

The 1939 Alabama Crimson Tide football team played its 46th overall and 7th season as a member of the Southeastern Conference (SEC). The team was led by head coach Frank Thomas, in his ninth year. Alabama played home games at Denny Stadium in Tuscaloosa and Legion Field in Birmingham, Alabama.

I report on the field in each year because Alabama has always used a number of different fields in its 46 years. Sometimes they keep using them. Sometimes they start using others. See Chapter 3 about Alabama's Fields and Stadiums for more insights.

The 1939 team finished the season with a record of five wins, three losses and one tie (5–3–1 overall, 2–3–1 in the SEC).

1940 Coach Frank Thomas #18

The 1940 Alabama Crimson Tide football team played its 47th overall and 8th season as a member of the Southeastern Conference (SEC). This team was led by head coach Frank Thomas, in his tenth year. It played home games at Denny Stadium in Tuscaloosa and Legion Field in Birmingham, Alabama. UA finished the season with a record of seven wins and two losses (7–2 overall, 4–2 in the SEC).

The Crimson Tide opened the 1940 season with three consecutive, non-conference home victories. The first was on Sept 27 over Spring Hill W (26-0) played at Murphy High School. The next was on Oct 5 at Denny v Mercer W (20-0). The next was on Oct 12 v Howard at

Denny Stadium W (31-0). In its fourth game on Oct 19, Tennessee defeated the Crimson Tide in the Third Saturday in October rivalry L (12-27) in the SEC Conference opener.

UA rebounded with four consecutive conference victories at Kentucky on Nov 2 W 25-0); Tulane at Legion Field on Nov 9 W (13-6); Georgia Tech in Atlanta on Nov 16 W (14-13) and then on Nov 13, it was Vanderbilt at legion Field W (25-21). Alabama then closed its season with a loss against Mississippi State L (0-13) on homecoming day Nov 30 at Denny Stadium.

1941 Coach Frank Thomas #18

The 1941 Alabama Crimson Tide football team played its 48th overall and 9th season as a member of the Southeastern Conference (SEC). The team was led by head coach Frank Thomas, in his 11th year, and played home games at Denny Stadium in Tuscaloosa and Legion Field in Birmingham, Alabama. They finished the season with a record of nine wins and two losses (9–2 overall, 5–2 in the SEC)

With a victory in the Cotton Bowl Classic over Texas A&M. Alabama also claims a share of the 1941 national championship due to its selection as national champion by the Houlgate System.

The Crimson Tide opened the 1941 season on Sept 27 with a non-conference victory over Southwestern Louisiana W (47-6) at Denny Stadium. UA lost on Oct 4 in its second contest of the season to Mississippi State L (0-14). UA rebounded very well with six consecutive victories over Howard on Oct 11 W (61-0); at Tennessee on Oct 18 W (9-2); Georgia on Oct 25 W (27-14), Kentucky Nov 1-- W (30-0); at Tulane in New Orleans on Nov 8—W (19-14) and then on Nov 15 at Legion Field v Georgia Tech W (20-0).

As they entered their game at Vanderbilt, the Crimson Tide was nationally ranked at #7 in the AP Poll, but were upset L (0-7) in Nashville. Alabama then closed the regular season on Nov 28 with a road victory over Miami W 21-7) and on January 1, 1942, they defeated Texas A&M W (29-21) in the Cotton Bowl Classic Bowl Game.

This game has been determined by the pundits to be one of the most significand football games in Crimson Tide History.

1942 Cotton Bowl Classic

In the 1942 Cotton Bowl Classic against Texas A&M in Dallas Texas before 38,000 excited fans, Alabama was outgained 309 yards to 75 and earned just one official first down, but were able to win the game 29–21 nonetheless.

It was amazing.

Alabama's defense was tougher than nails as it forced 12 turnovers (seven interceptions and five fumbles). The Crimson Tide scored touchdowns on events such as a 72-yard punt return and a 12-yard interception return. They also two touchdowns after recovering A&M fumbles on the A&M 21 and 24-yard lines and on another occasion, they kicked a field goal after they intercepted a pass on the Texas A&M 17. Who says you can't win when your offense does not produce?

UA bona fide National Championship claim

As we have discussed in other places in this book, the NCAA of today recognizes consensus national champions as the teams that have captured a championship by way of one of the major polls since the 1950 college football season. Prior to 1950, however, teams were claiming national championships. Before 1950, national championships were chosen by a variety of selectors.

In the 1980s, Alabama chose to claim the 1941 championship as one of its 16 claimed and recognized national championships. As such, Alabama claims a share of the 1941 national championship, with Minnesota. Each school was selected national champion by at least one selector. Specifically, Alabama was selected national champion in 1941 by the Houlgate System.

The Houlgate System was a mathematical ranking system devised by Dale Houlgate that was syndicated in newspapers between 1927 and 1958 to determine the national champion. It was respected in its day for the job that it did.

This championship claim may or may not be true on multiple fronts but regardless present day football genius and Alabama Coach Nick Saban, if he can continue under the extreme pressure of being flawless, is destined to put Alabama way ahead of all college teams for National Championship Wins. Saban is a born winner.

Some pundits did not like the often-scribed Alabama claim to a championship in 1941.

Let me go through one of the rants against this so we know the disputers think they have the facts down pretty well. Here it is:

"The AP ranked Alabama 20th in the nation in this season with 14 teams having better records above them. Once again, it is the Football Thesaurus that retroactively awards the Tide this title. Alabama finished third in the SEC that year, while Mississippi State won the SEC title. It completely baffles me that 'Bama claims a national title in 1941."

The explanation is simple. No team, especially on with such a history of greatness wants to miss out on an opportunity in any year to gain or to have gained the national championship.

I think UA has a right to claim what may rightfully be theirs. It was a great year for the Thomas-led team for sure and most listings show Alabama as having gained the title in 1941. Nothing is fair when men sit down with beers and cigars, and cigarettes—and smoke to decide things. Look at the 10-0-0 year (7-0-0) in the SEC, in which Alabama did not get even a piece of the championship. In an imperfect system, things come out imperfect.

Nobody can deny Alabama is either the best or one of the best football teams that there ever was and it is because, not in spite of their university officials' acute awareness and dedication to the support of their teams. Let a defining authority make the decisions but surely in a world of claimants and no valid referees, Alabama has its rights to the 1941 college championship title. I dare you to prove conclusively otherwise.

1942 Cotton Bowl – A Year of Contention

This game is considered one of the greatest ever played by the Crimson Tide.

Frank Thomas' 1941 Crimson Tide did not end the season undefeated. The Tide had an 8-2-0 record after losses to the Vanderbilt Commodores and the Mississippi State Bulldogs. So, when the Tide went into the 1942 Cotton Bowl against the Texas A&M Aggies, it didn't have the same feeling of importance as perhaps other games with undefeated teams in the Rose Bowl had in the past.

Alabama wasn't favored in the game and Texas A&M ended up looking like the better team on the stat sheet... in everything but the final score. The Aggies had 13 first downs to Alabama's 1, but Alabama carried the day.

Alabama defeated Southwest Conference champion Texas A&M Aggies.

Alabama claims a national championship for 1941 because some champion selectors picked Alabama as the champion that year after their Cotton Bowl win. This seems crazy by today's standards considering Mississippi State won the SEC that year.

At the time, though, the selectors could pick whomever they wanted as the national champion. It's not a clear championship by any means, but Alabama isn't completely inventing it either.

1942 Coach Frank Thomas #18

The 1942 Alabama Crimson Tide football team played its 49th overall and 10th season as a member of the Southeastern Conference (SEC). The team was led by head coach Frank Thomas, in his 12th year at the helm. UA played home games at Denny Stadium in Tuscaloosa, Legion Field in Birmingham and sometimes at the Cramton Bowl in Montgomery.

They finished the 1942 season with a record of eight wins and three losses (8–3 overall, 4–2 in the SEC). They also secured a victory in the Orange Bowl over Boston College. It was another fine Frank Thomas season.

1943 Orange Bowl v Boston College – Game Notes

After their loss to Georgia Pre-Flight in their regular season finale, on November 30 Alabama accepted an invitation to play in the Orange Bowl at Burdine Stadium in Miami Florida before 25,200 against the Boston College Eagles.

At that time, the final AP Poll was also released with Alabama in the No. 10 position and Boston College in the No. 8 position. Both teams had fine seasons and had played respectable teams. In the Orange Bowl, the Crimson Tide overcame a 14–0 first quarter deficit to defeat the Eagles 37–21.

BC took a 14–0 lead with first-quarter touchdowns scored on a 65-yard Mike Holovak pass to Ed Doherty and on a 33-yard Holovak run. Alabama came back with three consecutive touchdowns in the second quarter to take a 19–14 lead on a 14-yard Russ Mosley pass to Wheeler Leeth pass; a 17-yard Johnny August pass to Ted Cook; and a 40-yard Tom Jenkins run.

The Eagles chose not to play dead. They scored their final points of the game on a 1-yard Holovak touchdown run before the Crimson

Tide took a 22–21 halftime lead on a 15-yard George Hecht field goal.

UA went on to shut-out the Eagles for the rest of the game and score on a 15-yard August run in the third and on a 1-yard Jenkins run in the fourth. Joe Domnanovich then tackled Harry Connolly for a safety to make the final score 37–21. It was a great game.

1943 Coach Frank Thomas #18

Due to the World War II effort, there was no football season for UA in 1943

The 1943 Alabama Crimson Tide football team was prepared to represent the University of Alabama in the 1943 college football season. However, the season was canceled due to the effects of World War II.

In February 1943, the Army instituted a policy that prohibited their cadets from participation in intercollegiate athletics. Unsure if a season would occur, head coach Frank Thomas proceeded through spring practice as if it would be played. By summer, only two Alabama players were available to compete on the squad as a direct result of the Army prohibition on its trainees competing in intercollegiate athletics.

On August 23, 1943, the University announced its decision to cancel the 1943 season. The cancellation marked only the third time since the inaugural 1892 season that Alabama did not field a football team.

Although not officially sanctioned by the University, UA fans got to see some football that year. An independent team called the Alabama Informals was organized in October 1943. Coached by former Crimson Tide player Mitchell Olenski, the Informals were composed of 17-year-old and draft deferred students ineligible for military service.

The Informals were permitted to play their games at Denny Stadium and utilize the equipment of the Crimson Tide football team. The squad lost to Howard, defeated the Marion Military Institute twice and finished the season with an overall record of two wins and one loss (2–1). What a nice gesture to help the people's morale from the University of Alabama.

At the conclusion of the season, SEC officials met in an effort to bring a full football schedule back for the 1944 season. By May 1944, all SEC schools, with the exception of Vanderbilt, indicated they would field teams for the 1944 season. Football officially returned on September 30, 1944, when the Crimson Tide played LSU to a tie in their season opener. Frank Thomas was still the coach of the Crimson Tide.

1944 Coach Frank Thomas #18

The 1944 Alabama Crimson Tide football team has been referred to over years as "Alabama", "UA" or "Bama, or The Tide, or Tide").

This 1944 team played the 50th overall and 11th football season as a member of the Southeastern Conference (SEC). The team was led by head coach Frank Thomas, in his 13th year, (though he was employed by UA in the non-functional 1943 season).

Though the field houses and the stadiums grew to more capacity. UA still played its home games at Denny Stadium in Tuscaloosa and Legion Field in Birmingham and occasionally at the Cramton Bowl in Montgomery. They finished the 1944 season with a record of five wins, two losses and two ties (5–2–2 overall, 3–1–2 in the SEC) and they lost the Sugar Bowl to Duke.

After a hard-fought tie, T (27-27) against LSU on Sept 30 to open the season, Alabama then defeated both Howard and Millsaps. On Oct 7, Howard went down w (63-7) and on Oct 14, Milsaps went down even easier W (55-0).

The Crimson Tide dueled Tennessee on Oct 21 to a scoreless tie in the fourth week in their traditional "Third Saturday in October" rivalry T 0-0). Then, on Oct 27, the Crimson Tide defeated Kentucky at the Crampton Bowl W (41-0) before they suffered their only regular season loss against Georgia L9 7-14 on Nov 4.

Alabama then closed the season with wins over both Ole Miss on Nov 11 W (34-6) and Mississippi State W (19-0) on Nov 18.

All of this great football playing secured UA a position in the Sugar Bowl where despite continued great play it was not enough to beat Duke L (26-29)

The 1944 squad was an unusual group in that its football career had to take a full year hiatus because of the war in 1943. And, so this return of football at Alabama after a one-year lay-off was a really big thing.

However, as the war effort was ongoing at that time, the 1944 team was composed of players who were either too young and / or were physically unable to enlist in the military.

As the squad was generally smaller than both previous Alabama squads and many they competed against, coach Thomas called this and his 1945 team the "War Babies." God bless their efforts while the US efforts were underway.

The Sugar Bowl – A Fitting Tribute

On November 25, UA officials announced that Alabama had accepted a bid to play in the 1945 Sugar Bowl against the Duke Blue Devils. What an accomplishment for a bunch of scrappers doing their best while the boys were fighting the war.

In the game, the Crimson Tide were barely defeated L (26-29) before 66,822 fans at Tulane Stadium. Duke score a late, game-winning touchdown. Take nothing away from Duke, please as its efforts were for the greater honor and glory of their fine university.

The Blue Devils took an early 7–0 on a 14-yard George Clark run before a pair of one-yard, Norwood Hodges touchdown runs gave the Crimson Tide a 12–7 lead at the end of the first. Alabama extended its lead further to 19–7 after Harry Gilmer threw a 12-yard touchdown pass to Ralph Jones. Duke responded with a pair of short, Tom Davis touchdown runs to take a 10–19 lead into the fourth quarter.

Harry Gilmer QB # 52 with Coach Frank Thomas

In 4Q, Hugh Morrow gained a touchdown on a 78-yard interception return; however, the Crimson Tide lost the game after Gilmer took a safety and George Clark scored the game-winning points on a 20-yard run. For a bunch of great scrappers playing big man football, this UA team played like big men throughout the season. They were ready for a better game nonetheless the next season.

1945 Coach Frank Thomas #18

The 1945 Alabama football team played the Crimson Tide's 51st overall and 12th season as a member of the Southeastern Conference (SEC). The team was led by head coach Frank Thomas, in his 14th year, and played their home games at Denny Stadium in Tuscaloosa, Legion Field in Birmingham and at the Cramton Bowl in Montgomery.

They finished with a perfect season (10–0 overall, 6–0 in the SEC) and with a victory in the Rose Bowl over USC. This team was the second season of the "War Babies" as coined by head coach

Thomas. They kicked butt (a "b" word recognized by many as an acceptable alternative to the "a" word). After Wallace Wade and Frank Thomas, Alabama was moving from just being a great team to being a great tradition at Alabama University and the United States. Wow!

The Crimson Tide opened the season on the road on Sept 29 with a victory over Keesler AAF W (21-0) at Flier Field in Beloxi, MS. Military teams were always loaded and for its first game of the year, the War Babies et al were outstanding in this game and for the season.

Jackson Army Air Base, where I had my own Basic Training prior to MP School at Fort Gordon GA, in the Vietnam Era, for its own reasons had to cancel this game at Denny Stadium. Keesler were fine opponents in place of the Jacksons.

Alabama then defeated LSU W (26-0) in Baton Rouge before their first home win of the season at the Cramton Bowl on Oct 13 over South Carolina W (55-0). To beat the military teams with over-age players looking for patriotic relief, a team had to be pretty darn good and well inspired. No military team was looking for a cake walk. Alabama gave them all a game and sometimes more than expected.

After victories over both Tennessee W (25-7) on Oct 20, and Georgia W (28-14) at Legion Field on Oct 27, the Crimson Tide routed both Kentucky on Nov 3 W (60-19) and on Nov 17 at Vanderbilt on the road W (71-0) to extend their record to 7–0.

Au was on a roll for having played hardball football with underclassmen for years. Bama then closed the season with a pair of games at Denny Stadium, which by the way kept growing over the years, where they defeated the Pensacola NAS W (55-6) on Nov 24. and then on Dec 1 -- Mississippi State W (55-13) to complete an undefeated regular season.

One month later, Alabama, having been invited and having agreed to participate in the game, won the Rose Bowl over USC to finish the season undefeated. A great team had shown its consistency and greatness.

No football season is easy. Football is not an easy game. It is not for wimps. Participants must be willing to give it up at all times for the greater good of the team. Those teams that understand that win National Championships. Alabama seems to make seasons easy because at an institutional level in the classroom and on the field UA is dedicated to excellence and winning as opposed to the alternative. You have to want to win to win! If nobody else claims that exhortation as their own, I would be pleased to accept the honors. Viva Alabama!

The 1945 season was the fourth perfect season in Alabama history, following the perfect seasons of 1925, 1930 and 1934. Those reading these accounts know how many "almost there's" there were over the years but this was the real deal. Frank Thomas, years before Bear Bryant stood for Alabama. He had the winningest program in the nation. Bravo UA!

However, despite its clear dominance of opponents, Alabama did not win the national championship in 1945. In a world swept up with patriotism and a military team that had run roughshod over all of the best in US Universities from across the country, that honor went to the Army Cadets team that went 9–0 and outscored its opponents by a 412–46 margin. The Crimson Tide finished second in the AP poll behind the Cadets. Nobody complained. We were winning the war. The Crimson Tide may have beaten Army in its finest year but who is going to ask that question? There was no UA – Army game.

During the War, most Americans were not thinking of how great were the Crimson Tide or the Army Football Team. The people were so pleased that when the boys left the football field they manned-up enough to defeat the mortal WWII enemies of the US. That, of course is why we all can play football at the college level in freedom today. Amen!

However, years later, the issue of 1945 champion was brought up again and this time 71 years had passed. Somehow Oklahoma presented a case and it was retroactively declared National Champions for 1945. The Cowboys went 9-0 in 1945, finishing the season with a 33-13 win over St. Mary's in the Sugar Bowl.

Unfortunately for Oklahoma State, it was one of a few teams to go undefeated in 1945.

Army finished the season ranked No. 1 at 9-0, with 10-0 Alabama checking in at No. 2, a 7-1-1 Navy at No. 3 and 9-0-1 Indiana at No. 4. The Cowboys had to settle for No. 5.

As if all this isn't enough, if this stands, Oklahoma State is now the first school to win a national title in both football and basketball in the same season, as the school's basketball team won its second consecutive basketball title in 1945. The 2006 Florida team thought it owned this distinction Sorry, it's now the second to do it. Interesting what a group of men can do after 71 years.

This 1946 Rose Bowl Game has been determined by the pundits to be one of the most significand football games in Crimson Tide History.

The 1946 Rose Bowl

On November 23, University officials accepted an invitation to participate in the 1945 Season's Rose Bowl on January 1, 1946. The opponent was USC. The Crimson Tide defeated the Trojans 34–14 to complete a perfect season.

Alabama took a 34–0 lead into the fourth quarter before the Trojans scored their first points. Alabama touchdowns were scored on a pair of one-yard Hal Self runs, a five-yard Lowell Tew run, a one-yard Norwood Hodges run and on a 20-yard Self pass to Harry Gilmer.

The victory improved Alabama's all-time record against USC to 2–0. This edition of the Rose Bowl also marked the final one that did not feature a matchup between teams from what are now both the Big Ten Conference and the Pac-12 Conference until Miami played in the 2002 Rose Bowl.

This was the case as the Pacific Coast Conference and the Big Nine Conference entered into an agreement to place their conference champions in the Rose Bowl effective for the 1946 season.

1946 Rose Bowl – The Wooden Horse Arises

This game is highlighted here in this section because it has been identified as one of the greatest Alabama games of all time.

The 1946 Rose Bowl featured Alabama facing the mighty USC Trojans. USC had won eight straight Rose Bowls coming into the game against Alabama, but all that changed on January 1, 1946.

Alabama led USC 20-0 at the half and USC didn't make a first down until the third quarter. Frank Thomas' 1946 Alabama Crimson Tide football team was so dominant in their victory over the Trojans that they began to be called "The Wooden Horse" in reference to the wooden horse the Greeks used to defeat the ancient Trojans in Homer's Iliad.

Alabama dominated on the offensive side of the ball as well, racking up 351 yards of offense compared to USC's 41. The Tide were of course led by the legendary Harry Gilmer at quarterback.This was the last Rose Bowl to take at large teams instead of picking PAC and B1G schools exclusively. You might say that Alabama's 34 -14 drubbing of the Trojans taught the PAC that perhaps they should be trying to play northern teams instead of SEC teams.
This is perhaps the earliest example of a team regretting wanting Bama.

Coach Thomas with his Rose Bowl stars: Harry Gilmer, Thomas Whitely, Gordon Pettus and Henry Self.

1946 Coach Frank Thomas #18

The 1946 Alabama Crimson Tide football team played in the 52nd overall and 13th season as a member of the Southeastern Conference (SEC). The team was led by head coach Frank Thomas, in his 15th year, and played their home games at Denny Stadium in Tuscaloosa, Legion Field in Birmingham and at the Cramton Bowl in Montgomery. They finished with a record of seven wins and four losses (7–4 overall, 4–3 in the SEC).

After the Crimson Tide opened the season with four consecutive victories over Furman at Legion Field on Sept 20 W (26-7), at Tulane on Sept 28 W (7-6), at South Carolina Oct 5 W (14-6), and Southwestern Louisiana on Oct 12 at Denny Stadium W 54-0), Alabama's 14-game winning streak was snapped when they lost at Tennessee L (0-12) on the "Third Saturday in October on Oct 19.

One week later, on Oct 26, the Crimson Tide faced off against Kentucky and their new young coach, Bear Bryant. The Crimson Tide won by a score of W (21–7), before they lost consecutive games at #5 Georgia L (0-14) on Nov 2, and at #19 LSU L (21-31) on Nov 9. Alabama then closed the season on with a victory over Vanderbilt W (12-7) on Nov 16, a loss at Boston College L (7-13) on Nov 13 (in their first game ever played in New England, and an upset victory over #19 Mississippi State W (24-7) on homecoming Nov 30 in the season finale.

Over the course of the 1946 season, Frank Thomas was riddled with health issues that ultimately led to his resignation as head coach. In January 1947, Harold Drew was named as the 17th head coach of the Crimson Tide.

Mississippi State Game Notes Denny Stadium

On what was both homecoming and the final game of the season before 25,000 at Denny Stadium, Alabama upset the Mississippi State Maroons 24–7. After a scoreless first quarter, Alabama took a 10–0 halftime lead after a six-yard Hugh Morrow field goal and a two-yard Lionel W. Noonan touchdown run in the second quarter.

They extended their lead further to 17–0 in the third after John Wozniak returned a blocked punt 38-yards for a touchdown.

The game then concluded with a pair of fourth-quarter touchdowns. The first was scored by Alabama on a one-yard Harry Gilmer run and the second for State on a short Wallace Matulich run. The victory improved Alabama's all-time record against Mississippi State to 23–7–2.

Coach Thomas' resignation

The struggles of the 1946 team might have been caused in part by the deteriorating health of coach Frank Thomas. High blood pressure left him bedridden for most of the 1946 season, unable to stand for long periods, and forced to ride in a trailer to conduct many Alabama practices. After the 1946 season his ill health forced his resignation when he was only 48 years old, and Thomas later died in Tuscaloosa on May 10, 1954.

During his fifteen seasons as head coach at Alabama, Thomas won four SEC championships and compiled an overall record of 115 wins, 24 losses and seven ties (115–24–7) record, for an .812 winning percentage.

Prior to the conclusion of the season, speculation began as to who would succeed Thomas as the head coach of the Crimson Tide. In early November, sources indicated that former Thomas player, and then head coach at Kentucky, Bear Bryant was to become the next head coach of the Crimson Tide.

On November 11, Bryant stated that he had not been in contact about the Alabama job and indicated his focus was on the Wildcats. After an exhaustive search, on January 14, 1947, former Thomas assistant and then head coach at Ole Miss, Harold Drew was introduced as the new head coach of the Crimson Tide.

Frank Thomas – A Great One's Great One!

Being a football coach is a demanding life. Sometimes it is an unrequited life though the impact on young players surely makes it worthwhile. While researching this particular chapter—for this book, I was caught up in the mastery and the mystery of Frank

Thomas. History will prove that one of the finest coaches in the history of football has the name of *Frank Thomas*.

All of the writers (me) and readers (you) as you have just read the facts can recognize that Frank Thomas is unquestionably worthy of major accolades. One of his star players, the late Coach Paul "Bear" Bryant would surely attest to that. Within the story of Frank Thomas, it is easy to find a gentleman, who was respected and loved by many, and many more to come.

I would like to thank Tidefans.com for the opportunity to reprint an parts of the following article from their site. It best captures the essence of Frank Thomas – the same essence that I gained in researching this great man and his great football legacy.

http://www.tidefans.com/forums/showthread.php?t=109961. Please enjoy this and remember that there are a lot of good guys out there. There just are not a lot of great guys in the tradition of Frank Thomas. I am honored to have learned about him and to have written about him. Bill Brown captures his essence perfectly throughout his essay and especially in his closing remarks. Alabama people are especially loyal to their favorite team. And, as the essay portrays, the loyalty is well deserved.

A Look Back: Alabama Football Coach Frank Thomas
by Bill Brown (selmaborntidefan)
August 8, 2010

Imagine for just a moment that your life was over at 55 years old. When you looked back over the course of that all-too-brief life you could count up memories of those whose life you'd come in contact with. Perhaps you had played quarterback for the Fighting Irish of Notre Dame and their legendary coach, Knute Rockne. You were a roommate with the most famous collegiate football player in history, a guy whose mythical story would resonate down through the years off the lips of a President. Or maybe you yourself had been privileged enough to coach the greatest college football coach who ever lived, Bear Bryant. Or maybe you had won a couple of Rose Bowls and a national championship.

[Thomas played quarterback for coach Knute Rockne at University of Notre Dame from 1920 to 1922. According to Rockne, Thomas was the smartest player he ever coached.[citation needed]Thomas's roommate and best friend at Notre Dame was George "The Gipper" Gipp].

Any one of those accomplishments would be a legacy of the highest order. But what if you – all by yourself – did all of those things in a brief life? If so then your name is Frank Thomas, perhaps the greatest obscure coach in collegiate football history.

WHO?

Frank Thomas may be the most anonymous great coach in the history of college football. When any list of the ten greatest football coaches comes up there are seven who always – without fail – make that list: Bryant, Woody Hayes, Schembechler, Eddie Robinson, Bobby Bowden, Joe Paterno, and Knute Rockne. The other three spots rotate among such slightly lesser mortals as Lou Holtz, Barry Switzer, Darrell Royal, Tom Osborne, Bud Wilkinson and a host of others. But how does Thomas compare to the seven coaches cited among the greatest?

His winning percentage is higher than six, trailing only Rockne. And Rockne can credit Thomas in part, whom Knute called the smartest player he had ever coached, with the fact he's higher. Thomas had an 8-1-1 record as the 1922 starting QB for the Fighting Irish. Thomas, as coach, won an astounding 79.5% of his games.

He won two Rose Bowls, the same number as Hayes or Schembechler, two men whose teams mostly took turns going to the game for some 20 years – one longer than Thomas's entire coaching career. Paterno won one and the others combined have won zero. Thomas also won a national championship, something that Schembechler never accomplished. Thomas also never had a losing season, and his only .500 season was his first as head coach at Chattanooga. In fact, except for that first year and a miserable 1939, Thomas's teams always won at least three more games than they lost every year. When it comes to considering the greatest college coaches ever perhaps the writers need to do a little more homework.

Although he was the most successful coach at Alabama up to that time, Wallace Wade had had a number of disagreements with

Alabama President George Denny. Prior to his 1930 swan song at Alabama, Wade had made up his mind to get out of town when the year was over. Before the season even began Wade had signed a contract to coach Duke University in 1931. Wade recommended Thomas to President Denny as his successor. Wade then proceeded to make matters as difficult as humanly possible by putting a team that NFL Hall of Famer Mel Hein, whose Washington State Cougars lost the 1931 Rose Bowl to Wade, said was the best college team he ever saw.

That Tide team revolutionized the forward pass. Wade waltzed off to Duke, where he was so successful they only named the stadium after him, with a 9-0 record and a victory in the Rose Bowl. Wade had set some impossible standards for Thomas to keep. Wade stepped down at a football awards dinner after a brief statement that he couldn't say what was on his mind. To emphasize his unhappiness, Wade left the silver tray he had just been presented on the dais.

On July 15, 1930, Frank Thomas signed his contract to become the new football coach at the University of Alabama. Denny then gave Thomas the basic speech that has been the standard for all Tide coaches even before Thomas: football is 90 percent material and 10 percent coaching; you will be given the 90 percent and held strictly accountable for the 10 percent. The problem facing Thomas, however, was huge: how in the world do you function knowing you are being compared every single day to a legend? Thomas answered that question better than any coach in the history of college football.

Starting from his meeting with George Denny, Thomas reeled off a record of 115-24-7. That astounding accomplishment included three undefeated seasons and another one marred only by a tie. It also included three Rose Bowl appearances that ended with two wins. To make it all the more glorious, Thomas only returned one starter for his 1931 team (Johnny Cain who was primarily a punter).

Thomas did almost everything right in 1931. He went 9-1 with the sole blemish coming at the hands of Bob Neyland's Tennessee Volunteer juggernaut that topped him, 25-0. Building off his success, Thomas hit the recruiting trail and over the next 2 years went 15-3-1.

Unfortunately, one of the losses was to Tennessee. Thomas also oversaw the beginning of Alabama's play in the Southeastern Conference in 1933, the same year the Tide shut out five opponents. This set up Thomas's best team (perhaps) at Alabama, the 1934 national championship team.

1934

John MacCallum, author of "Southeastern Conference Football," states that the 1934 Alabama team was the greatest single-platoon team to ever come out of the South. It featured a future major league baseball player named Dixie Howell, a future NFL Hall of Fame tight end named Don Hutson, and a lesser talented "Other End" who would one day wear the same hat as Thomas (the coaching one, not the Hound's-tooth), Arkansas-born Paul W. "Bear" Bryant. Many old-timers consider Hutson the greatest receiver in the history of football at any level because he could catch a pass anywhere at any time. Hutson was so talented that he played on the Bama baseball and track teams.

…

Thomas's system was the old Notre Dame system and was the same basic running pattern every team has used since. Thomas never felt the need to run fancy gadget plays when a power running game would accomplish the same thing. Thomas's greatest legacy is probably the coaching career of Bear Bryant. But it almost didn't happen. Bryant got angry one time and vented his anger by suggesting he was going to leave Alabama and go play for LSU. Assistant Coach Hank Crisp, who did not know Bryant was just blowing off steam, told Bryant to pack his trunk and get out. Bear wound up doing some heavy persuading so he could keep his scholarship and never again did he mention quitting. Bryant himself would later use such psychology as a master motivator.

Bryant also stated that Thomas was actually the opposite of most successful coaches. Bear noted that Thomas yelled so infrequently that when he did yell it certainly got your attention.

THE "LEAN" YEARS

As hard as it may be to believe now, Thomas's teams only made it to one bowl game between 1935 and 1941, the 1938 Rose Bowl, where they were shut out, 13-0. Thomas made the mistake of believing what he heard. Rumor had it that nobody could run on the Cal Golden Bears, so Thomas tried the passing game. He would later say that he found out far too late that he COULD run but his team could NOT pass. Thomas also did something unheard of today – he smoked cigars on the sidelines during the game. His greatest asset is said to have been his ability to adjust to unique situations. And Thomas believed that he could prevail no matter how much or how little material he had. The best example came in 1944. His record was only 5-1-2, but that was good enough for the Sugar Bowl, played that year. An unusual set of circumstances surrounded the end of Thomas's career.

After the Japanese attack on Pearl Harbor drew the United States into World War 2, football took a back seat most places. There were a couple of places, however, that thrived on the suddenly altered playing field – intellectual schools (Duke, Georgia Tech, Vandy) and the service academies (Army, Navy; Air Force did not yet exist) suddenly found the playing field slanted in their favor. The situation was so bad that football crazy Alabama did not even field a team in 1943. Thus, Thomas getting his team to the Sugar Bowl with mostly inexperienced players against a Duke team at normal strength by virtue of its Navy V-12 personnel was nothing short of a miracle. And Thomas nearly pulled off a bigger one in the actual game, losing only by a score of 29-26. But the game paid rich dividends for the future.

Thomas built his game plan around new QB Harry Gilmer, whose leaping delivery was both astounding and confusing. Gilmer only threw 8 times against Duke, but he completed every one of them. His last pass would have been a game-winning TD but the receiver, Ralph Jones, was brought down by the last man who had a chance at him. The game, however, set up Thomas and the Tide for a great 1945.

THE END OF THE CAREER

Talent returned to the Tide as the war wound down in 1945. And Harry Gilmer was still flinging passes while leaping into the air. Gilmer led the Tide to a perfect 9-0 record capped by a scintillating

34-14 win over the USC Trojans – a team that up until that day had never lost a Rose Bowl.

It might be noted that Thomas and Bear Bryant probably disagreed about nearly everything involved in the preparation for a game. Bryant had practices that extracted the manhood from everyone on the field while Thomas's practices were short and to the point. Thomas believed 'slave driving' was wrong while that very thing is a hallmark of what made Bryant great. Thomas and Bryant did agree; however, that ability was not everything and a little luck was necessary to win national championships.

Frank Thomas may have been the unluckiest successful coach that has ever walked the field in Tuscaloosa. After the Rose Bowl win his health began to deteriorate. He suffered from high blood pressure and an un-named (in those days) heart condition (probably congestive heart failure). Under physician orders he coached the 1946 team from the back of a trailer while sitting down. Unsurprisingly, they went 7-4. And Thomas knew his days as an Alabama coach were over. He resigned the coaching position in 1946 but stayed on as the Alabama Athletic Director until 1951. That same year Thomas was inducted into the College Football Hall of Fame but his health was so far gone that he received his plaque from the confines of a wheelchair.

THE END OF HIS LIFE

Thomas died, probably due to lung cancer, on May 10, 1954 at Druid City Hospital in Tuscaloosa. He was 55 years old. His coaching record was 141-33-9 for a winning percentage of .795, 12th highest among all coaches, and higher than any coach in Alabama history. He was succeeded as head coach by the same man who took over for him at Chattanooga, Harold "Red" Drew.

THE OBSCURE LEGACY

Thomas built a career that is among the greatest of any coach in any sport and yet most people outside of the state of Alabama do not even know who he is. Mention the name Frank Thomas even within the state of Alabama and every person under 40 is probably going to name a former baseball player who won a pair of MVPs with the Chicago White Sox in the early 1990s. Why isn't Frank Thomas better known given his record of accomplishment? He coached during the same era as Red Blaik and Bob Neyland and with the exception of Neyland was the cream of the crop in Southeastern football. What made such a fate befall Thomas?

There are several reasons we could pursue. The first one is the fact that almost nothing of Thomas's coaching career exists on videotape. In this era of 16-hour Saturday coverage – and that's just the games – very little video exists of Thomas' time at the Capstone. This should not be underestimated when making an evaluation. But another main reason is that Thomas is simply a great coach in a long line of great coaches. His accomplishments are undercut because they occurred between two phenomenally great eras in Alabama football, Wallace Wade and – only 11 years after Thomas quit – Bear Bryant.

In a bizarre sense, the success of Bear Bryant at Alabama makes every other coach's accomplishments pale in comparison. Add the fact that Bryant coached as both television was coming of age and social change was rampant (some of which he was at the center of) and he casts a long shadow that swallows everything else that has ever occurred in Tuscaloosa. Bear Bryant won six national championships to Thomas's one. But we should note that Thomas had the higher winning percentage (.795 to .780) and had just as many undefeated seasons (3) as Bryant did. The insane success enjoyed by Wade and Bryant overshadow Thomas's career.

Another problem, of course, is that Thomas died at a relatively young age. His coaching career ended when he was only 48 years old. Many college coaches don't even get their dream job by that age. Bryant was 48 when he won his first national championship by which point he had been coaching 18 years; Thomas only coached 19 total. Thomas also lost a year – and who knows how many wins? – to a human tragedy known as World War II. He also coached mostly during the Great Depression at a time when football attendance (and interest) paled in comparison to what followed the 1950s.

Ask an Alabama fan who the greatest Crimson Tide coach was and the answer is known by everyone: Paul "Bear" Bryant. I'm inclined to agree with that assessment. But I would be willing to bet you if Bear himself had a vote, he would probably choose Coach Frank Thomas.   Thank you, Bill Brown.

Chapter 9 Coaches Harold Drew & J. B. Whitworth 1947-1957

Harold Drew & Jennings Whitworth were post Frank Thomas and pre-Bear Bryant

Year	Coach	Conference	Record	SEC
1947	Harold Drew # 19	SEC	8-3-0	5-2-0
1948	Harold Drew	SEC	6-4-1	4-4-1
1949	Harold Drew	SEC	6-3-1	4-3-1
1950	Harold Drew	SEC	9-2-0	6-2-0
1951	Harold Drew	SEC	5-6-0	3-5-0
1952	Harold Drew	SEC	10-2-0	4-2-0
1953	Harold Drew	SEC	6-3-3	4-0-3
1954	Harold Drew	SEC	4-5-2	3-3-2
1955	Jennings Whitworth #20	SEC	0-10-0	0-7-0
1956	Jennings Whitworth	SEC	2-7-1	2-5-0
1957	Jennings Whitworth	SEC	2-7-1	1-6-1

1947 Alabama Crimson Tide -- Harold Drew, Coach

1947 Coach Harold Drew #19

The 1947 Alabama Crimson Tide football team played its 53rd overall and 14th season as a member of the Southeastern Conference The team was led by head coach Harold Drew, in his first year, and played their home games at Denny Stadium in Tuscaloosa and Legion Field in Birmingham, Alabama. They finished with a record of eight wins and three losses (8–3 overall, 5–2 in the SEC) and with a loss in the Sugar Bowl.

The 1947 season was the first for Harold Drew as head coach for the Crimson Tide. As noted, Drew was hired as the replacement for long-time head coach Frank Thomas after he resigned his post due to personal health conditions in January 1947.

1948 Coach Harold Drew #19

The 1948 Alabama Crimson Tide football team played the Crimson Tide's 54th overall and 15th season as a member of the Southeastern Conference (SEC). The team was led by head coach Harold Drew, in his second year, and played their home games at Denny Stadium in Tuscaloosa, Legion Field in Birmingham and Ladd Stadium in Mobile, Alabama. They finished with a record of six wins, four losses and one tie (6–4–1 overall, 4–4–1 in the SEC).

Alabama opened the season on Sept 25 with a loss to Tulane L (14–21), the first for Alabama to open a season since 1903. The Crimson Tide closed their season with a homecoming victory over Florida on Nov 27 and a W (55–0) win over Auburn at legion Field on Nov 4 in the renewal of their Iron Bowl rivalry.

This Iron Bowl game has been determined by the pundits to be one of the most significand football games in Crimson Tide History.

The Iron Bowl Tradition being brought back was big for both schools. This meeting against Auburn marked the resumption of their rivalry with the Tigers after a 41-year hiatus. The two schools had met regularly from 1892 through 1895 and then regularly from 1900 through 1907.

However, trivial disputes led to the series being discontinued in 1908. Their disputes centered on disagreements on how much per diem to allow players for the trip to Birmingham, how many players each school should bring and where to find officials.

By the time all these matters were resolved, it was too late to play in 1908, and the series ended by default and was simply not scheduled again. By 1947 pressure to renew the Iron Bowl had grown to the point that the state legislature threatened to withhold funding from the two schools unless they scheduled a game. In 1948 Alabama and Auburn finally agreed to meet on a football field.

Prior to the game, Alabama had not played Auburn since their 6–6 tie in 1907. In the renewal of the dormant series, Alabama defeated Auburn 55–0 at Legion Field, in what remains the most lopsided win by either team in the history of the series.

The Crimson Tide took a 7–0 lead in the first quarter after Gordon Pettus threw an eight-yard touchdown pass to Butch Avinger. Alabama then extended its lead to 21–0 at halftime with a pair of second-quarter touchdowns. Points were scored on a 20-yard Ed Salem pass to Clem Welsh and then on a six-yard Welsh reverse. The Crimson Tide then scored six second half touchdowns and continued to hold the Tigers scoreless in the 55–0 rout.

Third-quarter touchdowns were scored by Salem on a 17-yard run and on a 53-yard Salem pass to Rebel Steiner. Alabama then closed the game out with three touchdowns in the fourth quarter. Points were scored on a 20-yard Salem pass to Howard Pierson, a punt blocked by Larry Lauer and recovered in the end zone by Tom Salem and on a 20-yard Don Spurrell interception return. The victory improved Alabama's all-time record against Auburn to 5–7–1.

1948 Iron Bowl – More information

This game is recognized as one of the greatest Alabama games of all time.

The 1948 Iron Bowl was the first time Auburn and Alabama had faced each other in football since 1907. That's 41 years in the state of Alabama without an Iron Bowl, something that sounds unthinkable now.

In 1948 though, the Iron Bowl was brought back to life. Students of Alabama and Auburn actually went into the woods and buried a hatchet together to show that feelings had changed… and they might have for that one afternoon.

Auburn and Alabama is a rivalry in sports like no other; it's just not something that can be shook on and forgotten. You have to assume that the 55-0 beat down that the Alabama Crimson Tide put on the hapless Auburn Tigers that day also didn't do anything to help relations.

The Iron Bowl was being played, and Alabama was winning it big, once again all was right in the world.

1949 Coach Harold Drew #19

The 1949 Alabama Crimson Tide football team played its 55th overall and 16th season as a member of the Southeastern Conference (SEC). The team was led by head coach Harold Drew, in his third year, and played their home games at Denny Stadium in Tuscaloosa, Legion Field in Birmingham and Ladd Stadium in Mobile, Alabama. They finished with a record of six wins, three losses and one tie (6–3–1 overall, 4–3–1 in the SEC).

Alabama lost the Iron Bowl on Dec 3 to Auburn in a squeaker L (13-14). In this game, Alabama closed its season with the L 13-14) loss to Auburn in the Iron Bowl after Ed Salem missed an extra point that would have tied the game with less than two minutes left.

1950 Coach Harold Drew #19

The 1950 Alabama Crimson Tide football team played its 56th overall and 17th season as a member of the Southeastern Conference (SEC). The team was led by head coach Harold Drew, in his fourth year, and played its home games at Denny Stadium in Tuscaloosa, Legion Field in Birmingham and Ladd Stadium in Mobile, Alabama. They finished with a record of nine wins and two losses (9–2 overall, 6–2 in the SEC).

Although they finished ranked in the top 20 of both major polls, the Crimson Tide did not receive a bid to play in a bowl game after the season.

The Iron Bowl

One year earlier UA was upset by Auburn 14–13. So, this was sweet. Alabama scored touchdowns in all four quarters and shutout the Tigers 34–0 at Legion Field. Bobby Marlow scored the first three touchdowns for the Crimson Tide on a 26-yard reception from Ed Salem in the first, and on runs of seven and two yards in the second and third quarters. A 31-yard Larry Chiodetti run in the third and one-yard Jim Burkett run in the fourth quarter provided the final 34–0 margin. The victory improved Alabama's all-time record against Auburn to 6–8–1.

1951 Coach Harold Drew #19

The 1951 Alabama Crimson Tide football team played its 57th overall and 18th season as a member of the Southeastern Conference (SEC). The team was led by head coach Harold Drew, in his fifth year, and played their home games at Denny Stadium in Tuscaloosa, Legion Field in Birmingham, Ladd Stadium in Mobile and at the Cramton Bowl in Montgomery, Alabama. They finished with a record of five wins and six losses (5–6 overall, 3–5 in the SEC).

1952 Coach Harold Drew #19

The 1952 Alabama Crimson Tide football team played its 58th overall and 19th season as a member of the Southeastern Conference (SEC). The team was led by head coach Harold Drew, in his sixth year, and played their home games at Denny Stadium in Tuscaloosa, Legion Field in Birmingham, Ladd Stadium in Mobile and at the Cramton Bowl in Montgomery, Alabama. They finished with a record of ten wins and two losses (10–2 overall, 4–2 in the SEC) and they gained a nice victory over Syracuse in the Orange Bowl.

After a 5–6 campaign for the 1951 season, Alabama bounced back in 1952 to have its best season of the decade and finished 10–2. However, losses to Tennessee, for the fifth consecutive year without a victory, and Georgia Tech cost Alabama the SEC title. The Crimson Tide ended the season in its first bowl game in five years, against Syracuse in the Orange Bowl. The 61–6 Alabama victory set a school record for most points scored in a bowl game and an Orange Bowl record for points scored until the 2012 Orange Bowl.

The 55-point margin of victory stood as the all-time record for margin of victory in a bowl game through the 2008 GMAC Bowl. Freshman quarterback Bart Starr, playing with the varsity, appeared in seven games as the backup to Clell Hobson. Starr went on to have a legendary Hall of Fame career as quarterback of the Green Bay Packers.

On January 1, 1953 Alabama was invited to the Orange Bowl in Miami FL, to play Syracuse. The Crimson Tide manhandled the Orangemen in a 61-6 bloodbath shown on CBS TV.

1953 Coach Harold Drew #19

The 1953 Alabama Crimson Tide football team played its 59th overall and 20th season as a member of the Southeastern Conference (SEC). The team was led by head coach Harold Drew, in his seventh year, and played their home games at Denny Stadium in Tuscaloosa, Legion Field in Birmingham, Ladd Stadium in Mobile and at the Cramton Bowl in Montgomery, Alabama. They finished with a record of six wins, three losses and three ties (6–3–3 overall,

4–0–3 in the SEC), as SEC Champions and with a loss against Rice in the Cotton Bowl Classic.

1953 was one of the more unusual seasons in Alabama history. Alabama won only six games all year, and only four of seven conference games. However, the other three conference games were ties, and a 4–0–3 record was good enough to win Alabama the SEC title. It was Bama's first conference championship since 1945 and last until 1961. For their championship, Alabama accepted an invitation to play in the Cotton Bowl Classic.

In their matchup against Rice in the Cotton Bowl on January 1, 1954, one of the strangest plays in the history of college football occurred. In the second quarter, the Owls had the ball on its own five-yard line up 7–6 after they recovered an Alabama fumble.

On their first play of the drive, Rice running back Dicky Moegle swept around the right side, broke free, and appeared to be on his way to a 95-yard touchdown run—until Tommy Lewis of Alabama, who was on the sideline, ran into the field of play and tackled Moegle at the Alabama 40. Officials awarded Moegle a 95-yard touchdown run, and Rice won the game W (28–6).

1954 Coach Harold Drew #19

The 1954 Alabama Crimson Tide football team played its 60th overall and 21st season as a member of the Southeastern Conference (SEC). The team was led by head coach Harold Drew, in his eighth year, and played their home games at Denny Stadium in Tuscaloosa, Legion Field in Birmingham, Ladd Stadium in Mobile and at the Cramton Bowl in Montgomery, Alabama. They finished with a record of four wins, five losses and two ties (4–5–2 overall, 3–3–2 in the SEC).

Notes on Iron Bowl

It had not been since the 1949 season that Alabama was defeated by the rival Auburn Tigers 28–0 at Legion Field. Auburn led 7–0 at halftime with the only first half touchdown scored on a one-yard Bobby Freeman run in the first quarter. After a 41-yard Freeman run gave the Tigers a 14–0 lead in the third, a pair of fourth-quarter touchdowns gave Auburn the 28–0 victory. The final points came on a one-yard Joe Childress run and a three-yard Freeman run. The loss brought Alabama's all-time record against Auburn to 9–9–1.

More on Bart Starr

In May 1954, Bart Starr was in love and he eloped with Cherry Morton. The couple chose to keep their marriage a secret. Colleges often revoked the scholarships of married athletes in the 1950s, believing their focus should remain on sports. His wife remained in Jackson, Alabama, while Starr returned to the University of Alabama.

That summer, Starr suffered a severe back injury during a hazing incident for his initiation into the A Club. Concerned about the repercussions of ratting on the culprits, he covered up the cause by creating a fake story about being hurt while punting a football. He rarely played during his junior year due to the injury. The back injury disqualified him later from military service, and would occasionally bother him the rest of his football career.

Post script on Coach Harold Drew

Harold D. Drew was not Wallace Wade or Frank Thomas or Bear Bryant but he was not a bad coach. His successor on the other hand was a bad coach—the worst in Alabama history. As we discussed, Drew coached the University of Alabama football program from 1947-54, leading the Crimson Tide to 54 wins, 28 losses, and 7 ties. His tenure was highlighted by a 1952 major defeat of Syracuse in the Orange Bowl W (61-6) and a victory in the SEC Championship game in 1953.

Drew's successor, J.B. "Ears" Whitworth, led the Crimson Tide to its worst three-year stretch in school history, posting a 4–24–2 record before being fired following the 1957 season.

1955 Coach Jennings B. Whitworth #20

The 1955 Alabama Crimson Tide football team played its 61st overall and 22nd season as a member of the Southeastern Conference (SEC). The team was led by head coach Jennings B.

Whitworth, in his first year, and played home games at Denny Stadium in Tuscaloosa, Legion Field in Birmingham and at Ladd Stadium in Mobile, Alabama. They finished with a record of zero wins and ten losses (0–10 overall, 0–7 in the SEC).

Whitworth replaces Drew in 1955

After a disappointing season of 4–5–2, Red Drew was replaced by J.B. Whitworth as coach of Alabama. As noted, Drew was not a bad coach by anybody's facts.

Whitworth conducted a youth movement in Alabama for the 1955 season and only two seniors started for the team. While supposedly healed from the back injury, Starr rarely played in his senior season either. Starr played briefly in the Blue–Gray bowl of 1955.

How Bart Starr Got to the Packers

Johnny Dee, the basketball coach at Alabama, was a friend of Jack Vainisi, the personnel director of the Green Bay Packers. Dees recommended Starr as a prospect to Vainisi. The Packers were convinced that Starr had the ability to succeed in the NFL and would learn quickly. They were in no hurry, however, and waited until the 17th round of the 1956 NFL Draft. Bart Starr was selected by the Packers, with the 200th pick.

Starr spent the summer of 1956 living with his in-laws and throwing footballs through a tire in their backyard, in order to prepare for his rookie season. The Packers offered $6500 to sign Starr and he accepted, with the added condition, requested by Starr, that he receive $1000 up front.

The moral of the story is that a great coach would have had Bart Starr on the field, not on the bench. Look at Whitworth's record. 0-10. Sophomore Albert Elmore was Whitworth's QB. Although he was relegated to a role as a backup senior quarterback in 1955, Bart Starr completed 55 of 96 passes for 587 yards and showed flashes of the brilliance he would enjoy as one of the NFL's greatest players. He threw a touchdown pass in the Miami game. Alabama did not score much in Starr's Senior Season -- 1955, and few scores were from passing.

On December 2, 1954, Harold Drew resigned as head coach of the Crimson Tide, and Jennings B. Whitworth was introduced as his successor. Whitworth brought a new system that was more oriented towards the running game. As a result, senior quarterback Bart Starr and the other Tide seniors saw little playing time. Whitworth, for his part, was only allowed to hire two assistants and required to retain the rest of Coach Drew's staff.

To put it mildly, Alabama football hit rock bottom in 1955, going 0–10, the worst season in school history. It was only the third winless season in the history of the Crimson Tide, the others being the 0–4 teams in 1893 and 1895 when the program was just starting.

For the season, Alabama only averaged 4.8 points per game and the opposition averaged 25.6. The Tide was shut out four times, the opposition never scored fewer than 20 points, and the smallest margin of defeat was 15 points in a 21–6 loss to Vanderbilt. Those of us looking on from the stands wonder how this coach got two more years.

1955 Alabama Crimson Tide Football Team Jennings B Whitworth Coach

Since all scores are losses, I will show the games in a columar fashion. None of the games were even close.

0-20 September 24   at No. 13 Houston Texas
6-21 October 1 at Vanderbilt
0-21 October 8 v TCU @ Denny Stadium
0-20 October 15 v Tennessee@ Legion Field
7-26 October 22 v Mississippi State @ Denny Stadium
14- 35October 29 at Georgia
7-27 November 5 v Tulane @ Ladd Stadium
2-26 November 12 v #11 Georgia Tech @ Legion Field •
12-34 November 18   at Miami Burdine Stadium
0-26 November 26 v #10 Auburn Legion Field (Iron Bowl)

1956 Coach Jennings B. Whitworth #20

The 1956 Alabama Crimson Tide football team played its 62nd
overall and 23rd season as a member of the Southeastern Conference
(SEC). The team was led by head coach Jennings B. Whitworth, in
his second year. UA played home games at Denny Stadium in
Tuscaloosa, Legion Field in Birmingham and at Ladd Stadium in
Mobile, Alabama. They finished with a record of two wins, seven
losses and one tie (2–7–1 overall, 2–5 in the SEC).

1957 Coach Jennings B. Whitworth #20

The 1957 Alabama Crimson Tide football team played its 63rd
overall and 24th season as a member of the Southeastern Conference
(SEC). The team was led by head coach Jennings B. Whitworth, in
his third year, and played their home games at Denny Stadium in
Tuscaloosa, Legion Field in Birmingham and at Ladd Stadium in
Mobile, Alabama. They finished with a record of two wins, seven
losses and one tie (2–7–1 overall, 1–6–1 in the SEC).

Paul "Bear" Bryant New Coach

 On October 24, University officials announced the contract of head
coach Whitworth would not be renewed when it expired December
1 after the season. On December 3, former Maryland, Kentucky and
then Texas A&M head coach and former Alabama player Paul Bear
Bryant was hired as both the head coach of the football team and
athletic director at Alabama.

On December 3, the University formally introduced then Texas A&M head coach and former Crimson Tide player Paul William "Bear" Bryant as the new head coach of the Crimson Tide. At the time of the announcement, Bryant also became athletic director as the replacement for Hank Crisp. He signed a ten-year contract to serve as Alabama's head coach. With a ten-year contract, there was no doubt that Bear Bryant would turn around the UA program and place it on the road to success.

Wrap Up on Coaches Harold Drew & Jennings B. Whitworth From Wiki Audio

Drew and Whitworth (1947–1957)

In January 1947, Harold Drew was hired as the head football coach of the Alabama Crimson Tide. In his first year, "Red" Drew led the 1947 Alabama team to an 8–3 record, a berth in the 1948 Sugar Bowl, and a number eight ranking in the final AP poll. In November 1948, he led Alabama to a victory over Georgia Tech that The Tuscaloosa News called "the upset of the season."

In November, he led the Crimson Tide to a 55–0 victory over Auburn, a score which remains the most lopsided in the history of the Alabama – Auburn football rivalry. In August 1951, Drew led the East team to a 15–6 victory in the Third Annual All-American High School game in Memphis. He also led the 1952 team to a 10-1-2 record and a 61–6 victory over Syracuse in the 1953 Orange Bowl.

Alabama's 55-point margin of victory remains the largest in the history of the Orange Bowl; it was also the highest point total in Orange Bowl history until West Virginia scored 70 points in the 2012 Orange Bowl. When the Orange Bowl bid was announced in November 1952, former Alabama athletes organized to urge the University to sign Drew to a long-term contract, and The Tuscaloosa News reported:

The invitation also is a fine tribute to Coach Harold (Red) Drew and his staff. We doubt if there is a coaching staff in the country that has done a better job than the one done by the Crimson

Tide staff in getting Alabama ready for the Georgia Tech and Maryland games.

Drew was selected as the SEC Coach of the Year in 1952, and he was given a two-year contract extension in December of that year. The following year, he led the 1953 team to a Southeastern Conference (SEC) championship and a berth in the 1954 Cotton Bowl Classic.

However, the 1954 team finished in sixth place in the SEC with a 4–5–2 record. With the poor showing of the 1954 team, rumors began to spread that Drew would not return as the head coach. On December 2, 1954, Drew was fired as the head coach and replaced with J. B. Whitworth. Drew was retained as Alabama's head track coach and associate professor of physical education. Drew stayed on as Alabama's track coach for 23 seasons and through at least 1964.

At the end of his tenure as Alabama's head football coach, Drew's salary was reported to have been about $12,000 per year. In eight years as Alabama's head football coach, Drew compiled a 51-28-7 record. He was inducted into the Alabama Sports Hall of Fame in 1970.

Alabama had grown into a major football power and enjoyed consistent success over the past three decades, but Drew's successor, J.B. "Ears" Whitworth, would lead the Crimson Tide to its worst three-year stretch in school history. From 1955 to 1957, Whitworth coached Alabama, where he posted a 4–24–2 record that included a 14-game losing streak from 1955 to 1956.

In his first year at Alabama, Whitworth was only allowed to hire only two of his own coaches and forced to retain the rest of former coach Harold Drew's assistants. This included athletic director Hank Crisp, Whitworth's boss, who was in charge of the defense.

Whitworth brought assistant coach Moose Johnson with him from Oklahoma A&M. Following successive 2–7–1 seasons in 1956 and 1957, Whitworth was fired and replaced by Bear Bryant.

Chapter 10 Coach Paul "Bear" Bryant - 1ˢᵗ 15 Yrs. 1958-1972

Paul "Bear" Bryant is Alabama's Most Renowned and Most Winning Coach

"No coach has ever won a game by what he knows; it's what his players know that counts." -Coach Paul "Bear" Bryant

Year	Coach	Conference	Record	SEC
1958	Bear Bryant #21	SEC	5-4-1	3-4-1
1959	Bear Bryant	SEC	7-2-2	4-1-2
1960	Bear Bryant	SEC	8-1-2	5–1–1
1961*	Bear Bryant	SEC	11-0-0	7-0-0
1962	Bear Bryant	SEC	10-1-0	6-1-0
1963	Bear Bryant	SEC	9-2-0	6-2-0
1964*	Bear Bryant	SEC	10-1-0	8-0-0
1965*	Bear Bryant	SEC	9-1-1	6-1-1
1966	Bear Bryant	SEC	11-0-0	6-0-0
1967	Bear Bryant	SEC	8-2-1	5-1-0
1968	Bear Bryant	SEC	8-3-0	4-2-0
1969	Bear Bryant	SEC	6-5-0	2-4-0
1970	Bear Bryant	SEC	6-5-1	3-4-0
1971	Bear Bryant	SEC	11-1-0	7-0-0
1972	Bear Bryant	SEC	10-2-0	7-1-0

* National Championships (6 in total for the Bear)

NCAA football national champ. BEAR BRYANT Alabama

1958 Coach Paul "Bear Bryant #21

The 1958 Alabama Crimson Tide football team played its 64th overall and 25th season as a member of the Southeastern Conference (SEC). The team was led by head coach Bear Bryant, in his first year, and played their home games at Denny Stadium in Tuscaloosa, Legion Field in Birmingham and at Ladd Stadium in Mobile, Alabama.

UA finished 1958 with a record of five wins, four losses and one tie (5–4–1 overall, 3–4–1 in the SEC). As they finished the season above .500, Alabama gained its first winning season since 1953, and their five victories gave Bryant more wins in one season than former head coach Jennings B. Whitworth had achieved in previous three. At the end of the prior season, On December 3, 1957, University Officials formally introduced then Texas A&M head coach and former Crimson Tide player Bear Bryant as the new head coach of the Alabama Crimson Tide.

After its victory over Memphis State, Alabama players voted to accept any potential bowl bid if one was extended to the team. As they entered their final game of the season against Auburn, officials from the Bluegrass Bowl announced that the Crimson Tide was their top choice to participate in the inaugural event regardless of the outcome against the Tigers. Although the Crimson Tide were their top choice, on December 1, bowl officials announced that Florida State and Oklahoma State would participate in the game. It's not nice to fool a "Bear."

It was reported that prior to the announcement, the game was to have been seen a rematch of Alabama against Vanderbilt, but that no deal had been reached. After the Crimson Tide declined the invitation, Florida State accepted it.

Even great men make mistakes. Greater men admit them. Years later, Bryant stated he regretted he did not accept the bid as it would have allowed for additional practice time at the conclusion of the season.

1959 Coach Paul "Bear Bryant #21

The 1959 Alabama Crimson Tide football team (in other forms known as "Alabama", "UA" or "Bama") played its 65th overall and 26th season as a member of the Southeastern Conference (SEC). The team was led by head coach Bear Bryant, in his second year, and played its home games at Denny Stadium in Tuscaloosa, Legion Field in Birmingham and at Ladd Stadium in Mobile, Alabama. This year's team finished with a record of seven wins, two losses and two ties (7–2–2 overall, 4–1–2 in the SEC). Additionally, the team suffered a loss against Penn State in the inaugural Liberty Bowl.

1960 Coach Paul "Bear" Bryant #21

The 1960 Alabama Crimson Tide football team played its 66th overall and 27th season as a member of the Southeastern Conference (SEC). The team was led by head coach Bear Bryant, in his third year, and played its home games at Denny Stadium in Tuscaloosa and Legion Field in Birmingham, Alabama. They finished 1960 with a record of eight wins, one loss and two ties (8–1–2 overall, 5–1–1 in the SEC) Alabama was invited and accepted an invitation to play Texas in the Bluebonnet Bowl. The result was a tie. Great game.

Immediately after its victory over Auburn in the season finale, Bryant accepted an invitation to play in the Bluebonnet Bowl against Texas. As played against the Longhorns, each team only scored a single field goal in this 3–3 tie. Tommy Brooker connected on a 30-yard field goal for Alabama in the third and Dan Petty tied the game in the fourth for Texas with his 20-yard kick. The tie brought Alabama's all-time record against Texas to 0–4–1. The long-term difference for Alabama was that the "Bear" had arrived. Long live the Bear. Bear Bryant had another 22 seasons in him before he would choose to retire after the 1982 season.

1961 Coach Paul "Bear" Bryant #21

The 1961 Alabama Crimson Tide football team played its 67th overall and 28th season as a member of the Southeastern Conference (SEC). The team was led by head coach Bear Bryant, in his fourth year, and it played home games at Denny Stadium in Tuscaloosa, Legion Field in Birmingham and Ladd Stadium in Mobile, Alabama. The team finished the season undefeated with eleven wins (11–0 overall, 7–0 in the SEC). Alabama added a victory over Arkansas in the Sugar Bowl for good measure and they became the 1961 NCAA consensus national champions.

At 11-0, it was unmistakable that the Bear had done it. The 1961 national championship was the first of the six that Bear Bryant would win as head coach of the Crimson Tide. 1961 was the beginning of a nice and very sweet legacy for Alabama as Bear Bryant a favorite son, would bring many victories home one by one.

1962 Sugar Bowl – Nine Heart Attacks

This game is recognized as one of Alabama's greatest games of all time. Expanded narrative provided by bamahammer.

Alabama legends Pat Trammel and Bear Bryant had led Alabama to a perfect regular season, but the Sugar Bowl wouldn't be as easy. Alabama was facing the Arkansas Razorbacks of the Southwest Conference under their own legendary coach Frank Broyles and they were determined to make it hard on the Tide.

Jan. 1, 1962: Sugar Bowl (New Orleans, LA)

This team was an Alabama defensive juggernaut though. Bear Bryant said "they played like it was a sin to give up a point." The Bear wasn't exaggerating either; over 10 games Alabama only allowed 22 points in 1961. Before the bowl game Alabama hadn't allowed a point in 5 games.

The first half of the game went Alabama's way, and the Tide was able to put 10 points on the board. Alabama's first score came on the sixth play of the game. This wasn't an offensive minded team though and those would be the only points Alabama would score in the contest.

Alabama depended on their defense to win the game and was able to hold off Arkansas with a few well-timed interceptions. Bear Bryant described the experience by saying that he "had about nine heart attacks out there."

Arkansas did manage to get a field goal in the third quarter and Alabama ended the game with a 10-3 victory.

Alabama was once again named national champions; so the 1962 Sugar Bowl is just more proof that defense wins championships.

1962 Coach Paul "Bear" Bryant #21

The 1962 Alabama Crimson Tide football team played its 68th overall and 29th season as a member of the Southeastern Conference (SEC). The team was led by head coach Bear Bryant, in his fifth year, and played their home games at Denny Stadium in Tuscaloosa and Legion Field in Birmingham, Alabama. They finished this season with ten wins and one loss (10–1 overall, 6–1 in the SEC) and with a victory over Oklahoma in the Orange Bowl.

The Crimson Tide opened the season on Sept 22 with a win over Georgia W (35-0) at Denny Stadium before 54,000. Many saw this as an opportunity for another National Championship for the Bear and it was. They missed it by a hair. Bear would get his next championship through the great QB play of a sophomore on the 1962 team—Joe Willie Namath

I loved watching Joe Namath play as a kid. He was from his own mold. Bear Bryant saw a lot in Joe Namath as he chose him above the rest of the QB talent he had to run the Crimson Tide as its on-field general. Yet, when necessary, Bear would mete out sanctions v Joe when he did not measure up to Alabama's discipline standards.

After a successful twelve-year career, Namath was inducted into the NFL Hall of Fame in 1985.

Looking back: Joe Namath's debut was stellar as Alabama routed Georgia 35-0 in 1962

By Creg Stephenson | cstephenson@al.com
Submitted on October 01, 2015 at 6:30 AM;
Updated October 08, 2015 at 8:20 AM

Few players in the history of college football have had a more spectacular debut than Joe Namath.

Alabama began its season against Georgia on Sept. 22, 1962, rolling to a 35-0 victory behind a sophomore quarterback making his varsity debut. Namath completed 10 of 14 passes for

179 yards and three touchdowns as the Crimson Tide opened defense of its national championship in dominating fashion before what was then a record crowd of 54,000 at Birmingham's Legion Field.

Namath threw scoring passes of 52 yards to Richard Williamson (who died just last week) and 10 and 12 yards to Cotton Clark. Alabama head coach Paul "Bear" Bryant pulled Namath midway through the third quarter, with Jack Hurlbut handling quarterback duties the rest of the way.

Clark also ran for a touchdown, as did Hudson Harris, part of a 273-yard rushing night for Alabama. The Crimson Tide defense, led by All-America linebacker Lee Roy Jordan, limited Georgia to just 116 total yards.

The win was Alabama's 12th straight, and 19th in a row without a loss (a 3-3 tie with Oklahoma in the Bluebonnet Bowl being the only blemish). The Crimson Tide's defense extended its streak of not allowing a touchdown to 34 consecutive quarters.

…

Despite Namath's season-long brilliance and Alabama's continued defensive dominance, the Crimson Tide ultimately failed to defend its national championship. Alabama dropped a late-season game to Georgia Tech 7-6 and finished 10-1 after beating Oklahoma 17-0 in the Orange Bowl. Southern Cal and Ole Miss claimed that season's national titles.

…

Of course, Alabama's domination on the field that night in 1962 is only half the story. The game would have lasting fame not only for launching Namath's legend as well as other reasons…

1963 Coach Paul "Bear" Bryant #21

The 1963 Alabama Crimson Tide football team played its 69th overall and 30th season as a member of the Southeastern Conference (SEC). The team was led by head coach Bear Bryant, in his sixth year, and played their home games at Denny Stadium in Tuscaloosa, Legion Field in Birmingham and Ladd Stadium in Mobile, Alabama. They finished season with nine wins and two losses (9–2 overall, 6–2 in the SEC) and with a victory over Ole Miss in the Sugar Bowl.

Additional Notes:

After their loss in the Iron Bowl on November 30, Alabama officially accepted an invitation to play the SEC champion Ole Miss Rebels for the first time since the 1944 season in a Sugar Bowl that featured a pair of SEC teams. As each team entered the game, Mississippi finished in the No. 7 position and Alabama in the No. 8 position in the final AP poll of the season.

With starting quarterback Joe Namath still suspended, the Crimson Tide offense struggled, but four Tim Davis field goals proved to be enough for Alabama to win 12–7 over the Rebels. Davis gave the Crimson Tide a 12–0 lead as then entered the fourth quarter after connecting from 31-yards in the first, 46 and 22-yards in the second and 48-yards in the third quarter.

Ole Miss responded in the fourth quarter with their only points on a five-yard Perry Lee Dunn touchdown pass to Larry Smith that made the final score 12–7. For his four-field goal performance, Davis was named the Sugar Bowl MVP. The victory improved Alabama's all-time record against Ole Miss 17–3–2.

1964 Coach Paul "Bear" Bryant #21

The 1964 Alabama Crimson Tide football team played its 70th overall and 31st season as a member of the Southeastern Conference (SEC). The team was led by head coach Bear Bryant, in his seventh year. UA played home games at Denny Stadium in Tuscaloosa, Legion Field in Birmingham and Ladd Stadium in Mobile, Alabama.

UA finished the season with ten wins and one loss (10–1 overall, 8–0 in the SEC). They were SEC champions. They picked up a loss after the season to Texas L (17-21) on January 1, 1965 in the Orange Bowl. The major wire services at that time awarded national champions prior to the start of bowl season. Therefore, Alabama was also recognized as national champions by the AP and UPI before their loss to Texas.

After the bowl games, the Football Writers Association of America as stated in 1964 college football season named the undefeated Arkansas Razorbacks as the national champions. The Razorbacks had defeated Texas during the regular season. So, it was a split decision.

Bear Bryant & Joe
<<<Namath

After the season, Joe Namath was selected as the first overall pick by the New York Jets in the 1965 AFL Draft. In addition to Namath, eleven other lettermen from the 1964 squad were drafted into the National Football League.

Coach Bear Bryant, right, quarterback Joe Namath and Alabama lost to Texas in the first Orange Bowl played at night, in 1965. Credit University of Alabama

1965 Coach Paul "Bear" Bryant #21

The 1965 Alabama Crimson Tide football team played its 71st overall and 32nd season as a member of the Southeastern Conference (SEC). The team was led by head coach Bear Bryant, in his eighth year. It played home games at Denny Stadium in Tuscaloosa, Legion Field in Birmingham and Ladd Stadium in Mobile, Alabama. They finished this season with nine wins, one loss and one tie (9–1–1 overall, 6–1–1 in the SEC), as SEC champions and with a victory over Nebraska in the Orange Bowl. Alabama was also recognized as national champions by the AP Poll after their Orange Bowl win.

1966 Orange Bowl Notes:

For the second year in a row, Alabama played in the Orange Bowl. In the 1966 edition of the game, the Crimson Tide defeated the Nebraska Cornhuskers 39–28 and finished the season 9–1–1 and as AP national champions.

The NCAA recognizes consensus national champions as the teams that have captured a championship by way of one of the major polls since the 1950 college football season. As they entered the Orange Bowl, the Crimson Tide was ranked fourth by the AP behind Michigan State, Arkansas and Nebraska.

After losses by the Spartans and Razorbacks in their bowl games, coupled with an Alabama victory over Nebraska in their contest, the Crimson Tide vaulted into the No. 1 position in the final AP poll of the season and therefore won the national championship. Michigan State was also recognized as national champions by various other selectors for the 1965 season, including the UPI.

1966 Coach Paul "Bear" Bryant #21

The 1966 Alabama Crimson Tide football team played its 72nd overall and 33rd season as a member of the Southeastern Conference (SEC). The team was led by head coach Bear Bryant, in his ninth year, and played their home games at Denny Stadium in Tuscaloosa, Legion Field in Birmingham and Ladd Stadium in Mobile, Alabama. They finished season undefeated with eleven wins (11–0 overall, 6–0 in the SEC), as SEC co-champions and with a victory over Nebraska in the Sugar Bowl.

Before the season even began, Alabama was recognized as national champions from the Associated Press for the 1965 season after they defeated Nebraska in the Orange Bowl and finished with an overall record of 9–1–1. In February 1966, SEC commissioner Bernie Moore penalized Alabama for scholarship violations with its freshman squad. Moore found that Alabama awarded 42 freshman scholarships instead of the 40 allowed by the league. As such, the Crimson Tide were penalized with a scholarship reduction of two to 38 for the 1966 recruiting class.

In the January 1 game that followed, Alabama defeated Nebraska W (34-7) in the Sugar Bowl and finished the season undefeated.

Although they were the only undefeated and untied college team at the conclusion of the football year, Alabama was not selected as national champions for the season. On the 1966 squad, Green Bay Packers head coach Vince Lombardi stated: "I don't know, we haven't played Alabama yet" when asked how it felt to have the world's greatest football team for the season after his Packers won their 5th Super Bowl. Sometimes the pundits get it plum wrong!

Notes on Bowl Game & National Championship

This Sugar Bowl has been determined by the pundits to be one of the most significand football games in Crimson Tide History.

For the second year in a row, Alabama played Nebraska in a bowl game, and for the second consecutive year. Alabama defeated the Cornhuskers. As we look at this year's Sugar Bowl, the Crimson Tide defeated Nebraska 34–7 and finished the season undefeated.

UA opened with a 17–0 lead in the first quarter on touchdown runs of one-yard by Leslie Kelley, 14-yards by Ken Stabler and on a 30-yard Steve Davis field goal. Bama then extended the lead to 24–0 at halftime after a six-yard Wayne Trimble touchdown run in the second quarter.

Lefty Ken Stabler in the 1967 Sugar Bowl Alabama dominated 34 - 7. Stabler scored TDs on runs of 1 and 14 yds. Stabler was selected as the MVP.

After a 40-yard Davis field goal in the third for the Crimson Tide, Nebraska scored its only points early in the fourth quarter on a 15-yard Bob Churchich touchdown pass to Dick Davis that made the score 27–7. The Crimson Tide then closed the game with a 45-yard Stabler TD pass to Ray Perkins (Coach #22)- made final score 34–7.

For his stellar performance, Ken Stabler, who later was my father-in-law's favorite pro player with the Broncos, was recognized as the game's MVP. The victory improved Alabama's all-time record against Nebraska to 2–0.

As noted several times in this book, the NCAA recognizes consensus national champions as the teams that have captured a championship by way of one of the major polls since the 1950 college football season. Although Alabama was the only team with a perfect record at the end of the season as Notre Dame and Michigan State tied in their meeting, they were not recognized as national champions.

Keith Dunnavant suggests in his book about the 1966 season, that the continued segregation of the Alabama football team (the Crimson Tide did not integrate until Wilbur Jackson and John Mitchell made the 1971 team), as well as violent resistance by white Alabamians to the Civil Rights Movement, cost the Crimson Tide support with voters in 1966 and led to the third-place finish. Many believe that football and politics are two different things and should be kept separate.

The 1966 squad was retroactively recognized as national champions by Berryman and Sagarin (ELO-Chess) but Alabama does not claim either in their official national championship total.

1967 Sugar Bowl – Dominance Denied

This game is recognized by the major pundits as one of the greatest Alabama football games of all time.

Alabama is very often described as being a "dominant" football team, and what they did to Nebraska in the 1967 Sugar Bowl was clearly a show of dominance.

Alabama put a beating on Nebraska, winning the game 34-7 with Nebraska's 7 coming in the fourth quarter after the game was all but decided.

The thing about the 1967 Sugar Bowl is that Alabama didn't end up winning the national championship. Even though Alabama had a perfect season, beat some really great teams, and Notre Dame had tied Michigan State in the regular season the Tide was denied a national championship.

Alabama had been awarded the national championship the last two season, in 1965 Alabama was given a national championship even though they lost their bowl game.

Perhaps this was the awarding bodies trying to correct the mistake of 1965… or perhaps this was some of the first Bama hate from the media. Whatever the reason, Alabama did not get a national championship that they most certainly should have been awarded in 1966.

Instead Notre Dame and Michigan State claim the 1966 national title. If you were looking for a reason to dislike the Michigan State Spartans…

So, when you're complaining about the playoff and the bowl system now, just remember how bad it was after the 1967 Sugar Bowl.

1967 Coach Paul "Bear" Bryant #21

The 1967 Alabama Crimson Tide football team (played its 73rd overall and 34th season as a member of the Southeastern Conference (SEC). The team was led by head coach Bear Bryant, in his 10th year, and played its home games at Denny Stadium in Tuscaloosa, Legion Field in Birmingham and Ladd Stadium in Mobile, Alabama. They finished the season with eight wins, two losses and one tie (8–2–1 overall, 5–1 in the SEC) and with a loss against Texas A&M in the Cotton Bowl Classic.

During the spring practice sessions, five African American students attempted to walk-on to the football team. Two of the five, Dock Rone and Andrew Pernell participated in the annual A-Day Game. Although none of the five made it to the varsity squad, their participation as part of the team marked the beginnings of the desegregation of the football program that culminated in the signing of Wilbur Jackson to an athletic scholarship in 1970.

This Iron Bowl Game has been determined by the pundits to be one of the most significand football games in Crimson Tide History.

1967 Iron Bowl – The Run in the Mud

This game is another one that the pundits have described as one of Alabama's best football games ever and so we show their textual description about the game. Here it is:

This is an Alabama legend. The 1967 Iron Bowl is one of those moments in Alabama football history that grabs the imagination and will bring chill bumps to your skin even after all this time.
The 1967 Iron Bowl is of course Kenny Stabler's famous "run in the mud."

The 1967 Iron Bowl was played under the lights at Legion Field. It's strange to us now since we are used to the 7pm CBS start, but this was the first Iron Bowl to ever be played at night.

It had been raining all evening and so Legion Field had naturally (as opposed to artificially, perhaps using sprinklers) been turned to mud. It was a defensive battle with Alabama holding off Auburn at the goal line several times. Auburn was able to get a field goal in the third quarter to take a 3-0 lead… then Kenny Stabler happened.

On an option play, Kenny "the Snake" Stabler kept the ball bobbing and weaving around Auburn Tigers all the way down to the end-zone. Alabama would win the game 7-3.

Bear Bryant simply said "I could watch that all night" about Stabler's run. The 1967 Iron Bowl had it all, Alabama vs Auburn, mud and blood, defense, and a win on a big play by Kenny "The Snake" Stabler.

The infamous Ken Stabler Run in the Mud

Discriminatory scholarship policies were a violation of Title VI of the Civil Rights Act of 1964. In February 1967, Dock Rone, an African American student enrolled at the University from Montgomery, met with coach Bryant about potentially trying to make the football team as a walk-on. At that time, Coach Bryant believed a non-scholarship, African American walk-on would help pave the way to complete integration of the football team.

On April 1, the football team opened spring practice. Rone then became the first African American to wear the Alabama uniform. An additional four African American students reported to practice, but were unable to participate at that time as they had not yet been academically cleared to play.

These African American students that reported were Melvin Leverett of Prichard, Arthur Dunning of Mobile, Andrew Pernell of Bessemer and Jerome Tucker of Birmingham. By the second practice all except for Tucker were declared academically eligible to compete on the football squad and joined the team on April 3.

Throughout spring practice, Rone played as an offensive lineman and Leverett, Dunning and Pernell played as backs. On May 5,

Rone and Pernell participated in the annual A-Day Game and became the first African American players to play at Denny Stadium as members of the Crimson Tide football team.

Although Rone was on track to potentially become the first African American player on scholarship at Alabama, in the summer that followed family problems forced him to leave school. Three years later, Wilbur Jackson became the first African American to sign and play under athletic scholarship for the Alabama football team.

Cotton Bowl Notes

After Texas A&M upset Alabama 20–16 in the 1968 Cotton Bowl Classic, Bear Bryant carried the Aggies head coach Gene Stallings (later a great Alabama coach) off the field to celebrate the victory as he was both a former player and assistant coach under him. After Alabama scored first on an eight-yard Ken Stabler touchdown run, A&M responded with a 13-yard Edd Hargett touchdown pass to Larry Stegent that tied the game 7–7 at the end of the first quarter.

In the second quarter, UA scored first on a 34-yard Steve Davis field goal and Texas followed with a seven-yard Hargett touchdown pass to Tommy Maxwell that made the halftime score 13–10.

Each team then scored their final points in the third quarter. The Aggies scored first on a 20-yard Wendell Housley touchdown run followed by Ken Stabler on an eight-yard touchdown run that made the final score 20–16. The loss put Alabama's all-time record against Texas A&M to 1–1.

1968 Coach Paul "Bear" Bryant #21

The 1968 Alabama Crimson Tide football team played its 74th overall and 35th season as a member of the Southeastern Conference (SEC). The team was led by head coach Bear Bryant, in his 11th year, and played their home games at Denny Stadium in Tuscaloosa, Legion Field in Birmingham and Ladd Stadium in Mobile, Alabama. They finished the season with eight wins and three losses (8–3 overall, 4–2 in the SEC) and with a loss against Missouri in the Gator Bowl.

1969 Coach Paul "Bear" Bryant #21

The 1969 Alabama Crimson Tide football team played its 75th overall and 36th season as a member of the Southeastern Conference (SEC). The team was led by head coach Bear Bryant, in his 12th year, and played their home games at Denny Stadium in Tuscaloosa and Legion Field in Birmingham, Alabama. They finished season with six wins and five losses (6–5 overall, 2–4 in the SEC). UA also suffered a loss against Colorado in the Liberty Bowl.

1970 Coach Paul "Bear" Bryant #21

The 1970 Alabama Crimson Tide football team played its 76th overall and 37th season as a member of the Southeastern Conference (SEC). The team was led by head coach Bear Bryant, in his 13th year. Alabama played home games at Denny Stadium in Tuscaloosa and Legion Field in Birmingham, Alabama. They finished this season with six wins five losses and one tie (6–5–1 overall, 3–4 in the SEC) and with a tie against Oklahoma in the Astro-Bluebonnet Bowl.

1971 Coach Paul "Bear" Bryant #21

The 1971 Alabama Crimson Tide football team played its 77th overall and 38th season as a member of the Southeastern Conference (SEC). The team was led by head coach Bear Bryant, in his 14th year, and played its home games at Denny Stadium in Tuscaloosa and Legion Field in Birmingham, Alabama.

They finished the season with eleven wins and one loss (11–1 overall, 7–0 in the SEC), as SEC champions. They finished the season with a loss to Nebraska in the Orange Bowl, dampening their championship hopes.

The 1971 squad had a number Alabama football firsts to their credit. This was the first team that African Americans contributed as members of the Alabama varsity squad, with John Mitchell being the first to actually see playing time.

1971 also marked the first season the Crimson Tide utilized the wishbone offense that Alabama became noted for throughout the remainder of Bryant's tenure as head coach at Alabama.

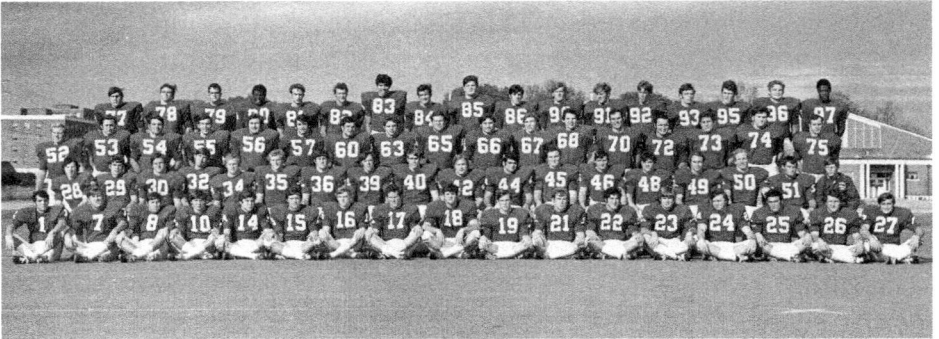

Alabama Football 1971 Coach Bear Bryant

Although several African American students had competed during spring practice in 1967, Wilbur Jackson was the first African American awarded a scholarship to play for Alabama. He competed as a member of the freshman squad in 1970 and played for the varsity team in 1971.

For the 1971 season, John Mitchell became the first African American to play on the varsity squad for the Crimson Tide during the regular season after he transferred from Eastern Arizona College.

1971 Tennessee – The Start of a Streak

This game has been determined by the pundits to be one of the most significand football games in Crimson Tide History.
It had been 3,347 days since Tennessee last beat Alabama in football, but Alabama's longest win streak vs. the Volunteers was logged in another time at 4,015 days long.

The 1971 matchup between Alabama and Tennessee would start an eleven-year winning streak for the Crimson Tide of Alabama over their rivals from the north.

In October of 1971 Alabama faced Tennessee in Legion Field in Birmingham, one of the Tide's favorite places to beat a rival. The Crimson Tide would end up on top that day too, defeating Tennessee W (32-15).

Maybe the win was due to Alabama's moving to the run focused wishbone, or maybe it was all about motivation...

Alabama QB Terry Davis Scampers with the ball in Tide Win

Before 1971 Tennessee had won 4 straight against Alabama and for the first time in history the Vols had taken a lead in the series. So, every Tennessee win from that point forward would have just increased their lead. Alabama and its pride in winning could not permit that notion to stand.

By the end of the streak Alabama had acquired a ten-game lead, today as research shows, that lead stands at 14 games.

The Crimson Tide on Nov 13 defeated Miami W (31-3) on homecoming and set up a match-up between undefeated teams for the first time in the history of the Iron Bowl on Nov 27 to close the regular season.

With both teams ranked in the top five, Alabama defeated Auburn W (31–7) and captured the outright SEC football championship. Playing again for the National Championship, the Crimson Tide could not pull it off and were defeated by #1 Nebraska in the Orange Bowl on January 1 1972.

!972 Orange Bowl Action

Some notes on the "wishbone" from Wikipedia

In 1968, Texas head coach Darrell Royal and his offensive coordinator Emory Bellard introduced what would become known as the wishbone offense. The wishbone was derived from the Split-T offense run at Oklahoma under Bud Wilkinson. In the formation, the quarterback lines up with a fullback and two tailbacks behind him, and on any play, may keep the ball, hand off to the fullback, or pitch to a tailback.

From the time, Bryant arrived at Alabama through the 1970 season, the Crimson Tide ran a pro-style offense. By 1969, Bryant began to recruit larger linemen and tailbacks, and after a pair of six win seasons in 1969 and 1970, Bryant saw the success of the wishbone for the Longhorns and decided to implement the offense for the 1971 season.

In spring 1971, Alabama assistants Mal Moore and Jimmy Sharpe traveled to Austin where they saw first-hand how the wishbone operated during Texas' final week of spring practice. During the second summer session at the University, both Moore and Sharpe began to work with players on the offensive change, and in August Royal and Bellard traveled to Tuscaloosa and led a coaching clinic for the Alabama staff on the wishbone.

In order to keep the change a secret, Bryant kept all of the Crimson Tide's practices closed from the public, screened the practice field from view with a canvas and hired security to keep people away.

The change to the wishbone was kept under such secrecy that when the media would visit practice, Bryant had the team practice the pro-style system that had been phased out. Alabama later opened the season with an upset victory over USC that was credited to the surprise switch to the wishbone that caught the Trojans off-guard.

The Orange Bowl

It was billed as #1 v #2 and it was nothing less. It was for all the marbles--the national championship. Alabama was dominated by the Nebraska Cornhuskers L (6-38) in the game. Nebraska came out like gangbusters and captured a 28–0 halftime lead by scoring a pair of touchdowns in each of the first two quarters. Jeff Kinney scored on a two-yard run and Johnny Rodgers on a 77-yard punt return in the first; Jerry Tagge scored on a one-yard run and Gary Dixon on a two-yard run in the second quarter.

Alabama then scored its only points on a three-yard Terry Davis touchdown run in the third and made the score 28–6. But, the Cornhuskers had not stopped playing. They closed the game with a 21-yard Rich Sanger field goal in the third and a one-yard Van Brownson touchdown run in the fourth that made the final score L 6-38). The loss brought Alabama's all-time record v Nebraska to 2–1.

1972 Coach Paul "Bear" Bryant #21

The 1972 Alabama Crimson Tide football team played its 78th overall season and 39th season as a member of the Southeastern Conference (SEC). The team was led by head coach Bear Bryant, in his 15th year, and played its home games at Denny Stadium in Tuscaloosa and Legion Field in Birmingham, Alabama. They finished the season with ten wins and two losses (10–2 overall, 7–1 in the SEC), as SEC champions and they suffered a loss to Texas in the Cotton Bowl Classic.

Chapter 11 Coach Bear Bryant - Last 10 Yrs. -- 1973-1982

Paul "Bear" Bryant is Alabama's Most Renowned and Most Winning Coach

"No coach has ever won a game by what he knows; it's what his players know that counts." -Coach Paul "Bear" Bryant

Year	Coach	Conference	Record	SEC
1973*	Bear Bryant #21	SEC	11-1-0	8-0-0
1974	Bear Bryant	SEC	11-1-0	6-0-0
1975	Bear Bryant	SEC	11-1-0	6-0-0
1976	Bear Bryant	SEC	9-3-0	5-2-0
1977	Bear Bryant	SEC	11-1-0	7-0-0
1978*	Bear Bryant	SEC	11-1-0	6-0-0
1979*	Bear Bryant	SEC	12-0-0	6-0-0
1980	Bear Bryant	SEC	10-2-0	5-1-0
1981	Bear Bryant	SEC	9-2-1	6-0-0
1990	Bear Bryant	SEC	8-4-0	3-3-0

* National Championship

1973 Coach Paul "Bear" Bryant #21

The 1973 Alabama Crimson Tide football team played its 79th overall and 40th season as a member of the Southeastern Conference (SEC). The team was led by head coach Bear Bryant, in his 16th year, and played their home games at Denny Stadium on the UA campus in Tuscaloosa and Legion Field in Birmingham, Alabama.

The Crimson Tide finished the season with eleven wins and one loss (11–1 overall, 8–0 in the SEC), as SEC champions and with a loss to Notre Dame in the Sugar Bowl. Although they did lose in the Sugar Bowl, Alabama was recognized as national champions by the Coaches' Poll (UPI) as their selection was made prior to bowl season at the time. UA had a great football year.

Sugar Bowl

Without the benefit of the Bowl Games, at the conclusion of the regular season, Alabama was selected as national champions in the UPI Coaches' Poll for 1073. Back then this poll was taken before the bowl games were played. However, the Crimson Tide would not win the AP championship as they lost 24–23 against Notre Dame, coached by Ara Parseghian in his tenth year with the Irish. It was a classic Sugar Bowl tough game. The two polling factions were not yet in synch as they were independent of the NCAA.

Notre Dame took a 14–10 by half-time with a big play coming on a 93-yard kickoff return for a touchdown by Al Hunter. Each team scored a touchdown in the third quarter. With this, the Irish were up 21–17 going into the fourth. Alabama took a 23–21 lead on a flea flicker touchdown pass from running back Mike Strock back to quarterback Richard Todd. However, Bill Davis missed the extra point and Alabama was up by only two.

Notre Dame drove the ball downfield and kicked a 19-yard field goal to go up 24–23 with 4:26 to go. Bama could not move the ball well enough to answer. However, the punt left Notre Dame backed up to their own goal. With time ticking away and Notre Dame facing a third and eight, Alabama had a chance to get the ball back in excellent field position.

Then, came the "but." But Irish QB Tom Clements threw a 35-yard pass to tight end Robin Webber and Notre Dame held on to win the game and the AP side of the national championship. Football games are often decided on razor-thin margins.

1974 Coach Paul "Bear" Bryant #21

The 1974 Alabama Crimson Tide football team played its 80th overall and 41st season as a member of the Southeastern Conference (SEC). The team was led by head coach Bear Bryant, in his 17th year, and played their home games at Denny Stadium in Tuscaloosa and Legion Field in Birmingham, Alabama. They finished the season with eleven wins and one loss (11–1 overall, 6–0 in the SEC), as SEC champions and with a loss to Notre Dame in the Orange Bowl.

Some Season Game highlights – Florida State

After their victory over Ole Miss, Alabama retained its #3 position in the AP Poll prior to its game against Florida State. Against the Seminoles, the Crimson Tide struggled and trailed until the final minute of regulation. The team moved close enough for a field goal try with time running out. Bucky Berrey toed the game-winning field goal for the 8–7 victory.

The Seminoles started the scoring early when they took the opening kickoff and drove 78-yards on nine plays for a 7–0 lead behind a six-yard Larry Key touchdown run. Florida State continued to hold their touchdown lead through the third quarter when the Crimson Tide scored their first points on a 44-yard Berrey field goal. With just 1:27 left in the game, Seminoles head coach Darrell Mudra elected to take an intentional safety instead of attempting a punt out of the end zone. Sometimes Avant-garde strategies fail like this one did.

The coach made this decision as Alabama had been close on a couple of previous attempts to block punts during the game. He did not want a block to occur in the end zone, and felt that he had the two points to spare to protect his victory. The safety would provide a free kick with no onrushing Bama linemen.

Down now 7–5, after the safety free-kick the Crimson Tide drove into field goal territory and Berrey hit the game winner from 36-yards out with only 0:33 left in the game. The victory improved Alabama's all-time record against Florida State to 2–0–1

Orange Bowl Notes

Playing for what should have been a second consecutive national championship against Notre Dame, Alabama played the Irish tough but just not enough. They were upset again by the Fighting Irish L (11-13) in the Orange Bowl.

UA had come back well after Notre Dame took a 13–0 lead behind touchdown runs of four-yards by Wayne Bullock in the first and nine-yards by Mark McLane in the second quarter. A 21-yard Danny Ridgeway field goal for Alabama made the halftime score 13–3.

After a scoreless third period, the Crimson Tide scored the final points of the game on a 48-yard Richard Todd touchdown pass to Russ Schamun that made the final score 13–11. It was a game that was as close as it could get. Well-played. The loss brought Alabama's all-time record against Notre Dame to 0–2.

1975 Coach Paul "Bear" Bryant #21

The 1975 Alabama Crimson Tide football team played its 81st overall and 42nd season as a member of the Southeastern Conference (SEC). The team was led by head coach Bear Bryant, in his 18th year, and played its home games at Denny Stadium in Tuscaloosa and Legion Field in Birmingham, Alabama.

Bama finished the season with eleven wins and one loss (11–1 overall, 6–0 in the SEC), as SEC champions and with a victory over Penn State in the Sugar Bowl.

The 1975 squad entered the season with the No. 2 ranking in the AP Poll and as one of the favorites to compete for the national championship. Their championship hopes were dashed after they were upset by an unranked Missouri team in their season opener at Legion Field 7-20 on Sept 8.

Under Bear Bryant, Alabama teams were always competitive and up there for the championships, but sometimes a few other teams had better records. Bryant was consistent. He did well with what he had and whenever he reloaded, Alabama dominated.

1976 Coach Paul "Bear" Bryant #21

The 1976 Alabama Crimson Tide football team played its 82nd overall and 43rd season as a member of the Southeastern Conference (SEC). The team was led by head coach Bear Bryant, in his 19th year, and it played its home games at the new Bryant–Denny Stadium in Tuscaloosa and the long-time Legion Field in Birmingham, Alabama. UA finished a fine season with nine wins and three losses (9–3 overall, 5–2 in the SEC) and with a victory over UCLA in the Liberty Bowl.

Watching the great Bear Bryant coach his teams in these years that we have covered one by one, a reader must remember the Bear's basic philosophy that "No coach has ever won a game by what he knows; it's what his players know that counts."

Coach Paul "Bear" Bryant preached that there is a mixture of player talent, player knowledge, coaching, and player experience in success on the field. By examining the Bear and his teams and other great coaches and their teams, I know that the element that Bryant never harped about but that he understood so well, was that luck has a role in every football game. Perhaps if the game were played with a round ball, the bounces would be more predictable? What do you think?.

Luck adds the element of suspense to the game and makes it even more enjoyable to watch. Even the best coaches find luck on their side at times. I see all these one-loss seasons over such a great coaching career and I know deep down it was not the coaching that failed – almost never – Bear Bryant was the best – no doubt from me! "Luck, be a Lady Tonight!"

Bear Bryant had so much chutzpah as a coach and so much good teaching skills that with his style and teaching and the luck of the AP and the UPI, as heralded as he has been, he would have been even more heralded. God bless the Bear!

We're not yet done on reporting about the greatest -- Bear Bryant in this book about Great Moments in Alabama Football!

Alabama and the people of Alabama understand football.

Bear Bryant defined Alabama football!

"Recognize a great man with major life achievements while he knows he is being recognized—why wait until he dies!"

You can quote me on that – Brian W. Kelly

Alabama did exactly that for their greatest coach, the "BEAR," Bear Bryant.

In September 1975, a bill sponsored by Alabama State Senator Bert Bank was passed by a margin of 88–0 to rename Denny Stadium to Bryant–Denny Stadium in honor of then head coach Bear Bryant.

The continually expanding Denny Stadium had received the go ahead for another great expansion from the Bear himself. It was expanded and was almost as big as it is now after the Bear Bryant recommended expansion.

Denny Stadium was then officially renamed as part of the halftime ceremonies to Bryant-Denny Stadium during the 1976 A-Day game. At the time of its re-dedication, Bryant was quoted as saying "this is a tremendous honor and I am proud and humble."

My own take on the name is that the people of Alabama knew whose name should be first but alphabetical order saved the day.

1977 Coach Paul "Bear" Bryant #21

The 1977 Alabama Crimson Tide football team played its 83rd overall and 44th season as a member of the Southeastern Conference (SEC). The team was led by head coach Bear Bryant, in his 20th year, and played their home games at Bryant–Denny Stadium in Tuscaloosa and Legion Field in Birmingham, Alabama. They finished season with eleven wins and one loss (11–1 overall, 7–0 in the SEC), as SEC champions and with a victory over Ohio State in the Sugar Bowl to make them national champions.

The Crimson Tide was invited to the Sugar Bowl to play on January 2, 1978 vs. Woody Hayes' No. 9 Ohio State at the Louisiana Superdome in New Orleans, UA prevailed v OSU W (35–6) before 76,811

1978 Coach Paul "Bear" Bryant #21

The days of wondering how good Alabama football actually is ended in 1978 for sure. But for the skeptics, it should have ended much sooner.

The 1978 Alabama Crimson Tide football team played its 84th overall and 45th season as a member of the Southeastern Conference (SEC). The team was led by head coach Bear Bryant, in his 21st year, and played their home games at Bryant–Denny Stadium in Tuscaloosa and Legion Field in Birmingham, Alabama.

They finished this championship season with eleven wins and one loss (11–1 overall, 6–0 in the SEC), as SEC champions and as national champions after a victory over Penn State in the Sugar Bowl. Alabama's costumed "Big Al" mascot officially debuted this season, appearing at the Sugar Bowl.

After the season. On January 1, 1979 Bama played # 1 Penn State at the Louisiana Superdome in New Orleans, LA on ABC TV and the Crimson Tide brought home a big V—W (14–7). Bear Bryant had upset another coach Joe Paterno opportunity for a National Championship.

Sugar Bowl Notes—The Goal Line Stand:

This game has been determined by the pundits to be one of the most significand football games in Crimson Tide History.

The anticipation for this game was high. Two legends were to take their teams and face off on National TV for the National Championship.

The 1979 Sugar Bowl against Penn State has gone down as a classic. What a game.

Alabama scored in the second quarter, then Penn State answered in the third, then Alabama took a 14–7 lead on a touchdown set up by a 62-yard punt return. Penn State had a chance to tie in the fourth, but quarterback Chuck Fusina threw an interception into the Alabama end zone.

Then Alabama had a chance to put the game away, but fumbled the

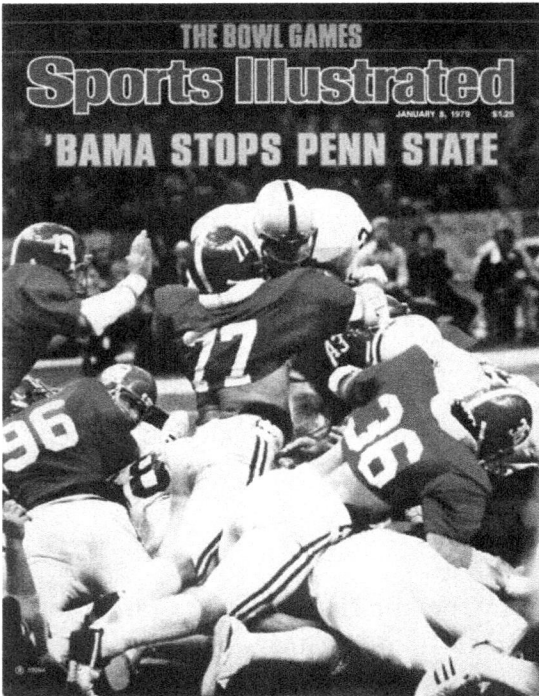

football back to Penn State at the Nittany Lion 19-yard-line with four minutes to go. Penn State drove to a first and goal at the Alabama eight. On third and goal from the one, the folklore says that Fusina asked Bama defensive lineman Marty Lyons "What do you think we should do?", and Lyons answered "You'd better pass."

On third down, Penn State was stopped inches short of the goal line. On fourth down, Penn State was stopped again, Barry Krauss met Mike Guman and threw him back for no gain. Alabama held on for a 14–7 victory.

The Crimson Tide split the national championship, winning the AP poll while Southern California won the UPI Coaches' poll. Roll Tide.

1979 Coach Paul "Bear" Bryant #21

The 1979 Alabama Crimson Tide football team played its 85th overall and 46th season as a member of the Southeastern Conference (SEC). The team was led by head coach Bear Bryant, in his 22nd year, and played its home games at Bryant–Denny Stadium in Tuscaloosa and Legion Field in Birmingham, Alabama. They finished the season undefeated (12–0 overall, 6–0 in the SEC) and they gained a victory over Arkansas in the Sugar Bowl. For their collective efforts, the Crimson Tide were recognized as consensus national champions for the 1979 season. Roll Tide!

Nobody touched the Bear Led Crimson Tide in 1979.

In 1979 the Alabama Crimson Tide capped off a decade of remarkable success with the program's seventh perfect season in college history after 1925, 1930, 1934, 1945, 1961, and 1966 (discounting the 1897 "season" in which Bama played and won only one game). The Tide defense recorded five shutouts and allowed only two teams to score in double digits. The offense scored thirty points or more seven times.

Despite this dominance, Alabama had three close calls. Against Tennessee on October 20, Alabama fell behind 17–0 in the second quarter before rallying to win W (27–17). Three weeks later, against LSU on November 10, all the Tide offense could scrape up was a single field goal, but it was enough to win W (3–0).

In the regular season, Iron Bowl finale on Dec 1 against Auburn, after leading 14–3 at the half Alabama let Auburn take an 18–17 fourth quarter lead before winning the Iron Bowl W (25–18). The Auburn and Tennessee games were the only two times in the 1979 season that Alabama trailed. A 24–9 victory over Arkansas in the Sugar Bowl on January 1, 1980 capped a 12–0 season and a unanimous national championship, Alabama's sixth wire service national title.

1980 Sugar Bowl Notes

On January 1, 1980, # 6 Arkansas was ready and they came serious to play # 2 Alabama at the Louisiana Superdome in New Orleans, LA before 77,846. The game was broadcast on ABC.

This game has been determined by the pundits to be one of the most significand football games in Crimson Tide History. Alabama's fine play eventually broke the backs of the Razorbacks as the Tide won the game 24-9.

Alabama's Steve Whitman (14) scores a touchdown against Arkansas in the Sugar Bowl at the Superdome in New Orleans Jan.1,1980 (Birmingham News file)

The two teams gained 696 yards between them. The double wing took the Hogs out of planned defensive schemes. Holtz addressed the change succinctly: "Alabama's defense is fourth best in the nation, and it's their major weakness. How could we know the nation's best team would play a perfect game?"

Amidst all the clamor and reasons why Alabama should be ranked No. 1, Bear Bryant was saying injuries may have kept his team from being one of the greatest of all time. "We hit some peaks," Bryant said, "against Baylor, and later against Tennessee, when we came back from being down 17-0. No team has ever done that against Tennessee. It was a team that did what it had to do. When Auburn went ahead of us, we marched 82 yards (actually 88). When the Sugar Bowl was hanging in the balance, we went 98 yards. Things like that say something about a football team."

That football team said something about Bear, too, who had coached in nine Sugar Bowls, most of anyone, and where he showcased four of the six national championships Alabama claimed under him. The victory, in Bryant's last Sugar Bowl appearance, was not only his 296th, bringing him within 20 of Amos Alonzo Stagg's record 314, but this was the 17th of Bryant's 22 teams at Alabama to finish in the Top Ten, an unmatched feat for a coach since the Associated Press began voting in 1936. Also, Southern Cal defeated Ohio State (17-16) that day, rectifying the AP voting and moving Bryant past Frank Leahy, who had won four AP national championships at Notre Dame in 1943-46-47-49.

Partial Recap excerpted from the book "Sugar Bowl Classic: A History" by Marty Mulé, who covered the game and the organization for decades for the New Orleans Times-Picayune.
https://www.allstatesugarbowl.org/site115.php

1980 Coach Paul "Bear" Bryant #21

The 1980 Alabama Crimson Tide football team played its 86th overall and 47th season as a member of the Southeastern Conference (SEC). The team was led by head coach Bear Bryant, in his 23rd year, and played their home games at Bryant–Denny Stadium in Tuscaloosa and Legion Field in Birmingham, Alabama.

They finished season with ten wins and two losses (10–2 overall, 5–1 in the SEC) and with a victory over Baylor in the Cotton Bowl. Though some zealot Alabama fans might say that 10-2 is unbecoming for Alabama, think about the lean years and this looks excellent. Alabama often achieves perfection but in its off years it achieves excellence while continually striving for perfection.

A 6–3 loss to Mississippi State ended Alabama's school record 28-game winning streak and all-time SEC record 27-game conference winning streak, and was Alabama's first loss to Mississippi State since 1957. It also cost the Tide a share of the SEC championship, the first time since 1976 they failed to win the SEC. Despite surrendering 35 points to Ole Miss, the Alabama defense still allowed only 98 points for the entire season.

1981 Coach Paul "Bear" Bryant #21

The 1981 Alabama Crimson Tide football team played its 87th overall and 48th season as a member of the Southeastern Conference (SEC). The team was led by head coach Bear Bryant, in his 24th year, and played its home games at Bryant–Denny Stadium in Tuscaloosa and Legion Field in Birmingham, Alabama. They finished season with nine wins, two losses and one tie (9–2–1 overall, 6–0 in the SEC), as SEC co-champions with Georgia and with a loss against Texas in the Cotton Bowl.

1981 Iron Bowl – 315 for the Bear

Bear Bryant wouldn't win any more national championships, but that doesn't mean he was done getting wins. The 1981 Iron Bowl would make 315 wins for Bear Bryant, which was at the time the record for most wins ever for a coach in college football.

It's fitting that Bear Bryant got to 315 wins in an Iron Bowl, and it's also fitting that the Bear did it in a game that was dominated by defense.

Alabama's offense struggled in the 1981 Iron Bowl, losing three fumbles and only passing for 81 yards. The Alabama Crimson Tide defense was in fine form though with three interceptions.

Alabama's offense finally started to click in the fourth quarter and with two eventual touchdowns Alabama beat Auburn 28-17 in Legion field to give Bear Bryant his 315th win.

315 wins may not be the record anymore, but it's just an amazing achievement. Add on top of that that the 315 came against some of the greatest teams in history like 1969's Ole Miss Rebels and 1979's Penn State Nittany Lions.

Alabama v Auburn action in 1981 Iron Bowl

Bear Bryant won six national championships and did it while running a passing attack, then a wishbone, then a double wing.

You can say a lot of things about Bear Bryant, but he wasn't ever anything but a winner.

Alabama had agreed to play in the Cotton Bowl against Texas on January 1, 1982. Alabama had never beaten Texas and there was a lot of hope that this would be the first win against this Bowl Nemesis for the Crimson Tide.

The 1982 Cotton Bowl

Alabama's Cotton Bowl Classic loss to Texas dropped the Tide's all-time record against the Longhorns to 0–7–1. This iteration was played before 73,243 in Dallas Texas at the Cotton Bowl.

Coach Bryant at the 1982 Cotton Bowl.

1982 Coach Paul "Bear" Bryant #21

The 1982 Alabama Crimson Tide football team played its 88th overall and 49th season as a member of the Southeastern Conference (SEC). The team was led by head coach Bear Bryant, in his 25th and final year, and played their home games at Bryant–Denny Stadium in Tuscaloosa and Legion Field in Birmingham, Alabama. They finished this season with eight wins and four losses (8–4 overall, 3–3 in the SEC) and with a victory over Illinois in the Liberty Bowl.

Alabama was 5–0 after they defeated Penn State 42–21, with the decisive play coming when a Penn State player blocked his own team's punt. But after that it was all downhill. Paul Bryant's last season as Alabama football coach saw a nine-game winning streak against Auburn and eleven-game winning streaks against Tennessee and LSU all come to an end. The loss to Southern Miss was Alabama's first loss in Tuscaloosa since 1963, breaking a 57-game win streak in Bryant–Denny Stadium. Coach Bryant retired after

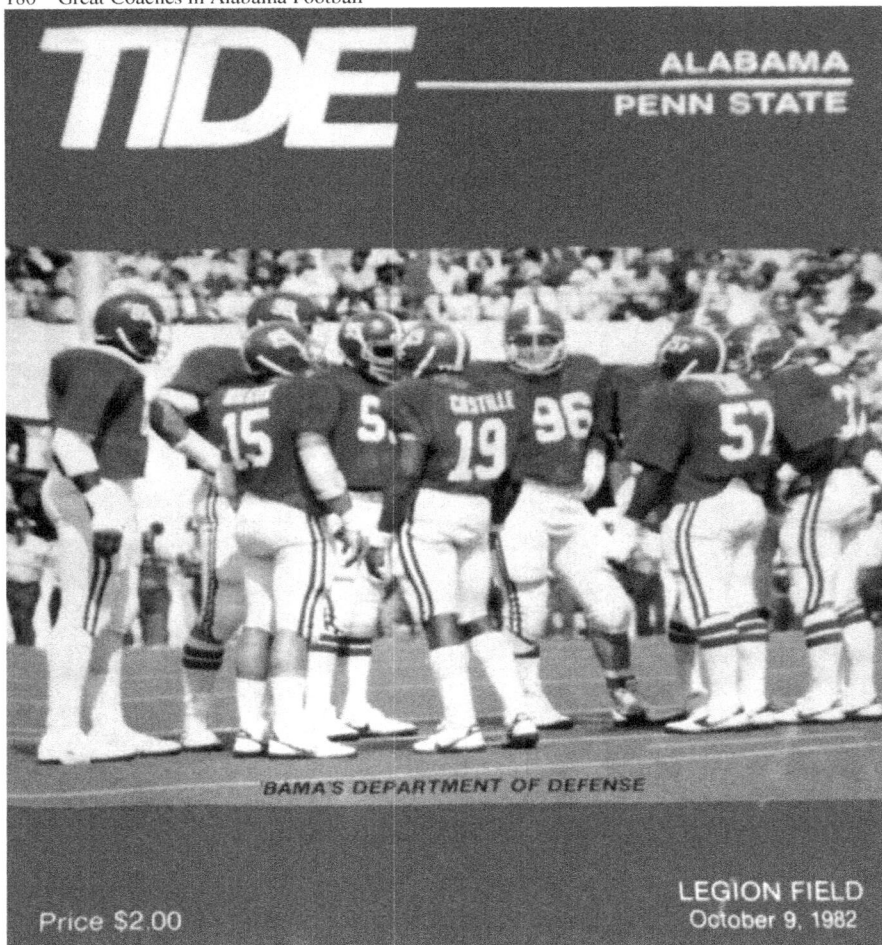

TIDE ———— ALABAMA
PENN STATE

BAMA'S DEPARTMENT OF DEFENSE

Price $2.00

LEGION FIELD
October 9, 1982

Alabama's bowl victory against Illinois and he died less than one month later, on January 26, 1983. He was a "Bear" for sure and a great and admirable man. He was not sick, his death came suddenly.

The season was a great season but the fact is great coaches bring about great expectations. No coach can create excellence every single year. Whether the Coach is Bear Bryant, Knute Rockne, Joe Paterno, Lou Holtz, or Nick Saban, it cannot be done. Yet, fans always expect the best every year. And, we should!

Well, that's just what I think but Nick Saban seems to be making me think that maybe he is not made from the same mold as other great coaches. Every week in recent years that Alabama faces a great opponent, I pity the opponent. Alabama has always been great. In the Saban years, I've seen some of the best football ever from any college football team.

Teams may line up to play the Crimson Tide, but almost without exception, they fall down and take the loss. Alabama, even when it gets handed a loss does not take it lightly.

Bear Bryant may have said '"I don't think there is a Texas whammy on Alabama...Their players and coaches beat us - not a whammy."

In the Bear's last season, On Sept 11 at Georgia Tech. Alabama won W (45-7). Then, on Sept 18, at Ole Missat the Mississippi Veterans Memorial Stadium in Jackson, MS, Alabama beat Mississippi W 42-14 before 62,385. Then, on September 25 at Bryant-Denny, UA defeated Vanderbilt in a close game W 24-21 before 60,210. On October 2 in a 7:30 p.m. game at Legion Field, UA defeated Arkansas State at Legion Field W 34-7.

Then, on October 9, A top ten Penn State team came in hoping to ruin the Bear's last season but even Joe Paterno could not take anything away from Bear Bryant on this early game on a Saturday afternoon. Bryant's UA dominated against the Nittany Lions at Legion Field under the cameras of CBS and 76,821 W (42-21).

Then, for Bear Bryant's 25th (Third Saturday in October) on October 16 at 1:00 p.m. at Tennessee's Neyland Stadium in Knoxville, a simple TD kept UA from winning this final meeting of the Bear and the Third Week people. The game went into the Crimson Tide Loss column L (28-35) before a whopping sell-out crowd of 95,342.

On October 23, Alabama invited Cincinnati to Bryant–Denny Stadium and beat the Bearcats W (21-3). On October 30, at Mississippi State's Veterans Memorial Stadium in Jackson, MS, the Crimson Tide defeated the Bulldogs W (20-12). Then, on Nov 6, # 11 LSU defeated UA at Legion Field L (10-20) in front of 77,230.

On Nov.13, Southern Miss played at Bryant–Denny Stadium and were just good enough to defeat the Crimson Tide L (29-38) before 60,210. On Nov 27 at 11:00 a.m., Alabama played Auburn at

Legion Field for the Bear's last Iron Bowl. It was very close L (22–23) before 76,300. The Bear took the season like all seasons in stride.

In the Bear Bryant Era, the last game was on December 29 at 7:00 p.m. v Illinois at Liberty Bowl Memorial Stadium in Memphis, TN It was played in the recently new Liberty Bowl. The Bear and the Alabama team got their last win in the Bear Bryant Era W (21–15) before 54,123 and a nationwide TV audience. It was the end of a major era in Alabama sports.

"No coach has ever won a game by what he knows; it's what his players know that counts." -Coach Paul "Bear" Bryant

You can't write about a fella for twenty-five years of his life and not become attached. I know I am going to miss Bear Bryant as I write the rest of this book but I have a feeling I'll find him again before I am done.

Let's take a quick look at Bear's last game.

The Liberty Bowl is held annually at Liberty Bowl Memorial Stadium in Memphis, Tennessee. The Bowl is the seventh oldest college bowl game and is one of the most tradition-rich and patriotic bowl games in America. Coaching in his final game, Paul Bryant and his Crimson Tide beat Illinois 21-15 at the Liberty Bowl played in Memphis, Tenn.

Chapter 12 Bear Bryant is Dead; Long Live the Memory of Bear Bryant!

Legend still missed by loyal fans

On Sep 11, 2016 - Paul W. "Bear" Bryant would have turned 103 years old. He had died about thirty-three years too soon to make this birthday. But, whether Bear liked it or not, even thirty years later, there would have been a grand celebration as his legacy at Alabama was so great, it has not been forgotten.

He is revered as all legacies are revered. Just as Knute Rockne and Frank Leahy, Nick Saban, Amos Alonzo Stagg, Woody Hayes, Pop Warner, and Tom Osborne are held in high esteem, so is Paul W. "Bear" Bryant. There is one difference. All of the coaches mentioned and those in the top 100 including the inimitable Bo Schembechler, are also rans to the winner. Yes, the consistent #1 voted football coach for years was and still is Alabama's own Bear Bryant. Even though the Bear would be over 103-years old today.

Some say that the emotions that connect player to coach, or fan to hero, are not easily handed down from one generation to another and to another. Yet, those who knew the Bear are still heard saying "We'll do anything just to hear Coach Bryant say, 'You did a good job. .... They also share a love for the University of Alabama.

Bear Bryant was a great coach wherever he coached – Maryland in 1945; Kentucky from 1946 to 1953; Texas A & M from 1954 1954 to 1957 and of course the Bear's favorite—Alabama, his home, from 1958 to 1982. His record of 323-85-17 in 38 seasons has been equaled and passed just once by Penn State's own immortal Coach Joe Paterno. History shows that Joe Paterno coached many more seasons to achieve his great record.

They say that if one coach has come to represent college football, to be associated with it more than anyone else, through success on the field and sheer force of personality, it is the man who needs to be known by only one name: Bear. Paul Bryant, legend has it, got the name Bear by literally wrestling a bear as a teenager at a carnival. The furry bear had no chance.

As an end at Alabama, he once played a game against Tennessee dragging a broken leg. After a stellar career as a player for the Crimson Tide, Bryant assisted at Alabama, then made his mark at various stops as a head coach to become one of the biggest personalities in American sports history, and the #1 football coach on the planet--ever.

Success came quickly, despite the fact that the man he replaced, Jennings Whitworth, had the worst record in Alabama football history—just 4-24-2 in three seasons. After such a dismal three years, Bryant could do nothing but succeed. He did a lot more than that. He excelled. Bear Bryant needed just one season to build his team -- just like Nick Saban -- and then Alabama took off to become a dominant force in American college football.

For most of the next quarter century, the Crimson Tide dominated college football everywhere, especially in the tough SEC. Bear did not wait long to bring home all the marbles. In 1961, Bryant led Alabama to an 11-0 season, a Sugar Bowl win and a split national title with Ohio State. The Crimson Tide would go on to share titles in three of five seasons, before going undefeated in 1965. Ironically, in this, one of the greatest years for any coach in any sport, undefeated and untied, Bear Bryant was denied a championship by pollsters for their own reasons.

Like many football dynasties, no college can win every game. And, so Alabama had a few dry spells, some more enduring than others, but the tea always came back with the Bear at the helm. Bryant's first big recovery was in the 1970s. There are two big reasons given for the comeback: 1) He switched to the wishbone, and most importantly, 2) Alabama football integrated its program and got from underneath a time when they had been kept down by administrative policies on recruiting. Wilbur Jackson became the first African-American scholarship player in the early 1970s.

From 1971-81, Alabama never finished worse than 11th in the AP poll. It shared a national title with Notre Dame in 1973, despite losing to the Irish in the Sugar Bowl. In this year, the champion was declared before the bowl games. This particular year was the last year the UPI crowned its champion before the bowls. After that UA won back-to-back titles in 1978-79 thanks to Sugar Bowl wins over Penn State and Arkansas.

The Bear stepped down after the 1982 season, and he did not get to enjoy his retirement for too long. He died one month after his final game. By the end of his Alabama career, he had won 82.4 percent of his games, gained six national championships and 13 SEC titles. And for some his crowning achievement was to dominate Alabama's rivals. He went 35-13-2 against rivals Auburn and Tennessee.

Bear Bryant was larger than life. He lived more years in his 69 years than just 69. He was a busy man in terms of the business of football and the business of life. He enjoyed to drink and he smoked heavily. He enjoyed life and he enjoyed his family. Besides family, he loved football and his teams the best.

Wright Thompson, Senior Writer for ESPN The Magazine notes that "Bryant surrounded himself with people he could trust, and he trusted nobody more than Billy Varner, a tough, barrel-chested African-American. Billy was always just around, in the office, on the road, on the sidelines. Over the years, various accounts have given him different titles, but essentially, he was a fixer. He took care of business, and he kept everything to himself, even after Bryant died."

Bear Bryant and his great friend Billy Varner <<< left courtesy of Paul W. Bryant Museum.

"… Billy saw him weak and insecure. He drove him to Birmingham one year before Christmas because Bryant got a letter from a sick girl and he wanted to surprise her. He saw him cry. "

When Bear Bryant died unexpectedly and the local paper interviewed him, Billy cried. "He could eat pheasant under glass with the president," he said, "or he could eat cheese and crackers with the boys out by the caddie shack, and he'd enjoy it all just the same. That's the man I'll always remember."

Nick Saban is from the Bear Bryant mold, and like Bear, and all Alabama fans, Saban does not take kindly to losing football games. Many are currently making a strong argument that Nick Saban may surpass Bryant's accomplishments. For Bear, I am sure that will be OK!

Even if Nick Saban passes Bear in championships over the next several years, and he probably will, nobody can surpass the almost mythical status that Bear Bryant holds between on-field success and the charismatic persona that made him the quintessential college football coach, and the greatest of all time.

When Bear Bryant went on to spend eternity with his maker, Mary Harmon Bryant didn't want to host an elaborate funeral for her husband, certainly nothing at the football stadium. She felt that her husband already had enough attention, she figured. She didn't want music or a long list of speakers giving eulogies.

People longed to pay respects to Bear Bryant

Yet, there were so many people who wanted to pay their respects that despite her deep wishes, the service and telecasts filled three churches in downtown Tuscaloosa. Hundreds of thousands lined the streets there and in Birmingham and along the path of Interstate 59 along which Paul "Bear" Bryant was taken to his final resting place at Elmwood Cemetery.

The people simply loved Bear Bryant and he meant a lot to them all so they just came out. They did not seek permission. Can you imagine the raucous in Alabama if the Bryant family had actually asked people to participate? We'd still be clearing the streets.

Nobody can say it all about a legend, especially a well-loved figure such as Bear Bryant. And, so, after I would like to show you some of Bear Bryant's favorite quotes for how to lead life, coach and play football. These were compiled by Ben George and posted on January 26, 2015. **http://tide1029.com/the-best-bear-bryant-quotes/**

"Bryant was known as a master motivator when he coached and many of his quotes continue to be used today. To help remember many of them, we've put together a list of the best Bear Bryant quotes:" Thanks Ben.

- "If you want to walk the heavenly streets of gold, you gotta know the password, 'Roll, Tide, Roll.'"
- "If you believe in yourself and have dedication and pride – and never quit – you'll be a winner. The price of victory is high but so are the rewards."
- "Have you called your mama today? I wish I could call mine."
- "I ain't never been nothin but a winner."
- "A good, quick, small team can beat a big, slow team any time."
- "If a man is a quitter, I'd rather find out in practice than in a game. I ask for all a player has so I'll know later what I can expect."
- "It's awfully important to win with humility. It's also important to lose. I hate to lose worse than anyone, but if you never lose you won't know how to act. If you lose with humility, then you can come back."
- "The first time you quit, it's hard. The second time, it gets easier. The third time, you don't even have to think about it."
- "If they don't have a winning attitude, I don't want them."
- "It's not the will to win that matters – everyone has that. It's the will to prepare to win that matters."
- "I don't guess anybody would think much of what Joe (Namath) did nowadays, including myself. But he was supposed to be a leader, so he had to live by the rules. It was the hardest thing I ever had to do, and it was to the greatest athlete I ever coached."

- "I don't have to apologize for who I play. I'm trying to win the game."
- "At Alabama, our players do not win Heisman Trophies, our teams win national championships."
- "You boys were eight and ten years old last time Alabama was on top. That was before any of you were paying much attention to it. What are you doing here? Tell me why you are here. If you are not here to win a national championship, you're in the wrong place. You boys are special. I don't want my players to be like other students. I want special people. You can learn a lot on the football field that isn't taught in the home, the church, or the classroom. There are going to be days when you think you've got no more to give and then you're going to give plenty more. You are going to have pride and class. You are going to be very special. You are going to win the national championship for Alabama."
- "In life, you'll have your back up against the wall many times. You might as well get used to it."
- "Don't give up at halftime. Concentrate on winning the second half."
- "Set goals – high goals for you and your organization. When your organization has a goal to shoot for, you create teamwork, people working for a common good."
- "In a crisis, don't hide behind anything or anybody. They're going to find you anyway."
- "I've had many a player tell me all through high school and right up until signing day that they were coming to Alabama, then they signed with somebody else."
- "Winning isn't everything, but it beats anything that comes in second."
- "There's no substitute for guts."

For those who would like to read further about the life and times of Coach Paul "Bear" Bryant, I recommend two articles that can be read on the Internet. Both articles were written near the time of Bear Bryant's death and his funeral so there is little guesswork. It is from the New York Times, written the day after his death January 27, 1983, by Joseph Durso. The second is a commemorative article written just about 25 years after the funeral by Tommy Dies of the Tuscaloosa News. Together they tell a great part of the Bear Bryant story but one thing we know for sure: There are lots more Bear

Bryant stories than these, and all of them are worthy of a gentle read.

New York Times

Here is a great Bear Bryant tribute article courtesy of the New York Times

BEAR BRYANT IS DEAD AT 69; WON A RECORD 323 GAMES

By JOSEPH DURSO
Published: January 27, 1983

http://www.nytimes.com/1983/01/27/obituaries/bear-bryant-is-dead-at-69-won-a-record-323-games.html?pagewanted=all

> Bear Bryant died of a heart attack yesterday in Tuscaloosa, Ala., only 37 days after he had retired as head football coach at the University of Alabama with the most victories in college football history.
> …

The picture on the prior page shows the Hearse carrying the last remains of Alabama coach Paul 'Bear' Bryant as it arrives at Elmwood Cemetery in Birmingham, Ala. Friday Jan. 28, 1983. (File Photo/ The Huntsville Times)

Alabama's Greatest Icon
The Tuscaloosa News

Wednesday Posted Jan 19, 2011 at 12:01 AM

From a 2011 perspective, we all know that "the death of Paul W. "Bear" Bryant nearly 25 years ago drew reaction from dignitaries far and wide." Tommy Dies of Tuscaloosa does a great job capturing the spirit of the tragedy.

By Tommy Deas Sports Writer

http://www.tuscaloosanews.com/article/DA/20110119/News/605297587/TL/

TUSCALOOSA | The death of Paul W. "Bear" Bryant nearly 25 years ago, drew reaction from dignitaries far and wide.

President Ronald Reagan issued a statement lauding the University of Alabama's late football coach as "a coach who made legends out of ordinary people." The Rev. Billy Graham sent his sympathies to the family. Football coaches including Ohio State's Woody Hayes, Oklahoma's Bud Wilkinson and Southern Cal's John McKay came from around the country to pay their respects.

...

Feel free to take the two links above to get the full story. The story is also told in my other popular book titled: about Great Moments in Alabama Football available on Amazon & Kindle.

Additional pictures, some with captions, others self-explanatory, are shown below through the end of this chapter. We all miss Bear Bryant.

Bear Bryant Funeral Procession

Bear Bryant's Home

The lyrics conveyed the feelings of Bryant's legion of fans:
"I'll never forget
The day that I heard the news
Bear Bryant has died
Funny, I thought he'd refuse
I watched as they laid him to rest
In old Alabama
Oh, how I cried
The day Bear Bryant died"

Buddie Buie – Heartfelt Bear Bryant Lyrics

Buie had written such chart-topping songs as "Spooky," "So Into You" and "Imaginary Lover," but this wasn't a commercial venture.

Reach Tommy Deas at tommy.deas@tuscaloosanews.com or at 205-722-0224. We all thank you Tommy!

Chapter 13 Post Bryant – Coaches Ray Perkins & Bill Curry, 1983-1989

"No coach in his right mind would want to take a team whose predecessor was a legend."

Year	Coach	Conference	Record	SEC
1983	Ray Perkins #22	SEC	8-4-0	4-2-0
1984	Ray Perkins	SEC	5-6-0	2-4-0
1985	Ray Perkins	SEC	9-2-1	4-1-1
1986	Ray Perkins	SEC	10-3-0	4-2-0
1987	Bill Curry # 23	SEC	7-5-0	4-3-0
1988	Bill Curry	SEC	9-3-0	4-3-0
1989	Bill Curry	SEC	10-2-0	6-1-0

1983 Alabama Football Team ready for coach Ray Perkins

"No coach in his right mind would want to take a team whose predecessor was a legend."

Can you imagine being asked to replace Jesus as the Savior of the world. For Alabama fans, that was Ray Perkins mission. Only a tough guy like Ray Perkins, a great coach could have straightened the ship that Bear left behind so that Alabama would again be the greatest.

Bear Bryant himself would not have agreed to such a task in my opinion. Ray Perkins in my opinion did a fine job but who could be the Bear who no longer was the Bear?

When Ray took over team, he knew he could win but nobody else did. He would have been more respected if he took over for Whitworth instead of Bryant. But, Perkins was no slouch and he could have done it… and in some ways, he really did. But you have to look! There are many great articles about Ray Perkins that I found in my research that tell what the folks at the time thought about this fine coach.

1983 Coach Ray Perkins #22

The 1983 Alabama Crimson Tide football team played its 89th overall and 50th season as a member of the Southeastern Conference (SEC). The team was led by head coach Ray Perkins, in his first year. Alabama played its home games at both Bryant–Denny Stadium in Tuscaloosa and Legion Field in Birmingham, Alabama. They finished the season with a fine record of eight wins and four losses (8–4 overall, 4–2 in the SEC).

Ray Perkins, who played as a wide receiver for Bear Bryant in the 1960s, was named as the new head coach at Alabama on December 14, 1982, to succeed Bryant after his 25-year tenure as Alabama's head coach.

1984 Coach Ray Perkins #22

The 1984 Alabama Crimson Tide football team played its 90th overall and 51st season as a member of the Southeastern Conference (SEC). The team was led by head coach Ray Perkins, in his second year. Alabama played its home games at both Bryant–Denny Stadium in Tuscaloosa and Legion Field in Birmingham, Alabama. The team finished the season with a record of five wins and six losses (5–6 overall, 2–4 in the SEC). This marked Alabama's first losing season since the Tide went 2–7–1 in 1957 under Jennings B. Whitworth, and this season ended Alabama's streak of 25 consecutive bowl appearances. For Crimson Tide supporters, all of this matters.

1984 Alabama Crimson Tide Coach Ray Perkins

1985 Coach Ray Perkins #22

The 1985 Alabama Crimson Tide football team played its 91st overall and 52nd season as a member of the Southeastern Conference (SEC). The team was led by head coach Ray Perkins, in his third year, and played their home games at both Bryant–Denny Stadium in Tuscaloosa and Legion Field in Birmingham, Alabama. They finished the season with a record of nine wins, two losses and one tie (9–2–1 overall, 4–1–1 in the SEC). The Perkins-coached team also gained a victory in the Aloha Bowl over USC.

It was an exciting season for sure beginning with the last-second, 20–16 comeback victory on Labor Day over Georgia to open the playing season for the Crimson Tide.

Additionally, the 1985 edition of the Iron Bowl against Auburn is regarded as one of Alabama's most dramatic victories in the history of the series. In the game, Alabama led 16–10 after three quarters, but saw four lead changes in the fourth quarter, including two in the final minute. It ended with Van Tiffin's 52-yard field goal as time expired to give Alabama a 25–23 victory. Tiffin's field goal is remembered simply as "The Kick" in Alabama folklore. See picture on next page.

This Iron Bowl game has been determined by the pundits to be one of the most significand football games in Crimson Tide History. Here comes the narrative from bamahammer:

1986 Coach Ray Perkins #22

The 1986 Alabama Crimson Tide football team played its 92nd overall and 53rd season as a member of the Southeastern Conference (SEC). The team was led by head coach Ray Perkins, in his fourth year, and played their home games at both Bryant–Denny Stadium in Tuscaloosa and Legion Field in Birmingham, Alabama. They finished the season with a record of ten wins and three losses (10–3 overall, 4–2 in the SEC) and with a victory in the Sun Bowl over Washington.

Classic SEC Football: Alabama Tops Auburn in 1985

Ray Perkins Moves On

Head Coach Ray Perkins coached at the pro and college levels for nearly 40 years, and is best known among college football fans as the man to succeed Bear Bryant as head coach at the University of Alabama. Perkins coached at Alabama for four seasons from 1983-1986 and accumulated a record of 32-15-1 during that time, including a 3-0 record in bowl games. Perkins eventually left Alabama following the 1986 season and signed a lucrative contract to take the head coaching job with the NFL's Tampa Bay Buccaneers. He was inducted into the Alabama Sports Hall of Fame in 1990.

Bill Curry Bama Head Football Coach for 1987

LA Times January 5, 1987 TUSCALOOSA, Ala. — Bill Curry signed a multiyear contract as football coach at Alabama Sunday, and Steve Sloan, a former Crimson Tide quarterback, accepted the athletic director's job at his alma mater.

Curry, 44, said that until he received the offer from Alabama, he never thought he would surrender the coaching job at Georgia Tech, his alma mater, that he held for seven years, compiling a 31-43-4 record.

1987 Coach Bill Curry #23

The 1987 Alabama Crimson Tide football team played its 93th overall and 54th season as a member of the Southeastern Conference (SEC). The team was led by head coach Bill Curry, in his first year, and played their home games at Legion Field in Birmingham, Alabama. They finished the season with a record of seven wins and five losses (7–5 overall, 4–3 in the SEC) and with a loss in the Hall of Fame Bowl to Michigan.

Due to a major renovation project that resulted in the completion of the western upper deck, Alabama played all of their home games at Legion Field instead of splitting them with Bryant–Denny Stadium for the 1987 season.

Alabama was invited to the Hall of Fame Bowl in Tampa Florida on January 2, 1988 and were beaten by Michigan L (24-28). It was the fifth loss of the season.

1988 Coach Bill Curry #23

The 1988 Alabama Crimson Tide football team played its 94th overall and 55th season as a member of the Southeastern Conference (SEC). The team was led by head coach Bill Curry, in his second year, and played home games at both Bryant–Denny Stadium in Tuscaloosa and Legion Field in Birmingham, Alabama. They finished the season with a record of nine wins and three losses (9–3

overall, 4–3 in the SEC) and with a victory in the Sun Bowl over
Army.

1989 Coach Bill Curry #23

The 1989 Alabama Crimson Tide football team played its 95th
overall and 56th season as a member of the Southeastern Conference
(SEC). The team was led by head coach Bill Curry, in his third year,
and played their home games at both Bryant–Denny Stadium in
Tuscaloosa and Legion Field in Birmingham, Alabama. They
finished the season with a record of ten wins and two losses (10–2
overall, 6–1 in the SEC), as SEC Co-Champions and with a loss in
the Sugar Bowl against national championship winner Miami.

Alabama won its first ten games on the way to its best record since
1980 and its first SEC championship since the 1981 season, its 19th
overall.

A major season highlight was Alabama's tough-fought 17–16 victory
on Oct 28 over Penn State. In this game, the Crimson Tide blocked
an 18-yard field goal try with 13 seconds left in the game for the win.

As good as the season was, it did not end as well. In the season
finale on Dec 2 against #11 Auburn—the first Iron Bowl ever played
in Auburn, Alabama—the Tigers beat Alabama 30–20. As a result,
Alabama, Auburn and Tennessee finished in a three-way tie for the
conference championship. Alabama would however receive the
conference's Sugar Bowl berth.

In the Sugar Bowl, Miami would defeat Alabama 33–25 in a close
hard fought match and would thus be named national champions. In
the week following the Sugar Bowl loss, on January 7, 1990, Bill
Curry resigned his position to take the head coaching job at
Kentucky.

Alabama's Curry Resigns

Published: January 8, 1990 by The New York Times

TUSCALOOSA, Ala., Jan. 7— Bill Curry, the football coach at the University of Alabama, announced today he would resign his job and seemed headed for the head-coaching post at Kentucky.

Curry was in Lexington, Ky., tonight and told WLEX-TV, "We're up here to meet with C. M. and other officials and hammer something out," a reference to the Kentucky athletic director, C. M. Newton.

Another Lexington station, WKYT-TV, reported that Curry, who spent three seasons at Alabama, told Newton earlier in the day that he would accept an offer to coach the Wildcats. The Kentucky coach, Jerry Claiborne, recently resigned.

Kentucky's Athletics Association scheduled a board meeting for Monday night to discuss the Curry situation. Efforts to reach Newton this afternoon were unsuccessful. Alabama finished the season with a 10-2 record and a share of the Southeastern Conference title, but lost the Sugar Bowl game to Miami.

Curry was voted the conference's coach of the year. Shortly after the Crimson Tide's 30-20 loss to Auburn on Dec. 2, Curry, who was 26-10 in his three seasons at Alabama, was offered a three-year contract extension. But the coach, who has two years left on his current contract, delayed accepting the offer.

Curry met Friday with Alabama's athletic director, Cecil Ingram, and its president, Roger Sayers, who gave him more time to consider an offer from Kentucky. Ingram and Sayers met with Curry after his return from a two-day trip to Lexington, where Newton offered him the Wildcats' coaching job.

The Louisville coach, Howard Schnellenberger, who had been mentioned in reports along with others as a possible successor to Curry, said tonight he wouldn't be interested in the job.

Chapter 14 Coach Gene Stallings -- 1990-1996

"You don't have to flaunt your success; but you don't have to apologize for it either." Stallings had a championship and a great coaching record for Alabama.

1990	Gene Stallings #24	SEC	7-5-0	5-2-0
1991	Gene Stallings	SEC	11-1-0	6-1-1
1992*	Gene Stallings	SEC	13-0-0	8-0-0
1993	Gene Stallings	SEC	9-3-1 (1-0)	5-2-1 (0-8)
1994	Gene Stallings	SEC	12-1-0	8-0-0
1995	Gene Stallings	SEC	8-3-0	5-3-0
1996	Gene Stallings	SEC	10-3-0	6-2-0

* National Championship

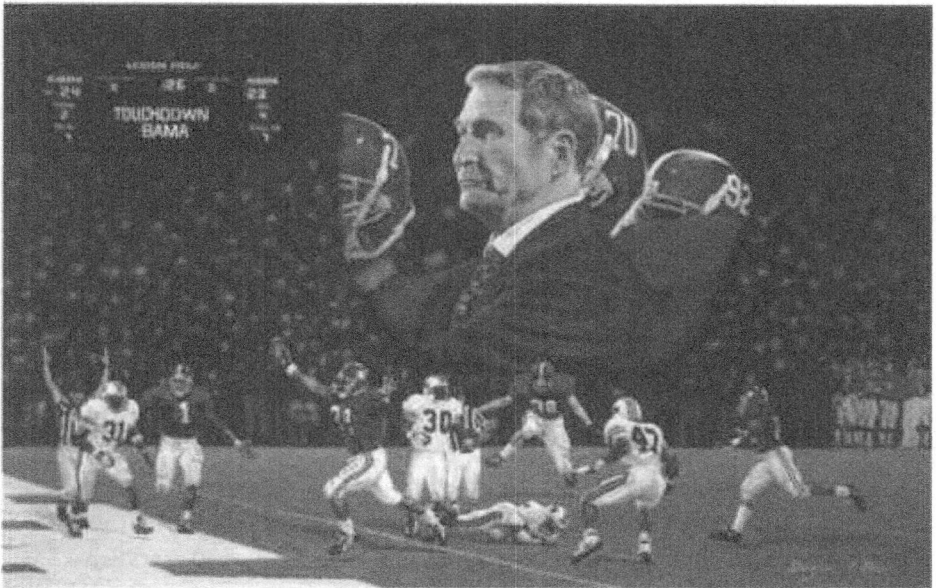

Artist Doug Hess

1990 Coach Gene Stallings #24

The 1990 Alabama Crimson Tide football team played its 96th overall and 57th season as a member of the Southeastern Conference

(SEC). The Crimson Tide was led by first-year head coach Gene Stallings, replacing Bill Curry who left for the University of Kentucky. The 1990 season got off to a really tough start for the Crimson Tide. The Tide and new coach Gene Stallings lost three games by a combined total of eight points. The season ended with a lopsided L (7-34) bowl loss to #18 Louisville in the Fiesta Bowl on January 1, and Alabama finished 7–5, 5-2 in the SEC.

1991 Coach Gene Stallings #24

The 1991 Alabama Crimson Tide football team played its 97th overall and 58th season as a member of the Southeastern Conference (SEC). The team was led by head coach Gene Stallings who was in his second season at Alabama. The team played their home games at Bryant-Denny Stadium, in Tuscaloosa, Alabama, and at Legion Field in Birmingham, Alabama.

The team substantially improved upon the 7–5 record from Stallings's first season as they ended with an 11–1 overall record, while going 6–1 in their conference games.

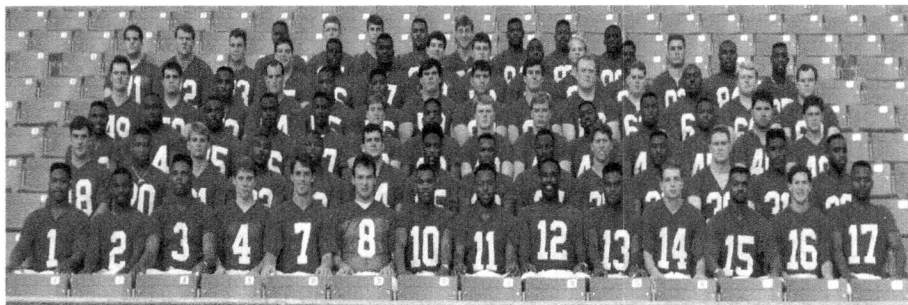

1991 Alabama Crimson Tide Team Picture

1992 Coach Gene Stallings #24

The 1992 Alabama Crimson Tide football team played its 98th overall and 59th season as a member of the Southeastern Conference (SEC). How about that folks? Alabama played almost 100 years of the finest football any college or university could ever hope to provide for its student fans, alumni fans, and just plain fans.

Like most Americans, Alabama as an institution saw winning as important right from the start. The University hired the coaches and picked the players for scholarship who understood their notion of winning. Losers have no conception of what winners are all about. Alabama is about winning in all facets – the classroom, the rec field and the competitive fields. Alabama knows how to spot winners. Bravo Alabama! Bravo Crimson Tide!

This was the team's third season under head coach Gene Stallings, one of the good guys. They played their home games at both Bryant–Denny Stadium in Tuscaloosa, Alabama and Legion Field in Birmingham, Alabama. They finished the season undefeated with a record of 13–0 (8–0 in the SEC) and as National Champions. It was a record that nobody could possibly improve upon.

The team was noted especially for its strong defense, which led the nation in fewest points allowed (9.2 per game during the regular season) and, in a strong bowl game performance, prevented defending national champion Miami from scoring an offensive touchdown. Gene Stallings knew how to motivate his great players to play at their best. He played for the Bear, and he was a fine coach.

The 1992 Crimson Tide won its twentieth Southeastern Conference title by defeating the Florida Gators 28–21 on December 5 in the inaugural SEC Championship Game. The team then capped off Alabama's eighth perfect season by winning the 1992 national football championship, defeating the heavily favored Miami Hurricanes W (34-13) in the 1993 Sugar Bowl on January 1, 1993. This was a matchup resulting from the first ever Bowl Coalition national championship game.

1992 SEC Championship Game, Alabama vs. Florida – The First Conference Championship Game

The inaugural SEC Championship Game was between Alabama and Florida. The 8-3 Gators had nothing to gain but a conference title, while the 11-0 Crimson Tide hoped for a trip to the Sugar Bowl, with a chance to play for the national championship on the line.

Alabama's Derrick Lassic scores one of his two touchdowns in the game

SEC Commissioner Roy Kramer had been criticized for creating a championship game in his newly expanded league. If a team in contention for a title stumbled in the championship game and lost the revenue of a title, what would that do to the league?

Skeptics of the game got a first look at this possibility when undefeated Alabama met three-loss Florida in Birmingham. Alabama beat Florida in dramatic fashion, securing their bowl game against Miami and reminding everyone that championship teams find ways to win. The format was soon adopted by the Big 12 and eventually all the major football conferences.

Florida quarterback Shane Matthews led the best offense in the SEC, while Alabama's defense was one of the best in the country. As the saying goes, defense wins championships.

The Gators scored first but Alabama responded with 21 unanswered points and led 21-7 in the third quarter. Florida wasn't done yet and scored twice to tie the game. Then Antonio Langham intercepted Shane Matthews for the game-winning touchdown.

The game (and Langham's pick-6) were recently the feature of an episode of SEC Storied, "The Play That Changed College Football." National championship contender Alabama was able to win a game over a quality opponent, which proved that the 12-team conference with a championship game was a valid format for major college football.

Alabama Celebrates After Winning 1992 SEC Championship

On January 1, 1993 at 7:30 p.m. Alabama had the privilege of playing in the Sugar Bowl in New Orleans against #1 ranked Miami for the National Championship. The game was played in the fabulous NO SuperDome. Alabama won the game W 34–13 before a total of 76,789 comfortable football fans.

1993 Sugar Bowl – Defense Really Does Win Championships

This game has been determined by the pundits to be one of the most significand football games in Crimson Tide History. Here comes the narrative:

Alabama faced #1 Miami in the Sugar Bowl for the national championship. The result was an emphatic 34–13 Alabama victory that completed the perfect season and won a national championship for the Crimson Tide.

Jay Barker managed only 18 yards passing in the Sugar Bowl and threw two interceptions, but the Tide running game punished Miami for 267 yards, including 135 rushing yards by Derrick Lassic. 1992 Heisman Trophy winner Gino Toretta threw for 278 yards but, critically, also threw three interceptions, all of which led to Alabama touchdowns. Like the Bear would say, it was mostly the student athletes who won the game but Lady Luck showed up on the side of the Tide.

On the opening possession, Alabama drove deep into Miami territory but could not get into the end zone, settling for a Michael Proctor field goal and a 3–0 lead. A 34-yard pass from Toretta to Kevin Williams set up a 49-yard field goal that tied the game. Jay Barker threw an interception in the first quarter that gave Miami the ball at the Alabama 39, but Lamar Thomas fumbled it right back after catching a pass from Toretta and the opportunity was wasted.

1993 Sugar Bowl Alabama v Miami

Barker's second interception killed a drive at the Miami 23 before the first quarter ended. In the second, Alabama drove down to the Miami 1, the key plays being runs of 24 yards and 10 yards by Lassic and a six-yard pass from Barker to Palmer to move the chains on a third down. However, after Lassic's 10-yard run he and Alabama were penalized 15 yards for unsportsmanlike conduct (Lassic had spun the ball on the ground as he got up), and the Tide was pushed back 15 yards.

Alabama settled for another Proctor field goal and a 6–3 lead. Sam Shade intercepted a Toretta pass in the second quarter and returned it to the Miami 31, setting up a five-play drive that ended in a 2-yard TD run by Sherman Williams, putting Alabama ahead 13–3. A late Miami field goal made it 13–6 at the half.

Early in the third, Tommy Johnson intercepted a Toretta pass and returned it 23 yards to the Miami 20-yard line. A Lassic TD followed soon after. On the first play from scrimmage after Lassic's touchdown, George Teague picked off another Toretta pass and ran it back 31 yards for another touchdown and a 27–6 Alabama lead

Later in the third, Toretta hit Lamar Thomas on what briefly appeared to be an 88-yard touchdown pass. George Teague somehow caught Thomas from behind, so the play briefly appeared to be an 82-yard completion, but instead Teague stripped Thomas of the football.

Miami retained possession of the ball due to an offsides penalty on Alabama, but Teague's feat in catching Thomas and stripping him of the ball prevented a Hurricane touchdown and sent the ball back deep in Miami territory. Miami was forced to punt three plays later.

Kevin Williams ran a punt back 78 yards for Miami in the fourth quarter to cut the deficit to 27–13, but Derrick Lassic's four-yard run with 6:46 to go for his second touchdown of the game closed the scoring. Alabama beat Miami 34–13 and finished 13–0.

It was Alabama's twelfth national championship and seventh by vote of either the AP Poll or Coaches' Poll. It was the first 13–0 season in Alabama history, and it was the eighth perfect season in Alabama history, following the perfect seasons of 1925, 1930, 1934, 1945, 1961, 1966, and 1979 (the 1897 season consisted of a single game which Alabama won).

1993 Coach Gene Stallings #24

The 1993 Alabama Crimson Tide football team played its 99th overall and 60th season as a member of NCAA Division I-A football competing in the Southeastern Conference (SEC) Western Division. The team was led by head coach Gene Stallings, who was in his fourth season at the position.

Alabama entered the season as the defending national champion, following their victory in the 1993 Sugar Bowl, and ranked #2 in the AP Poll, behind Florida State.

Alabama finished second in the SEC West in 1993, but played in the SEC Championship Game as Auburn was prohibited from post-season play because of NCAA violations. In the SEC Championship Game, Alabama lost 28–13 to the Florida Gators at Legion Field. Alabama received an invitation to the Gator Bowl versus North Carolina, winning 24–10 and finishing with a 9–3–1 record.

In 1995, the NCAA found Antonio Langham guilty of receiving improper benefits after signing with an agent following the 1992 season, forcing Alabama to forfeit all games in which Langham competed. Officially, Alabama finished the season with a 1–12 record, only winning their bowl game.

In the Gator Bowl Game on December v #12 North Carolina, # 18 Alabama defeated by the Tar Heels in Jacksonville, FL's Gator Bowl W (24–10) before 67,205

1994 Coach Gene Stallings #24

The 1994 Alabama Crimson Tide football team played its 100th overall and 61st season as a member of NCAA Division I-A football competing in the Southeastern Conference (SEC) Western Division. The team was led by head coach Gene Stallings, who was in his fifth season at the position. The team played their home games at Bryant-Denny Stadium in Tuscaloosa, Alabama, and Legion Field in Birmingham, Alabama.

Gene Stallings led the Crimson Tide to a perfect 11–0 regular season, only to see the Crimson Tide lose to the Florida Gators by one point in the SEC Championship Game. Highlights include a win over then unbeaten Auburn, and a dramatic victory over Georgia which is rebroadcast occasionally as part of the ESPN "Classic" series. Alabama beat Ohio State in the 1995 Florida Citrus Bowl to finish their 1994 season with a 12–1 record. 8-0 in the SEC

1995 Coach Gene Stallings #24

The 1995 Alabama Crimson Tide football team played its 101st overall and 62nd season as a member of NCAA Division I-A football competing in the Southeastern Conference (SEC) Western Division. The team was led by head coach Gene Stallings, who was in his sixth season at the position. UA played its home games at Bryant-Denny Stadium in Tuscaloosa, Alabama, and Legion Field in Birmingham, Alabama.

Gene Stallings led the Crimson Tide to an 8–3 record. Due to NCAA sanctions, no bowl appearance was made.

1996 Coach Gene Stallings #24

The 1996 Alabama Crimson Tide football team played its 102nd overall and 63rd season as a member of NCAA Division I-A football competing in the Southeastern Conference (SEC) Western Division. The team was led by head coach Gene Stallings, who was in his seventh and last season at the position. Alabama played its home games in two locations -- Bryant-Denny Stadium in Tuscaloosa, Alabama, and Legion Field in Birmingham, Alabama.

Gene Stallings led the Crimson Tide to a 10–3 record in his final year with the program. Though many try to deny Stallings his rightful honors, no coach wins every game. Stallings was a fine coach. He won a National Championship and almost another.

Chapter 15 Coaches Du Bose, Franchione, & Shula-- 1997-2006

No quotes can describe these mostly mediocre coaching records

Year	Coach	Conference	Record	SEC
1997	Mike DuBose #25	SEC	4-7-0	2-6-0
1998	Mike DuBose	SEC	7-5-0	4-4-0
1999	Mike DuBose	SEC	10-3-0	7-1-0
2000	Mike DuBose	SEC	3-8-0	3-5-0
2001	D. Franchione #26	SEC	7-5-0	4-4-0
2002	D. Franchione	SEC	10-3-0	6-2-0
2003	Mike Price #27	SEC	5 months --- No games	
2003	Mike Shula #28	SEC	4-9-0	2-6-0
2004	Mike Shula	SEC	6-6-0	3-5-0
2005	Mike Shula	SEC	10-2-0	6-2-0
2005	Shula Sanctions	SEC	0-2-0	0-2-0
2006	Mike Shula	SEC	6-7-0	2-6-0
2006	Joe Kines #29 Interim	SEC	0-1-0	0-0-0

1997 Coach Mike DuBose #25

The 1997 Alabama Crimson Tide football team played its 103th overall and 64rd season as a member of NCAA Division I-A football, competing in the Southeastern Conference (SEC) Western Division. The team was led by head coach Mike DuBose, former Defensive Coordinator, who was in his first season at the position. Alabama played its home games in two locations -- Bryant-Denny Stadium in Tuscaloosa, Alabama, and Legion Field in Birmingham, Alabama.

Du Bose's first season could be called a disaster. It was a tough year for the team and the fans. Alabama would finish with a record of 4–7 record and 2-6 in the SEC, in suffering the program's first losing season since the 1984 season. The loss against Kentucky marked Alabama's first ever overtime game, as overtime rules for college football had gone into effect the previous season. Prior to 1996, tie games were kept as ties.

It was a rare losing season for the crimson Tide. The pundits, the fans, and the Crimson White Student Newspaper knew there was something rotten in the state of Denmark. And in this story, Alabama was playing the role of Denmark.

1998 Coach Mike DuBose #25

The 1998 Alabama Crimson Tide football team played its 104th[th] overall and 65th season as a member of NCAA Division I-A football, competing in the Southeastern Conference (SEC) Western Division. The team was led by head coach Mike DuBose, in his second year with the Crimson Tide. Alabama played its home games in two locations -- Bryant-Denny Stadium in Tuscaloosa, Alabama, and Legion Field in Birmingham, Alabama.

This year, the team improved upon a 4–7 record from the 1997 season by finishing the 1998 campaign with a 7–5 record and an appearance in the Music City Bowl. The win against Ole Miss during the season marked Alabama's first ever overtime victory.

1999 Coach Mike DuBose #25

The 1999 Alabama Crimson Tide football team played its 105th[th] overall and 66th[th] season as a member of NCAA Division I-A football, competing in the Southeastern Conference (SEC) Western Division. The team was led by head coach Mike DuBose, in his third year with the Crimson Tide. Alabama continued to play its home games in two locations -- Bryant-Denny Stadium in Tuscaloosa, Alabama, and Legion Field in Birmingham, Alabama.

The DuBose-led team entered the season trying to build upon a 7–5 record from their 1998 season. The 1999 team had tremendous success. After a stunning last second upset loss to Louisiana Tech early in the year, The Tide eventually finished with a 9–2 regular season record (7–1 in the SEC).

This record included defeating Auburn on the road for the first time ever. For much of the 20th century, the game was played every year at Legion Field in Birmingham, with Alabama winning 34 games and Auburn 19. Four games were played in Montgomery, Alabama, with each team winning two. Since 2000, the games have been played at Jordan–Hare Stadium in Auburn every odd-numbered year and in Tuscaloosa every even-numbered year

Alabama went on to the 1999 SEC Championship Game where they defeated Florida for the second time for the year. Alabama then played Michigan in the 2000 Orange Bowl and suffered a heart-breaking 35–34 loss in overtime, due to a missed PAT. Ironically, Alabama had beaten Florida during the regular season by a single point in overtime, also due to a missed

After two poor DuBose-led seasons, this one started well and ended up as a fine season overall.

2000 Coach Mike DuBose #25

The 2000 Alabama Crimson Tide football team played its 106th overall and 67th season as a member of NCAA Division I-A football, competing in the Southeastern Conference (SEC) Western Division. The team was led by head coach Mike DuBose, in his fourth and final year with the Crimson Tide. Alabama continued to play its home games in two locations -- Bryant-Denny Stadium in Tuscaloosa, Alabama, and Legion Field in Birmingham, Alabama.

The team entered the season trying to build upon a fine 10–3 record from their 1999 season, which included a 34–7 victory in the SEC Championship over the Florida Gators. The 2000 team would not have the same success. Despite a preseason #3 ranking they eventually finished with a 3–8 record (3–5 in the SEC). It was almost inexplicable. But for sure Coach DuBose got the blame.

Mike Dubose Coached 2000 Alabama Crimson Tide

Mike Dubose Resigns

Alabama coach Mike DuBose, whose team has failed to approach lofty expectations in the fourth year of his turbulent tenure with the Tide, is resigning effective at the end of the season.

Athletic director Mal Moore made the announcement at a news conference today.

"We both agreed that new leadership is needed to move the program forward," Moore said.

Moore said DuBose would be paid his salary and benefits through January 2002 — one year beyond his stepping down as head coach — and there would be "no lump sum payment."

DuBose, 47, a former Alabama player and longtime assistant coach, is under contract through Jan. 31, 2004. His total annual compensation is $525,000.

The 1999 SEC Coach of the Year, DuBose has a 24-20 record in his fourth year as head coach at Alabama.

Moore said a search would be undertaken for an experienced head coach to replace DuBose, who had never been a college head coach when he took the reins of one of the country's most prominent football programs.

High Hopes for Season

DuBose led the Crimson Tide to the Southeastern Conference crown last year, a season that began under a cloud after DuBose nearly lost his job in an embarrassing sexual harassment scandal. But with the SEC title, he was touting his team as a national championship contender before the season, which opened with Alabama ranked No. 3 nationally.

The free fall began immediately. The Tide lost three of their first four games and have fallen to 3-5, losing all three nonconference games for the first time since 1955.

They are on the verge of their second losing season in DuBose's tumultuous reign. Alabama could still wind up in the SEC championship game by winning their final three games. [They did not.]

DuBose said after last Saturday's humiliating homecoming loss 40-38 to Central Florida that he did not plan to resign.

"If God intends me to do something, then I will do that," DuBose said. "Or if I look in the eyes of these young men and know I'm not doing the things I should be doing to help them be a better player, a better student and a better person. And I believe we're doing that."

Orange Bowl Appearance Last Year

After a 4-7 season in 1997, DuBose put together two winning seasons. He was named Southeastern Conference coach of the year after last year's team went 10-3, won the conference championship and went to the Orange Bowl.

After Alabama lost 21-0 to Southern Miss on Sept. 16, DuBose offered to resign at the end of the season. Moore did not accept the offer.

It wasn't the first-time questions about his future at Alabama have come up. Before the start of the 1999 season, DuBose was disciplined after he admitted to lying about a relationship with a woman on his staff who alleged sexual harassment. He received a pay cut but was allowed to retain his job.

2001 Coach Dennis Franchione #26

The 2001 Alabama Crimson Tide football team played its 107th overall and 68th season as a member of NCAA Division I-A football, competing in the Southeastern Conference (SEC) Western Division. The team was led by head coach Dennis Franchione, in his first season with the Crimson Tide. Alabama continued to play its home games in two locations -- Bryant-Denny Stadium in Tuscaloosa, Alabama, and Legion Field in Birmingham, Alabama. The team finished with a victory in the 2001 Independence Bowl and an overall record of 7–5.

2002 Coach Dennis Franchione #26

The 2002 Alabama Crimson Tide football team played its 108th overall and 69th season as a member of NCAA Division I-A football, competing in the Southeastern Conference (SEC) Western Division. The team was led by head coach Dennis Franchione, in his second and final season with the Crimson Tide.

Alabama continued to play its home games in two locations -- Bryant-Denny Stadium in Tuscaloosa, Alabama, and Legion Field in Birmingham, Alabama.

They finished the season with a record of 10–3 (6–2 in the SEC) to finish in first place in the SEC West; however, the team was ineligible to compete in the 2002 SEC Championship Game or a bowl game due to a two-year postseason ban imposed as part of the penalty for National Collegiate Athletic Association (NCAA) violations.

2003 Coach Mike Price #27 – 5 mos.
2003 Coach Mike Shula #28

<<< Mike Price

The 2003 Alabama Crimson Tide football team played its 109th overall and 70th season as a member of the Southeastern Conference (SEC) of NCAA Division I-A football, and its 12th season within the SEC Western Division. The team was led by head coach Mike Shula in his first- season with the Crimson Tide. Alabama continued to play its home games in two locations -- Bryant-Denny Stadium in Tuscaloosa, Alabama, and Legion Field in Birmingham, Alabama. They finished the season with a record of four wins and nine losses (4–9, 2–6 in the SEC).

Season Introduction

At the conclusion of the 2002 season, as noted above, Dennis Franchione resigned as head coach and took the same position with

Texas A&M. After a two-week-long coaching search, Washington State head coach Mike Price was hired as Franchione's replacement as UA's 27th Head Coach. Price then signed the 2003 recruiting class and led the Crimson Tide through spring practice. However, he was fired in May 2003 due to detrimental conduct as an employee of the University. Less than a week later, Mike Shula was hired as Alabama'a 28th head coach.

NCAA sanctions

The 2003 season was still impacted by sanctions imposed by the National Collegiate Athletic Association (NCAA) for violations that dated back as far as the late 1990s. On February 1, 2002, the NCAA lowered the boom. It imposed a two-year bowl ban; a reduction in athletic scholarships of 21 over a three-year period; and five years of probation.

On September 17, 2002, the NCAA rejected Alabama's appeal to reduce the severity of the sanctions. At the same time, the NCAA noted that it felt that the sanctions were quite appropriate. The bottom line was that it was only because of the cooperation of the University that the death penalty for the football program was not considered. Quite frankly, that is why so many fans and pundits find the NCAA quite often to exercise outrageous behavior.

The appeal was thus denied. And, so, for the 2003 season Alabama saw a smaller recruiting class and was ineligible for both the 2003 SEC Championship Game and for post-season bowl games. The latter penalty would end up essentially being meaningless due to the Tide's poor record during this period (4-9).

Dennis Franchione Resigns – One more look

In the post Bear Bryant Era and the Pre-Nick Saban Era, the 23 years from 1983 through 2006, Alabama had a tough time retaining coaches for a long duration. Gene Stalling's seven years at the helm —1990-1996 made him the only coach who lasted more than four years during this period.

With Franchione resigning after just two years and Price out even before the 2003 season began, Alabama's bad luck in coach retention continued. Mike Shula, in his first year this year, would last just four years. Four years had become the norm.

It was quite late in the 2002 season, when rumors got loud about head coach Dennis Franchione being ready to resign from Alabama to take the head coaching position with Texas A&M. The rumors as most rumors are, were true. On December 2, 2002, A&M head coach R. C. Slocum was fired after he served 14 seasons in the position. Three days later, Franchione left Tuscaloosa and formally accepted the Aggies coaching vacancy on December 6.

Immediately after the resignation of Franchione, athletic director Mal Moore started the search for his replacement. In the week of December 9, South Florida head coach Jim Leavitt was interviewed and then New Orleans Saints assistant coach Mike Riley was actually offered the Alabama coaching position, which he later declined.

<<<Mike Shula
After Riley turned down the position, Moore considered several other candidates. Included in the search were head coaches Les Miles of Oklahoma State, Rich Rodriguez of West Virginia and Mike Price of Washington State. On December 17, Price was officially named as the new head coach for the Crimson Tide. Price did not fully assume his duties

as head coach until January 4, after he coached Washington State in the 2003 Rose Bowl. Price appeared to be a good pick but he was let go in May for violations of Alabama conduct guidelines.

2004 Coach Mike Shula #28

 The 2004 Alabama Crimson Tide football team played its 110th overall and 71st season as a member of the Southeastern Conference (SEC) of NCAA Division I-A football, and its 13th season within the SEC Western Division. The team was led by head coach Mike Shula in his second season with the Crimson Tide. Alabama stopped playing home games in two locations -- Bryant-Denny Stadium in Tuscaloosa, Alabama, and Legion Field in Birmingham, Alabama.

This year, home games were played only in Bryant-Denny Stadium. The 2004 squad finished the season with a record of 6–6 following a loss to Minnesota in the Music City Bowl.
 (6-6, 3-5 in the SEC).

2005 Coach Mike Shula #28

The 2005 Alabama Crimson Tide football team played its 111thh overall and 72nd season as a member of the Southeastern Conference (SEC) of NCAA Division I-A football, and its 14th season within the SEC Western Division. The team was led by head coach Mike Shula in his third season with the Crimson Tide.

All Alabama home games were played at the revitalized Bryant-Denny Stadium on the campus in Tuscaloosa, Alabama. The 2005 squad finished the season with a record of 10-2, 6-2 in the SEC before Sanctions.

2006 Coach Mike Shula #28
2006 Coach Joe Kines #29

The 2006 Alabama Crimson Tide football team played its 112thh overall and 73nd season as a member of the Southeastern Conference (SEC) of NCAA Division I-A football, and its 15th season within the SEC Western Division. The team was led by head coach Mike Shula in his fourth and final season with the Crimson Tide. Joe

Kines, the Tides "D" Coordinator coached the Independence Bowl game after Shula was fired. Alabama lost the game L (31-34) v Oklahoma State.

<<< Joe Kines

All Alabama home games were played at Bryant-Denny Stadium on the campus in Tuscaloosa, Alabama. The 2006 squad finished the season with a record of 6-6, 4-4 in the SEC before sanctions. Despite a strong 5–2 start on the playing field, the Crimson Tide finished out the season by losing four of their final five games. The team thus closed its regular season at 6–6 (4–4, SEC). Almost as bad as the season was the fifth-straight loss to arch-rival Auburn in the Iron Bowl. This loss was more than UA Officials could take. Alabama coaches have one major job and that is to win football games, especially against traditional rivalries.

Following the loss Shula was fired as head coach and defensive coordinator Joe Kines served as interim head coach for the bowl game.

The Tide were defeated by Oklahoma State in the 2006 Independence Bowl L (31-34) to finish the season with a 6–7 (2–6) record. However, three years later even these measly six wins of the season were vacated as part of a penalty placed against Alabama by the NCAA for infractions committed during the season. As such, the official record for the 2006 squad is 0–7. Funny, how the losses were able to withstand the heavy hand of the NCAA sanctions.

Post Season Nick Saban

Following the Independence Bowl loss, on January 3, 2007, Alabama announced that Nick Saban was hired from the Miami Dolphins to serve as the programs 30th head coach.

In the weeks that followed, Saban worked to fill his staff for the 2007 season. As part of the A-Day (Spring Football) celebrations on April 21, 2007, the 2006 team captains Le'Ron McClain and Juwan Simpson were honored at the Walk of Fame ceremony at the base of Denny Chimes.

NCAA sanctions

In October 2007, the athletic department discovered a potential NCAA-violations present throughout the athletics program. The violations stemmed from athletes from several sports, including football, receiving improper benefits as a result of a failure in the distribution system of textbooks to student athletes from the university.

After a prolonged investigation, in June 2009 the NCAA ruled all athletes that received improper benefits related to the textbook distribution system were deemed ineligible. As such, as part of the penalties imposed on the football program, all victories which those included in the inquiry participated, were officially vacated from the all-time record. In this book, we opted to show the on-field results.

Chapter 16 Coach Nick Saban 2007-2017, etc.

"There are two pains in life. There is the pain of discipline and the pain of disappointment. If you can handle the pain of discipline, then you'll never have to deal with the pain of disappointment."

Year	Coach	Conference	Record	SEC
2007	Nick Saban # 29	SEC	7-6-0	4-4-0
2008	Nick Saban	SEC	12-2-0	8-0-0
2009*	Nick Saban	SEC	14-0-0	8-0-0
2010	Nick Saban	SEC	10-3-0	5-3-0
2011*	Nick Saban	SEC	12-1-0	7-1-0
2012*	Nick Saban	SEC	13-1-0	7-1-0
2013	Nick Saban	SEC	11-2-0	7-1-0
2014	Nick Saban	SEC	12-2-0	7-1-0
2015*	Nick Saban	SEC	14-1-0	7-1-0
2016	Nick Saban	SEC	15-0-0	8-0-0

* Championships

Nick Saban Leads Alabama Football Team onto the Field

We extend a big thank you to al.com for this great piece provided below on Nick Saban as he took over the reins of what had been a floundering Alabama Football Program. Nick Saban may not wrestle bears but he knows how to handle a ton of huge men—brutes for sure—who want to play great football for Alabama.

This fully copied and well attributed piece is a great perspective on the state of affairs at Alabama at the time and it is aptly titled. I

The day Rich Rodriguez said no to Alabama, Nick Saban said yes

By Kevin Scarbinsky | kscarbinsky@al.com
December 08, 2016 at 1:02 PM, updated December 08, 2016 at 1:13 PM

KEVIN SCARBINSKY COLUMNS

The day Rich Rodriguez said no to Alabama, Nick Saban said yes

Dec. 8, 2006, is not a date which will live in infamy in Alabama football history. Instead Dec. 8, 2006 is a date which should be remembered in this state as Rich Rod Day.

It's not a stretch to suggest that Rich Rodriguez did almost as much for Crimson Tide football as anyone who doesn't have a statue on the Walk of Champions.

And all he did was say no.

No to following Mike Shula as the Alabama coach after the 2006 season. No to accepting the Alabama job at the perfect moment in the program's history.

Because he said no, Nick Saban was able to say yes. That very same day.

Not completely, not directly and not in any detail, but the day the Rodriguez door closed for Alabama, the Saban door re-opened. More on that forgotten part of the story in a minute.

Had Rodriguez said yes, had he signed off on the deal his agent and Alabama had reached in principle, there's no way to know exactly where Alabama football would be today, but here's a hypothesis.

There's no way Alabama is celebrating its fifth SEC championship in the last 10 years and preparing for a playoff run at its fifth national title in this decade of dominance. There's no way Rodriguez is still the Alabama coach.

What really happened between Alabama, Rich Rod 10 years ago

Looking back at the moment Rich Rodriguez turned down Alabama 10 years ago, and the long-lasting impacts of that decision.

He didn't get the job done in three years at Michigan, where he had a losing record, and he's not getting it done after five years at Arizona, where he's yet to lose fewer than four games in a single season and is coming off a dud of 3-9 overall and 1-8 in the Pac-12.

It's impossible to imagine how he could've lasted in the cutthroat SEC as long as Saban has or approached Saban's incomparable record of success.

It's fun to look back on the series of events that put Rodriguez so close to the big office in Tuscaloosa. It was a historic coaching search that lasted more than a month, a story that was maddening and fascinating to chase at the time.

As we reported four days before Shula was fired, Alabama targeted Saban early. The first time Saban's agent, Jimmy Sexton, mentioned the possibility to him, Saban got angry. Not because he wasn't interested in returning to the college game. Because he didn't want to deal with distractions during his NFL season with the Miami Dolphins.

Despite his public denials, Saban privately was intrigued by the idea of becoming the Alabama coach. His camp conveyed that interest to the Alabama camp, but some Alabama decision-makers got cold feet.

They feared, if they agreed to Saban's demand to wait until after his NFL season ended, he might back out in the end, and they'd be left at the altar as they had been in previous searches by the likes of Butch Davis and Mike Riley.

So, Alabama turned to Rodriguez. On Rich Rod Day, with West Virginia supporters up to and including the governor showering him with love and inducements to stay, Rodriguez turned Alabama down.

Some athletics directors would've panicked. Not Mal Moore. That same day, as he realized the Rodriguez deal was falling apart, the Alabama AD turned back to his original target. As we reported at the time, a member of Moore's camp quickly reached out to Saban's camp to see if Saban was still interested in the Alabama job. Would it not be nice to have a camp?

Saban was at practice with the Dolphins at the time. Afterward, he returned a message and let Sexton know he was very much still interested. One person familiar with that conversation told me at the time that Saban said, "They wouldn't be in this mess if they'd listened to us. Get me the dang job."

Or words to that effect. Sexton communicated Saban's interest to Alabama that day, which turned out to be the bigger news on Rich Rod Day.

Here's the first line from my Dec. 9, 2006, column in The Birmingham News: Don't be shocked if the University of Alabama's long and winding search for a new head football coach ends up right where it began. At the doorstep of Nick Saban.

There would be more twists and turns from there to the journey's end, but Rich Rod Day was momentous in two ways. Alabama football got rejected by a coach who wasn't its first or best choice - and got encouraged to stay the course by the coach who was.

End of quote

Nick Saban is not only a great coach. Like the Bear and the immortals before him, he is also quite a man. It is now time that we explore the obvious as well some of the mysteries of the Nick Saban era here at Alabama.

As noted, in 2006, Athletic director Mal Moore had appointed defensive coordinator Joe Kines to serve as interim head coach to mark time until the after the Independence Bowl. In that way, the crimson Tide could take the time to gain a long-term coach, not a four-year max fly-by-night fill-in for the program.

UA under the last coach Mike Shula went on to lose its final regular season game in 2006 v Auburn L (15-22) in the Iron Bowl and then lost to Oklahoma State L (31-34) in the Independence Bowl to finish with a 6–7 overall record. The fans and the administration and the players wanted to be coached by the best coach there could possibly be. The team was languishing. Many are of the opinion and I am one of them that with Nick Saban, coaching the University of Alabama Football Team in 2007 and beyond, they got their wish.

On January 3, 2007, Alabama announced that Nick Saban was hired from the Miami Dolphins to serve as the program's 27th head coach. In the weeks that followed, Saban worked to fill his staff. The first hires came on January 9 with Kirby Smart hired from the Dolphins to serve as defensive coordinator; Kevin Steele from Florida State to serve as head defensive coach; and Lance Thompson from Central Florida to serve as linebacker's coach.

On January 11, Joe Pendry of the Houston Texans was hired to serve as an assistant head and linebackers coach. On January 12 Saban hired two more assistants. Ron Middleton was hired from the Tampa Bay Buccaneers to serve as both the tight ends and special teams coach and Bo Davis from the Dolphins was hired as defensive line coach. On January 13, Major Applewhite was hired from Rice to serve as both offensive coordinator and quarterbacks coach.

On January 16 Burton Burns was hired from Clemson to serve as both associate head and running backs coach. On February 19 Curt Cignetti was hired from NC State to serve as both receiver's coach and recruiting coordinator to fill the final position on Saban's inaugural coaching staff.

Head coach Nick Saban entered his first year as Bama's head coach for the 2007 season and there are few who do not admire his work

2007 Coach Nick Saban #30

The 2007 Alabama Crimson Tide football team played its 113th[h] overall and 74th season as a member of the Southeastern Conference (SEC) of NCAA Division I-A football, and its 16th season in the SEC Western Division. The team was led by head coach Nick Saban, a former head coach of rival LSU. This was Nick Saban's first of many seasons with the Crimson Tide.

All Alabama home games today and in the foreseeable future are played at Bryant-Denny Stadium on the UA campus in Tuscaloosa, Alabama. The 2007 squad tried to improve from a disappointing 2006 6-7 record with a 4-4 record in the SEC before sanctions. Nothing in life worth having is easy. So, it was with Mr. Saban's first year; but he did fine.

Despite a strong 6–2 start, the team finished out the season by losing four of its final five games. Alabama thus closed the regular season at 6–6 (4–4, SEC) and they lost for a sixth-straight time to rival Auburn in the Iron Bowl. Nick Saban had a baptism of fire as expectations were high; but he was up to it. He took notes on everything and he took notes on losing games and did not like reading them back to himself, so he fixed the problems.

The Tide ended the season positively by defeating Colorado in the 2007 Independence Bowl 30–24 to finish its first season under Nick Saban at a 7–6 overall with an SEC record of (4–4).

On November 3, 2007 #3 LSU came to Bryant-Denny Stadium and the Tigers lost L (34–41).

The Alabama–LSU football rivalry

In the game dubbed "Saban Bowl I", in which Nick Saban's new Alabama team faced a LSU Tigers team that featured several players that Saban himself had recruited during his tenure in Baton Rouge, the Tide found itself in an SEC shootout, but lost 41–34.

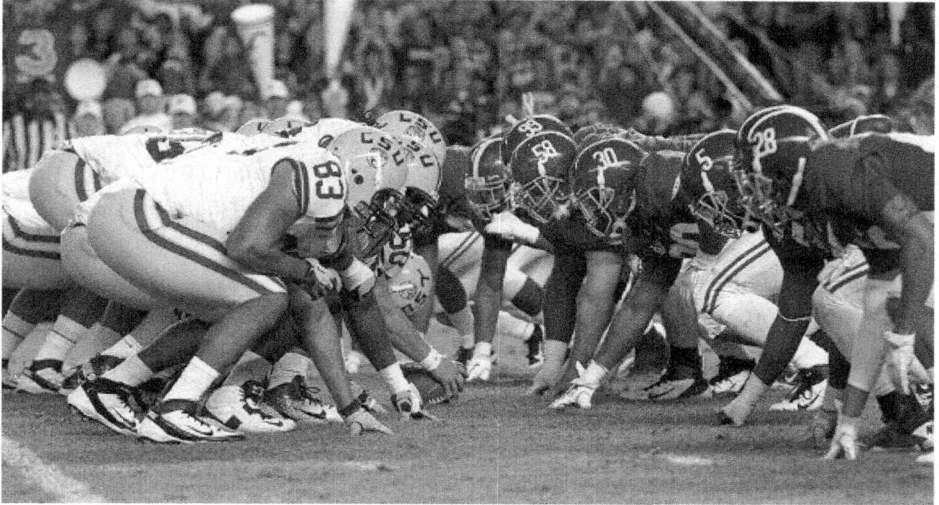

2008 Coach Nick Saban #29

The 2007 Alabama Crimson Tide football team played its 114th[h] overall and 75th season as a member of the Southeastern Conference (SEC) of NCAA Division I-A football, and its 17th season in the SEC Western Division. The team was led by head coach Nick Saban in his second year. All Alabama home games are played at Bryant-Denny Stadium on the UA campus in Tuscaloosa, Alabama. The 2008 squad improved substantially from the 7-6 record 4-4 in the SEC.

Alabama finished 2008 with an undefeated 12–0 regular season, their first since 1994. They won their first SEC Western Division Championship since 1999. They finished the season with a record of 12–2 (8–0 in the SEC) after losses to Florida in the SEC Championship Game and to Utah in the Sugar Bowl.

In February 2008, Alabama signed the No. 1 recruiting class per both Rivals and Scout. Spring practice began on March 13 and concluded with the annual A-Day game on April 12. Before a crowd of 78,200, the Crimson team defeated the White team by a score of 24–14 in Bryant–Denny Stadium. For their performances, Alfred McCullough earned the Dwight Stephenson Lineman of the A-Day Game Award and Terry Grant earned the Dixie Howell Memorial Most Valuable Player of the A-Day Game

2009 Coach Nick Saban #30

The 2009 Alabama Crimson Tide football team played its 115th overall and 76th season as a member of the Southeastern Conference (SEC) of NCAA Division I-A football, and its 18th season in the SEC Western Division. The team was led by head coach Nick Saban in his third year. All Alabama home games are played at Bryant-Denny Stadium on the UA campus in Tuscaloosa, Alabama. At 14-0; 8-0 SEC, and National Champions, the 2009 squad improved substantially from the prior year's 12-2 record 4-4 in the SEC.

Looking to build on the successes of the 12-2 2008 campaign, Alabama entered the 2009 season as the favorite to win the Western Division and meet the Florida Gators in the 2009 SEC Championship Game. Alabama closed the regular season with a 12–0 record including four wins against Top 25-ranked teams—and met the Gators for the SEC Championship in a rematch of the 2008 contest. Alabama was victorious by a final score of 32–13. The following day, final Bowl Championship Series (BCS) standings were unveiled. No. 1 ranked Alabama would meet No. 2 ranked Texas for the BCS National Championship. In the BCS National Championship Game, the Crimson Tide defeated the Longhorns 37–21 to capture their first-ever BCS Championship.

Alabama earned their third SEC championship since the inception of the SEC Championship Game in 1992, and their 22nd SEC title. The victory over Texas gave Alabama their 13th national championship in football (their eighth wire service title since the AP Poll began in 1936) and their ninth perfect season since 1925. The season included victories over the previous three national champions: Florida, Louisiana State University (LSU), and Texas.

The season marked the first time a player for Alabama won the Heisman Trophy: Mark Ingram won the award over Stanford running back Toby Gerhart. Other award winners included Rolando McClain, who won the Butkus Award and the Jack Lambert Award, and defensive coordinator Kirby Smart, who won the Broyles Award as the nation's top assistant coach. Also, six players were named to various All-America Teams with Terrence Cody, Mike Johnson, and Javier Arenas being consensus selections and Ingram and McClain each being unanimous selections.

Games of the 2009 Season

On Sept 5 # 7 Virginia Tech played the #5 UA team at the Georgia Dome in Atlanta, GA in the Chick-fil-A Kickoff Game W (34–24). Then on Sept 12, Florida International lost big at Bryant–Denny Stadium W (40–14) before 92,012. On Sept 19, North Texas lost big to UA at home W (53–7). On Sept 26 Arkansas made the trip to Bryant–Denny Stadium to be beaten by #3 Alabama W (35–7).

The recap of the season's games gets a little boring as Alabama brought the bacon home every game. Such as the game on Oct 3 v Kentucky at Commonwealth Stadium • Lexington, KY W (38–20), and the game on Oct 10 at #20 Ole Miss at Vaught–Hemingway Stadium in Oxford, MS W (22–3). On Oct 17, another win at home v #22 South Carolina at Bryant–Denny Stadium W (W 20–6). Then on Oct 24 on the (Third Saturday in October) UA just got by Tennessee at Bryant–Denny Stadium W (12-0).

This game has been determined by the pundits to be one of the most significand football games in Crimson Tide History. Here comes the second narrative by bamahammer:

2009 Tennessee – Rocky Block

The Alabama Crimson Tide was supposed to be unchallenged by first year head coach Lane Kiffin's Tennessee Volunteers. Instead, a sluggish offense set up a defensive struggle and a dramatic finish.

After coming into the season as an unknown at quarterback, Greg McElroy took over the starting job after the graduation of three-year starter John Parker Wilson. McElroy had a great September and went from potential problem to one of the most efficient passers in the SEC.

Then October came, and as the Tide got into the toughest stretch of their schedule, Greg McElroy started to struggle. He came into the Tennessee game not having thrown a touchdown in either of his last two starts. Mark Ingram had entered the national spotlight during McElroy's struggles, but the Volunteers had success containing Ingram.

Bama couldn't move the ball on its first two drives. An interception by Mark Barron gave the offense favorable field position, and instead of a punt Alabama was able to kick a field goal and take a 3-0 lead. Tennessee responded with a field goal, then Leigh Tiffin kicked two more and Tennessee missed one late in the second quarter. Alabama led 9-3 at the half.

Early in the fourth quarter, Tennessee's short field goal attempt to bring the score to 9-6 was blocked by Terrence Cody. Leigh Tiffin hit a long field goal on the next Bama possession to bring the Tide's lead to 12-3.

Then Mark Ingram lost his first career fumble, giving the Volunteers the ball near midfield with 3:29 to play. Tennessee scored on an 11-yard touchdown pass. The Volunteers successfully recovered an onside kick down 12-10. Tennessee set up for a 45-yard field goal as time expired, but Terrence Cody came up with his second block of the quarter to preserve a 12-10 Alabama win.

LSU came to Bryant Denny next. They were defeated by a #3 Bama team W (24–15). Next, on Nov 14 at Mississippi State's Davis Wade Stadium in Starkville, MS, #3 Alabama beat the Bulldogs W (31-3. On Nov 21 at Bryant Denny v Chattanooga, Alabama prevailed again in a shutout W (45-0). Finally, on Nov 27, Nick Saban got another chance to win another Iron Bowl, and Alabama brought home the victory over Auburn W (26-21) in another hard-fought battle.

This game has been determined by the pundits to be one of the most significand football games in Crimson Tide History. Here comes a more complete narrative from bamahammer:

On the game's last play, Daniel Lincoln's 44 field-goal attempt was blocked, far right, by Alabama's Terrence Cody. Cody blocked two field-goal attempts.

2009 Iron Bowl – The Drive

With just one win over Auburn since 2002, the Tide traveled to the Plains to try to finish their second straight perfect regular season. First year coach Gene Chizik's Tigers were more than ready to play. After forcing an Alabama punt on their first possession, Auburn scored on a 67-yard reverse to go up 7-0. It was the longest touchdown play Alabama had allowed under Nick Saban.

Auburn kicked off with an onside kick, recovered, and scored another touchdown on that possession to go up 14-0 in the first quarter. The Tide was on their heels, trailing by two possessions for the first time in the 2009 season.

Alabama responded with two second quarter touchdowns, and the teams went into the locker room at the half tied at 14 points each.

Auburn used another long touchdown early in the third quarter to gain another lead. Two drives ending in Leigh Tiffin field goals had Alabama down 21-20 at the end of the third.

With under 9 minutes to go in the game, Alabama got the ball on their own 21. Greg McElroy then led a 15-play drive to march 79 yards into the end zone and eat over 7 minutes of clock. McElroy completed seven straight passes, including the 4-yard touchdown pass to senior Roy Upchurch. Up 26-21, Alabama attempted the two-point conversion but did not convert.

Alabama's Roy Upchurch (5) reacts after scoring on a 4-yard pass from quarterback Greg McElroy late in the fourth quarter of an NCAA college football game against Auburn at Jordan-Hare Stadium in Auburn, Ala., Friday, Nov. 27, 2009. At right is Auburn's Neiko Thorpe (15). Alabama won 26-21. (AP Photo/Dave Martin)

Leigh Tiffin kicked off to Auburn. The Tigers made it to midfield quickly, but were unable to get within range. The time ran out on the Tigers comeback and the Tide's dreams of an undefeated matchup with Florida were a reality.

Alabama had won the Western Division SEC and so on Dec 5, the #2 Crimson Tide played a tough #1 ranked Florida team at 3:00 PM before a national audience and they won convincingly over the Gators at the Georgia Dome in Atlanta, GA in the SEC Championship Game W (32–13).

This SEC Championship Game has been determined by the pundits to be one of the most significand football games in Crimson Tide History. Here comes the narrative from bamahammer:

2009 SEC Championship Game, Alabama vs. Florida

After an embarrassing defeat at the hands of Urban Meyer's Gators in 2008, the Tide had another opportunity to win the SEC and advance to the program's first BCS National Championship Game.

Both teams entered the game undefeated, a first in the 15-year history of the SEC Championship Game. The game was advertised as a play-in game for the title game. Both teams also featured Heisman Trophy candidates on offense.

Alabama scored first, with a 48-yard field goal to end their first drive. The Tide led for the rest of the game.

Florida went in to the locker room at halftime down by only 6 points and got the ball to start the second half. The Gators punted on their first two possessions of the second half, but Alabama scored touchdowns on both possessions to put the game away.

Quarterback Greg McElroy used his 239 passing yards and 1 touchdown to claim MVP honors for the game. He also collected some broken ribs that didn't become public knowledge until after a lackluster performance in the national championship game. Now that's toughness built by Bama.

Mark Ingram's 3 touchdowns and 113 yards on 28 carries vaulted him to the top of the Heisman Trophy conversation. Ingram would go on to win the award by the narrowest margin in its history.

Alabama's win sent the team to Pasadena to face the Texas Longhorns with a national title on the line. I'm sure you don't need the reminder, but it's always fun to say – Alabama beat Texas 37-21 to claim the program's 13th national championship.

Mark Ingram bangs out some yardage in SEC Championship

Alabama, ranked at #1, was thus invited to the BCS Championship Game on January 7, 2010 at 7:39 p.m. vs. then #2 Texas in the Rose Bowl in Pasadena, CA in a game known as the (BCS National Championship Game. Alabama won W (37–21) before 94,906

This game has been determined by the pundits to be one of the most significand football games in Crimson Tide History.

National Championship Game Highlights from RollTide

1/7/2010 12:00:00 AM

Jan. 7, 2010

PASEDENA, Calif. - The No. 1-ranked Alabama football team held true to its ranking, defeating second-ranked Texas, 37-21, Thursday night in the 2010 BCS National Championship at the Rose Bowl in Pasadena. The 2009 national championship is the 13th in Alabama history.

"Our message to the team at halftime was that it's a 60-minute game," head coach Nick Saban said. "I'm proud of the way we hung in there and bounced back at the end of the game."

The Crimson Tide defense ended any hopes of a Longhorns comeback when Eryk Anders forced a fumble out of the hands of Texas quarterback Garret Gilbert with 3:08 remaining in the game.
Alabama would force two more turnovers and score two touchdowns to seal the 2009 national championship.

After Texas jumped out to a 6-0 lead on a pair of field goals in the first quarter, the Crimson Tide took the lead when sophomore Heisman Trophy winner Mark Ingram scored on a two-yard rush, putting Alabama up 7-6 with 14:18 remaining in the second quarter.
Freshman Trent Richardson joined in on the ground attack when he busted a 49-yard touchdown run at the 7:59 mark in the second quarter.

The long touchdown run stretched Alabama's lead to 14-6. Senior Leigh Tiffin would extend the Tide's lead further connecting on a 26-yard attempt. Two plays later Marcell Dareus intercepted Gilbert's shovel pass and returned it 28 yards for an Alabama touchdown. The 10-point swing gave the Crimson Tide a 24-6 lead heading into the half.

With Texas' offense scoring 11 unanswered points in the second half and pulling within 24-21, Anders swung into action, forcing a fumble at the three-yard line with Courtney Upshaw recovering for the Tide.

Ingram capitalized on the turnover, scoring on a one-yard touchdown run three plays later, putting Alabama up 31-21. Senior Javier Arenas came up with his second interception of the night with 1:55 remaining in the game. Richardson turned the turnover into points once again, scoring a touchdown on a two-yard run. Tiffin missed the extra point attempt, making the score 37-21.

Alabama Celebrates first BCS Championship under Nick Saban

With the win, Alabama head coach Nick Saban becomes the first head coach in major college football history to win a national championship at two different schools, also winning the BCS national championship in 2003 at LSU.

Saban also becomes the second head coach to win two BCS national championships, joining Urban Meyer of Florida.

The victory in Pasadena comes 84 years after Alabama won its first national championship in the 1926 Rose Bowl game and makes this the fifth Alabama team to end their national championship campaign at the Rose Bowl in Pasadena.

Alabama officials are tentatively planning a national championship celebration for Saturday, Jan. 16.

2009: How Sweet It IS!

2010 Coach Nick Saban #30

The 2010 Alabama Crimson Tide football team played its 116th overall and 77th season as a member of the Southeastern Conference (SEC) of NCAA Division I-A football, and its 19th season in the SEC Western Division. The team was led by head coach Nick Saban in his fourth year. All Alabama home games are played at Bryant-Denny Stadium on the UA campus in Tuscaloosa, Alabama. At 10-3; 5-30 SEC, The Squad had a fine year.

Alabama entered the season as defending national champions, and began the 2010 season as the preseason number one team in both the AP and Coaches' Polls.

Favored to win a second consecutive SEC championship and be in contention for the national championship, the Crimson Tide opened the season with five consecutive victories. Alabama appeared to be unstoppable but its luck had run out. After five great wins, The Crimson Tide completed the regular season with only nine victories and losses on Oct 9 to South Carolina L (21-35), and at LSU on Nov

6 L (21-24) and then at Auburn on Nov 26 L (27-28). The team finished fourth in the Western Division.

After the regular season, the Crimson Tide accepted an invitation to compete in the Capital One Bowl in Orlando. Against Big Ten co-champions Michigan State, Alabama won by a final score of 49–7 and captured both a third straight ten-win season and top ten finish.

UA v Michigan State

2011 Coach Nick Saban #30

The 2011 Alabama Crimson Tide football team played its 117th overall and 78th season as a member of the Southeastern Conference (SEC) of NCAA Division I-A football, and its 20th season in the SEC Western Division. The team was led by head coach Nick Saban in his fifth year. All Alabama home games are played at Bryant-Denny Stadium on the UA campus in Tuscaloosa, Alabama. They finished the season with a record of twelve wins and one loss (12–1, 7-1 in the SEC) and they were crowned consensus National Champions.

After the completion of the 2010 season, the Crimson Tide signed a highly-rated recruiting class in February 2011 and completed spring practice the following April. With seventeen returning starters from the previous season, Alabama entered their 2011 campaign ranked as the number two team in the nation and as a favorite to win the Western Division and compete for the SEC championship.

However, Alabama lost to the LSU Tigers in their regular season matchup, and as a result did not qualify for the 2011 SEC Championship Game. Despite not winning their conference championship, when the final Bowl Championship Series rankings were released, Alabama had the number two ranking to qualify for the 2012 BCS National Championship Game. In the rematch against LSU, the Crimson Tide defeated the Tigers 21–0 to capture their second BCS Championship in three years.

At the conclusion of the season, the Alabama defense led the nation in every major statistical category, and was the first to do so since the 1986 season. Additionally, several players were recognized for the individual accomplishments on the field. Barrett Jones won both the Wuerffel Trophy and the Outland Trophy; and Trent Richardson won the Doak Walker Award, was a finalist for the Heisman Trophy and was named the SEC Offensive Player of the Year.

Also, seven players were named to various All-America Teams with Dont'a Hightower being a consensus selection and Mark Barron, Jones and Richardson each being unanimous selections. In April 2012, eight members of the 2011 squad were selected in the NFL Draft, with an additional six signed as undrafted free agents to various teams.

Highlights of the Second LSU Game for the National Championship

On December 4, 2011, the final Bowl Championship Series standings were unveiled with a rematch between #1 LSU and #2 Alabama in the BCS National Championship Game. In the game, played on January 9, 2012 the Crimson Tide defeated the Tigers 21–0 to clinch their second BCS Championship in three years.

The first points of the game were set up after Marquis Maze returned a Brad Wing punt 49-yards to the LSU 26-yard line in the first quarter. Five plays later, Jeremy Shelley connected on a 23-yard field goal to give Alabama a 3–0 lead. After his first attempt was blocked by the Tigers' Michael Brockers, Shelley connected on second-quarter field goals of 34 and 41 yards to give the Crimson Tide a 9–0 halftime lead.

Shelley extended the Crimson Tide lead to 12–0 after he converted a 35-yard field goal on Alabama's first possession of the second half. He then missed a 41-yard field goal attempt wide right before he connected on a 44-yard attempt to give the Crimson Tide a 15–0 lead at the end of the third quarter.

Midway through the fourth quarter, the LSU offense crossed the 50-yard line for the first time of the game only to be pushed back to the 50 after Dont'a Hightower sacked Jordan Jefferson on a fourth down play to give possession back to Alabama. On that possession, the Crimson Tide scored the only touchdown of the game on a 34-yard Trent Richardson run to make the final score 21–0.

In the game, Alabama outgained LSU in total offense 384 to 92 yards, and the shutout was the first ever completed in a BCS game since the advent of the BCS in 1998. Jeremy Shelley established the all-time bowl record with seven field goal attempts and tied the all-time bowl record with five made. For their performances, Courtney Upshaw was named the defensive player of the game and AJ McCarron was named the offensive player of the game.

McCarron became the first sophomore QB to lead a team to a BCS National Title.

This BCS Championship game has been determined by the pundits to be one of the most significand football games in Crimson Tide History.

From Rolltide – 2012 BCS Bowl Game Highlights

1/9/2012 12:00:00 AM
Jan. 9, 2012
NEW ORLEANS –

A staunch defensive effort, combined with a record-setting night from kicker Jeremy Shelley, propelled the University of Alabama football team to its 14th national championship with a 21-0 victory over LSU Monday night in the BCS National Championship Game.

The Crimson Tide's defense held LSU to just 92 total yards and five first downs as Defensive Player of the Game Courtney Upshaw and Jerrell Harris each had seven tackles. As a unit, the defense had 11 tackles for loss, four sacks and an interception.

"I think it's a great team win," UA head coach Nick Saban said. "Our offense controlled the tempo of this game. We did a great job on special teams. It was just a great team win for every guy here, every fan that we have, every supporter of this program. This is great for Alabama."

Fifteen of UA's 21 points came from the leg of kicker Jeremy Shelley, who converted on a bowl-record five field goals from 23, 34, 41, 35 and a career-long 44 yards. The defense provided the offense with excellent field position all evening and quarterback AJ McCarron did a masterful job under center completing 23-of-34 passes for 234 yards to earn Offensive Player of the Game honors.

"We knew that he [McCarron] was going to have to play well because we knew that we were going to throw the ball," Saban said of his quarterback. "He showed great leadership and poise in making good decisions."

Thanks to Shelley, the Tide carried a 15-0 lead into the final quarter when LSU mounted its first legitimate charge after being held to just 55 yards in the previous three quarters. Upon crossing midfield for the first time all game, the drive stalled and left the Tigers facing 4th and 18 to gain on the UA 40. The Tide defense came through again as Dont'a Hightower sacked LSU's Jordan Jefferson and knocked the ball loose at the 50-yard line. Nick Gentry fell on the fumble to end the drive and set the UA offense up at midfield with 6:15 left in the contest.

Four plays later, Trent Richardson raced 34 yards for the first touchdown of the game and the Heisman Trophy semifinalist finished with 96 yards on 20 carries and 107 all-purpose yards.

Alabama put up the first points of the game when Shelley capped off a five-play, 20-yard drive with a 23-yard field goal with five minutes left in the first quarter. Shelley would come up big for the Tide on two more occasions in the first half, connecting from 34 and 41 yards to give Alabama a 9-0 lead at the break.

Alabama held LSU to one first down throughout the first half, while collecting 13 of its own. The Tide also collected 156 total yards compared to the Tigers' 26 total yards in the first 30 minutes.

The title is the Tide's 14th in program history adding to the national championships won in 1925, 1926, 1930, 1934, 1941, 1961, 1965, 1966, 1973, 1978, 1979, 1992, 2009 and 2011. The Crimson Tide finished the 2011 season with a 12-1 record. The combined record of UA's 14 national championship teams stands at 157-7-2.

2012 Coach Nick Saban #30

The 2012 Alabama Crimson Tide football team played its 118th overall and 79th season as a member of the Southeastern Conference (SEC) of NCAA Division I-A football, and its 21st season in the SEC Western Division. The team was led by head coach Nick Saban in his sixth year. All Alabama home games are played at Bryant-Denny Stadium on the UA campus in Tuscaloosa, Alabama.

The Tide finished the season with a record of thirteen wins and one loss (13–1, 7-1 in the SEC), as SEC champion and as consensus

national champion after it defeated Notre Dame in the Bowl
Championship Series (BCS) National Championship Game.

After they captured the 2011 national championship, the Crimson
Tide signed another highly-rated recruiting class in February 2012
and completed spring practice the following April. With twelve
returning starters from the previous season, Alabama entered the
2012 season as the defending national champions, ranked as the
number two team in the nation and as a favorite to win the Western
Division and compete for both the SEC and national
championships.

The Crimson Tide opened the season with nine consecutive victories
that included one over Michigan at a neutral site and a come-from-
behind victory on the road at Louisiana State University (LSU).

On Nov 10, #15 Texas A&M came to Bryant–Denny Stadium and
in a close match delivered the first loss of the season to the Crimson
Tide L (24–29). That would be the last loss of the season. Bama
would win its last four games.

In the SEC Championship Bowl, on Dec 1, #3 Georgia played # 2
Alabama in the Georgia Dome in Atlanta, GA W (32-28). Bama
won the overall SEC Championship.

Notre Dame was having a banner year and the Irish were ranked #1
before they met #2 Alabama in the BCS Championship game on
January 7, 2013 at 7:30 p.m. in Sun Life Stadium Miami Gardens,
FL. Alabama dominated the game and won handily over the Irish
W (42–14) before 80,120 fans and a nationwide TV audience.

At the conclusion of the season, the Alabama defense had led the
nation in total defense, scoring defense and rushing defense and
ranked 7th in passing defense. Offensively, the Alabama offense
ranked 12th in scoring offense, 16th in rushing offense, 31st in total
offense and 75th in passing offense.

Starting quarterback AJ McCarron was ranked first nationally in
pass efficiency. Additionally, several players were recognized for
their individual accomplishments on the field. Starting center Barrett
Jones won both the Rimington Trophy and the William V.
Campbell Trophy, and was named as the Academic All-America of

the Year; defensive coordinator Kirby Smart was named the 2012 American Football Coaches Association (AFCA) FBS Assistant Coach of the Year. Also, five players were named to various All-America Teams with Jones and C. J. Mosley being consensus selections and Dee Milliner and Chance Warmack being unanimous selections. Nick Saban knows how to produce winners and then coach them to win.

The 2012 SEC Championship game has been determined by the pundits to be one of the most significand football games in Crimson Tide History.

SEC Championship Game Roll Tide Recap

SEC Championship Game
No. 2 Alabama Outlasts No. 3 Georgia, 32-28

12/1/2012 12:00:00 AM

What a game! Some say it was the best game of 2012. It was certainly one of the most exciting games of all time. Two of the finest football programs put on a classic battle in the Georgia Dome. It was a rip-roaring showcase of national importance that pushed both teams to their limits, but somebody ultimately had to win. Second-ranked Alabama (12-1 overall) had just enough to outlast third-ranked Georgia (11-2 overall). The Crimson Tide beating the Bulldogs, 32-28, to win the 2012 Southeastern Conference Championship before a crowd of 75,624.

After the game, Alabama had over a month of practice drills before it would play in the National Championship Game against undefeated Notre Dame (12-0 overall). The BCS National Championship Game was scheduled for Monday, January 7, at Sun Life Stadium in Miami, Fla. Alabama defeated Notre Dame and won the National Championship but let's first discuss this fine game against Georgia.

BCS Championship Crimson Tide v Fighting Irish

Neither the NY Times staff nor any other pundits or reporters gave ND a break after this game. Notre Dame played poorly. All pundits had major praise for Nick Saban and his powerful Alabama Crimson Tide team. It was no contest.

This BCS National Championship Game has been determined by the pundits to be one of the most significand football games in Crimson Tide History.

All Alabama in Title Game

By GREG BISHOPJAN. 8, 2013

Newyorktimes.com

> MIAMI GARDENS, Fla. — They called the football game played here Monday night a national championship, a title clash for the ages, epic, monumental, historic.
>
> Then Notre Dame kicked the ball off.

Then Alabama drove down the field, unimpeded, as if out for a nighttime stroll. It all went downhill from there, for Notre Dame and for those interested in the most overhyped college football game in years. Instead, this national championship ended early, almost immediately, in a flurry of Alabama touchdowns that allowed the Crimson Tide to seize their third title in four seasons, 42-14, with all the ease predicted by the odds makers, sapping this game of all competitiveness or drama.

This was "Rudy," the sequel, after he stumbled onto Elm Street.

Alabama jumped to a 14-0 lead after one quarter and opened up a 28-0 advantage by the half, as Notre Dame fans streamed for the exits and the beer lines. Afterward, Alabama fans held newspapers with the headline "BAMA! AGAIN!" and chanted "S!E!C!", as defensive lineman Quinton Dial grabbed the school flag from a cheerleader and sprinted across the end zone.

The game itself brought to mind a famous quote from Mike Tyson. Everybody has a plan, he said — until getting punched in the face. On Monday, Alabama bludgeoned Notre Dame, repeatedly. It controlled the game with both lines, on offense and defense, putting on a clinic in power football. It ran all over a defense known for its ability to stop the run. Alabama (13-1) so dominated that it reminded sports fans that N.B.A. games were also available for viewing Monday night, and that Notre Dame's best chance for a national title is now in women's basketball. NT

This only strengthened the claim few at Alabama dared to make before Monday night: that Coach Nick Saban, who flopped in two forgettable seasons on this very field at Sun Life Stadium as coach of the Miami Dolphins, has created a college football dynasty. This was his fourth national championship and third since he left the Dolphins to return to college football at Alabama. One could easily argue it was also his most impressive.

In the locker room, surrounded by the teammates in gray championship hats and T-shirts, linebacker Nico Johnson blurted out words that only a senior could. For the underclassmen, Saban continued to ban the d-word. "OK, I can say it now," Johnson said. "This is a dynasty."

Only two other college coaches can claim at least four titles. One is John McKay of Southern California. The other is Paul Bryant, the coach known as Bear who made Alabama football famous.

Amari Cooper Scores – chased by ND Defenders

Now there is Saban, a coach who must contend with fewer scholarships than afforded coaches from the Bryant era and who faces far stiffer competition. Yet despite those limitations, Saban runs a program that resembles a 33rd N.F.L. team as closely as a college football powerhouse. This season, despite a close loss to Texas A&M, only reinforced that notion.

Saban spent all of last week scoffing at any comparison between himself and Bryant, and this from a man with a 9-foot-tall statue of himself outside his office. Those close to him knew what another championship meant. "There's no question," said Kirby Smart, his defensive coordinator.

"There's no question he is driven to be the greatest coach in the game."

Monday was another step, for Saban's legacy and for Alabama's program and for the Southeastern Conference, from which a team secured the national championship for the seventh straight season. As "Sweet Home Alabama" predictably blasted from the stadium speakers — Roll! Tide! Roll! — Mike Slive, the conference commissioner dodged confetti and smiled a smile that seemed to stretch from here to South Beach.

"You don't see something like this coming," he said. "One can enjoy it. But one cannot anticipate it."

The suspense this year ended almost immediately. Almost. Notre Dame (12-1) stuffed the Crimson Tide on their first play from scrimmage. On the next snap, quarterback A J McCarron found receiver Kevin Norwood for a 29-yard gain. Notre Dame compounded that with a face mask penalty, then compounded that with a defensive offsides. Its vaunted defense, led by linebacker Manti Te'o, was generally ineffective.

Running back Eddie Lacy finished off the drive with a 20-yard scamper into the end zone, his path largely unchallenged, his body largely untouched. It was the first time this season Notre Dame allowed a touchdown in the first quarter. The 82-yard drive was also the longest this year against the Fighting Irish.

The worst start Notre Dame could have imagined only worsened from that point. Officials ruled a completion incomplete that would have gone for a first down, and when the Irish appeared to recover a fumble on the ensuing punt, they were flagged for catching interference.

Alabama simply resumed its rush to judgment. McCarron continued to hand the ball to Lacy, who continued to plunge forward. The Crimson Tide mostly attacked the right side of Notre Dame's defense, which looked like a matador, with Lacy playing the role of bull.

"The toughness of our team came out in the beginning," defensive back Hunter Bush said. "We attacked them exactly as we wanted to."

By the time Alabama scored its second touchdown, on a pass from McCarron to tight end Michael Williams, the Crimson Tide boasted a 123-8 advantage in total yardage. By the time Alabama scored its third touchdown, a T. J. Yeldon run on the first play of the second quarter, the Fighting Irish had 23 yards — and the Crimson Tide had 21 points.

The most pertinent news in the rest of the first half came when Alabama actually did punt. Alabama wound up with two 100-yard rushers: Lacy had 140 yards on 20 carries, and Yeldon had 108 on 21. McCarron, meanwhile, played as if intent on earning a statue of his own. He threw four touchdowns and said afterward that he would return for his senior season and the chance to win a third straight national championship.

"Our offense did an exceptional job," Saban said, his face absent even a hint of emotion. While his players danced and hugged and shouted, Saban looked out at a mass of reporters and deadpanned, "I'm extremely happy." They would have to take his word for it.

As the game approached, the hype ballooned so as to dominate the national conversation about sports, until this felt less like a national championship game and more like a history lesson. Here they stood: Notre Dame and Alabama, golden helmets against red elephants, storied tradition opposite storied tradition, football in the heartland versus football in the South.

If college football released an encyclopedia, these schools would occupy two of the larger volumes. Alabama claimed 14 national championships before Saturday; Notre Dame had 11. Alabama employed Bryant; Notre Dame had Knute Rockne, Frank Leahy, Ara Parseghian, and Lou Holtz.

"A couple of us were joking the other day that it's 'Rudy' versus 'Forrest Gump,'" said receiver Robby Toma, in reference to two movies made about these football programs.

Before Saturday, the most-watched college football game took place between Texas and Southern California, in 2006, and it averaged 35.6 million viewers. This contest was expected to challenge and ultimately trump that number, at least until they played it.

The assembled expected a game as old-school as its participants. Even in this era of spread offenses and fancy passing, Alabama and Notre Dame won with size more than speed. They won with linemen, with bulk, with two defenses ranked among the top five in the nation.

"It's not about the crazy receiving numbers or passing yards or rushing yards," Notre Dame Coach Brian Kelly insisted. "This is about the big fellas, and this game will be decided unquestionably up front."

Kelly was right, of course, but not in the way he wanted to be. His team did score in the third quarter and end the shutout. It will eventually celebrate a season that brought the return of Notre Dame to college football's elite.

But not on Monday night. In this dud, Notre Dame flopped and Alabama triumphed and the SEC ruled again. The folks in Hollywood are unlikely to turn this season into any script, but Saban may get another statue anyway.

Alabama will be among the favorites for next season. And the season after that. And for as long as Saban is the coach. The former Alabama and N.F.L. running back Shaun Alexander said on the field after the game: "You know what makes this more exciting? I think next year's team will be better than this year's team."

So how many championships can Saban win? "Who knows?" Johnson said. "How many years can he coach?"

2013 Coach Nick Saban #30

The 2013 Alabama Crimson Tide football team played its 119th overall and 80th season as a member of the Southeastern Conference (SEC) of NCAA Division I-A football, and its 22nd season in the SEC Western Division. The team was led by head coach Nick Saban in his seventh year. All Alabama home games are played at Bryant-Denny Stadium on the UA campus in Tuscaloosa, Alabama.

Bama finished the season with a record of eleven wins and two losses (11–2 overall, 7–1 in the SEC) and with a loss in the 2014 Sugar Bowl to Oklahoma

2014 Coach Nick Saban #30

The 2014 Alabama Crimson Tide football team played its 120th overall and 81st season as a member of the Southeastern Conference (SEC) of NCAA Division I-A football, and its 23rd season in the SEC Western Division. The team was led by head coach Nick Saban in his eighth year. All Alabama home games are played at Bryant-Denny Stadium on the UA campus in Tuscaloosa, Alabama.

Alabama was 12–2 overall and 7–1 in SEC regular season. The Crimson Tide won the SEC Western Division title for the tenth time, advancing to their ninth SEC Championship Game, where they defeated Missouri 42–13. The Crimson Tide played in the inaugural College Football Playoff as the #1 seed, netting a berth in the CFP semifinal 2015 Sugar Bowl, where they were defeated by the #4 seed Ohio State Buckeyes 42–35.

Sugar Bowl V Ohio State from *Roll Tide*
NEW ORLEANS, La. - Ohio State running back Ezekiel Elliott rushed for 230 yards and two touchdowns on 20 carries,

including an 85-yard touchdown run, and Buckeyes quarterback Cardale Jones threw for 243 yards in only his second career start to lead No. 4 Ohio State (13-1 overall) to a 42-35 victory over No. 1-seedeed Alabama (12-2) in the College Football Playoff Semifinal at the Allstate Sugar Bowl before a crowd of 74,682 on Thursday night in the Mercedes-Benz Superdome (capacity: 72,500).

With the victory, Ohio State advanced to the College Football Playoff National Championship Game to take on No. 2 seed Oregon (13-1), which defeated No. 3 seed Florida State, 59-20, in the other CFP Semifinal at the Rose Bowl earlier in the day.

2015 Coach Nick Saban #30

The 2015 Alabama Crimson Tide football team played its 121st overall and 82nd season as a member of the Southeastern Conference (SEC) of NCAA Division I-A football, and its 24th season in the SEC Western Division. The team was led by head coach Nick Saban in his ninth year. All Alabama home games are played at Bryant-Denny Stadium on the UA campus in Tuscaloosa, Alabama.

UA finished the season with a record of 14 wins and 1 loss (14–1 overall, 7–1 in the SEC), as SEC champions and as consensus national champions after they defeated Clemson in the College Football Playoff (CFP) National Championship Game. Alabama also secured its 10th Associated Press (AP) national title.

2015 SEC Championship Game – Tide and Gators Yet Again

The Tide's 2015 SEC Championship Game win over the Florida Gators marked Alabama's second consecutive SEC Championship, a feat that no team in the SEC had accomplished since Steve Spurrier's 1995 and 1996 Florida Gators.

Alabama came into the game 11-1 and heavily favored. Florida had clinched the SEC East early in November, but their dominant defense hadn't been enough to overcome a struggling offensive in close games against South Carolina and Florida Atlantic and a loss to rival Florida State. The 10-2 Gators traveled to Atlanta as a double-digit underdog.

2015's game was the 8th meeting between Florida and Alabama in the SEC Championship Game, over twice as many as any other matchup in series history. In the last meeting (in 2009), underdog Alabama had upset Urban Meyer's #1 Florida Gators on the way to a national championship.

The first quarter was a defensive struggle, with the only points recorded on a Florida punt blocked through the back of the end zone for an Alabama safety.

Florida broke through with a punt return touchdown early in the second quarter to take a 7-2 lead, but the next two quarters were all Alabama. Derrick Henry's 189 yards on 44 carries boosted a Tide offense that couldn't find consistent success through the air and Alabama cruised to a 29-15 victory and a second straight conference championship.

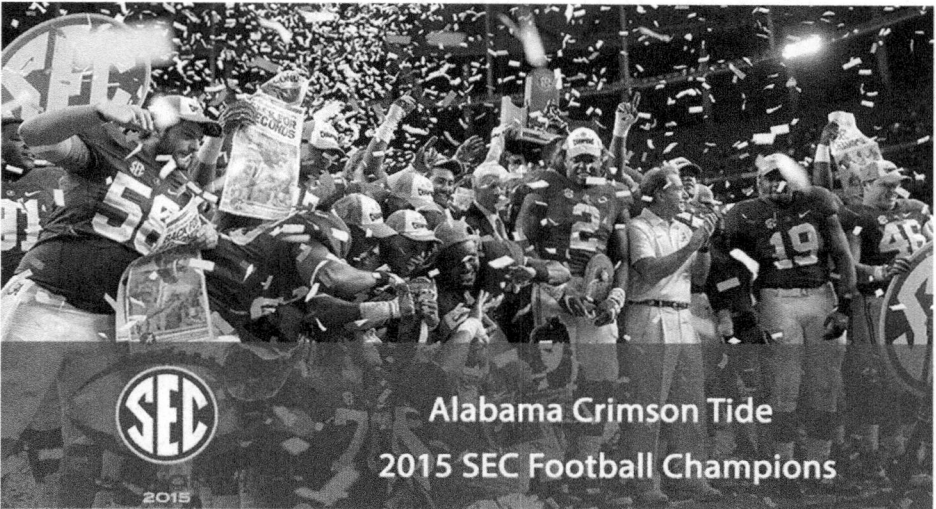

Alabama Crimson Tide
2015 SEC Football Champions

The next day, Alabama was announced as the #2 seed in the College Football Playoff, marking 2015 the tenth consecutive year where the SEC Champion was invited to play in the CFP Championship or the College Football Playoff.

Alabama was invited to the Cotton Bowl.

On Dec 31 at 7:00 p.m. v #3 Michigan State at AT&T Stadium in Arlington, TX in the Cotton Bowl Classic – also the CFP Semifinal, Alabama shut out Michigan State W (38–0). This entitled the Crimson Tide to fight for the National Championship on January 11.

On January 11, at the University of Phoenix Stadium in Glendale, AZ, the CFP National Championship contest featured #1 Clemson v # 2 Alabama. The game got underway at 7:30 P.M before 75,765. Alabama won in a back and forth shootout W (45-40).

This CFP Championship Game has been determined by the pundits to be one of the most significand football games in Crimson Tide History.

Clemson vs. Alabama final score: Crimson Tide win national championship in 45-40 classic

Alabama rolls again from SB Nation.

by Andy Hutchins Jan 12, 2016, 12:22am EST

In the desert, Alabama and Clemson played a doozy. When it was over, the Crimson Tide had a 45-40 victory, their fourth national title since 2009 and the glory of prevailing in one of the best national championship games ever.

Jake Coker threw for 335 yards and two touchdowns, Derrick Henry ran for 158 yards and three more scores, and Alabama poured on 24 points in the fourth quarter to hold off the Tigers, who kept it close with a phenomenal performance from Deshaun Watson (405 passing yards, four touchdowns and 73 more rushing yards) that topped even Vince Young's magisterial night for total yardage in a national title game.

The Crimson Tide came through in the fourth quarter with plays from players who weren't even their most reliable playmakers all year. Tide kicker Adam Griffith executed a beautiful surprise onside kick that set up the touchdown that put Alabama up for good. Kenyan Drake, Henry's backup, returned a kickoff 95 yards for a touchdown to put Alabama up by double digits for the first time. Tight end O.J. Howard had a career-high 208 receiving yards and two touchdowns. Howard also set up the Tide's final score with a huge catch-and-run.

Clemson played a great game against Alabama's fantastic defense, but got hammered repeatedly by big plays on defense and lost the special teams battle.

That more than provided the margin of victory and handed over the Tide's 16th national championship.
Three things to know

1. We got a phenomenal game, finally. The 2015 bowl season had largely been a bust up until Monday night, with just 14 of 40 bowls being decided by seven or fewer points. None of the New Year's Six bowls were decided by fewer than 14 points, either.

But this? This was a classic. Alabama and Clemson went back and forth for 12 great rounds and the winner prevailed by landing the last combination of the evening and withstanding a final flurry from the loser.

Few national title games this century were on par with this one - - maybe Ohio State upsetting Miami, Texas outdueling USC and Florida State surviving Auburn would be in the conversation. But for sheer quantity and variety of big plays, this one will stand the test of time.

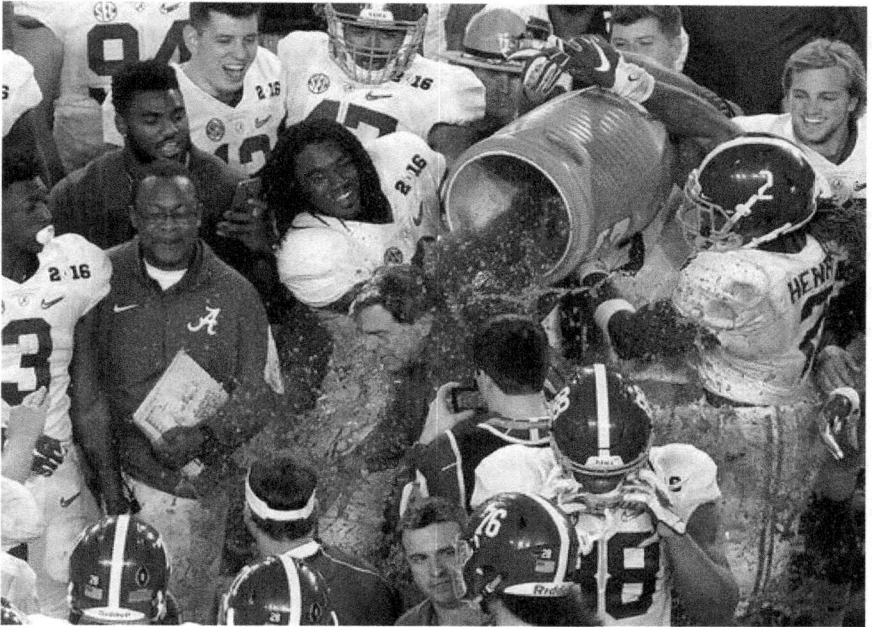

2. Deshaun Watson is college football's newest superstar. Clemson's Heisman finalist had a better passer rating than Heisman winner Marcus Mariota did in 2014 and improved throughout 2015 despite losing his leading receiver, Mike Williams, to a neck injury early in the year. Watson lost another elite talent, Deon Cain, prior to the Playoff. The quarterback still stepped up.

His performance on Monday put him on a plateau by himself:

2016 Coach Nick Saban #30

The 2016 Alabama Crimson Tide football team played its 122nd overall and 83rd season as a member of the Southeastern Conference (SEC) of NCAA Division I-A football, and its 25th season in the SEC Western Division. The team was led by head coach Nick Saban in his tenth year. All Alabama home games are played at Bryant-Denny Stadium on the UA campus in Tuscaloosa, Alabama.

UA finished the season with a record of 14 wins and 1 loss (14-1) overall, 8-0 in the SEC), as SEC champions and as a 2nd place finish in the national champions CFP series they were defeated by Clemson L (31-35) in the College Football Playoff (CFP) National Championship Game. Alabama was trying for its 10th Associated Press (AP) national title. Next year for sure!

SEC Championship

On December 3 @ 3:00 p.m. the opponent from the other division was #15 Florida. The #1 Crimson Tide was playing the Gators in the Georgia Dome in Atlanta, GA in what is known as the (SEC Championship Game. UA won handily against an always-tough Gators team, W (54–16). Alabama became the SEC Champion.

The SEC Champ was invited to the Peach Bowl. On Dec 31 at 2:00 P.M. vs. No. 4 Washington, #1 Alabama played in the Peach Bowl at the Georgia Dome in Atlanta, GA (Peach Bowl – CFP Semifinal)

The Peach Bowl

The pundits noted after the Peach Bowl game between the Alabama Crimson Tide and the Washington Huskies went almost exactly according to script. Alabama Crimson Tide's combination of speed and power on both sides of the ball proved too much for the Washington Huskies in a 24-7 UA victory to secure a spot in the College Football Playoff National Championship.

Things did not start out well for Alabama, as Washington struck first when Jake Browning hit Dante Pettis for a 16-yard touchdown in the first quarter. Alabama thus found itself trailing in a game, though there was plenty of time to make things right. It was a first for

Alabama as throughout the 2016 season, the Crimson Tide virtually never played from behind.

It wouldn't take long for Alabama to make its comeback by tying the game at seven. The Tide scored on the ensuing possession. Bo Scarbrough, a great running back, capped off the Tide's 78-yard drive by doing what he always does best:

Alabama would later settle for a field goal after an Anthony Averett turnover from Wide Receiver John Ross. This 10-7 lead would not be relinquished for the rest of the game. The game was basically over at that point for Washington. Things would slow down for both teams as the next six drives ended in punts.

One of the big keys to Alabama's success all season long has been creating points off turnovers. The Crimson Tide entered the Peach Bowl with 14 non-offensive touchdowns, so it was hardly a secret they would be aggressive and Washington needed to protect the ball.

Unfortunately for the Huskies, Browning made a critical mistake with less than two minutes remaining in the second quarter by trying to force a throw after getting pressured that Ryan Anderson picked off and returned for a touchdown.

A three-point deficit against Alabama would normally be manageable but Alabama got very stingy. It wound up not making a difference either way because Washington's offense was completely stymied in the second half.

Browning had his worst game of the year with 150 yards on 20-of-38 passing with one touchdown and two interceptions, compounded by the fact the Huskies could only muster 44 rushing yards on 29 carries.

Washington's pass defense did step up to keep Alabama from creating big plays down the field. Crimson Tide quarterback Jalen Hurts threw for a season-low 57 yards on just seven completions, but he did get support from the running game.

Scarbrough finished with 180 yards on 19 carries and two touchdowns, marking the third straight game in which he's broken the 90-yard barrier.

Alabama head coach Nick Saban explained the team has been working to include Scarbrough in the game plan more often because of his recent success.

"Bo's been playing pretty well for us the last three or four games," Saban said, per the Associated Press (via ESPN.com). "We wanted to play him more. He's hard to tackle. He's big and powerful. He's playing with a lot of confidence."

Alabama was on the verge of winning its fifth national championship since 2009. If there were a dynasty in any sport, pro or college, at this moment, the Crimson Tide stand tall over everyone else because of their nearly decade-long run of dominance.

Post-Game -- CFP Championship Game – The Full Recap

Uncommitted football fans across the world enjoyed one of the best football games of all-time on Monday evening January 9, 2007, from 8:00 PM to way past bedtime at 12:25 AM. For the committed Clemson fans the victory was sweet after waiting a year for a rematch. For the committed Crimson Tide fans, the loss was simply heartbreaking.

In this game, the song lyrics, *what a difference a day makes* took a back seat to *what a difference a few seconds make*. The Crimson Tide came literally one second away from a repeat title. With Alabama holding a three-point lead after rolling down the field and scoring on a Jalen Hurts' 30-yard touchdown run with just 2:01 remaining, Clemson took the second-last kickoff of the game and refused to be stopped.

Deshaun Watson was the game's super-hero. However, Watson had to perform all night to get the win and he had the ball in his hand as the game ended after a Clemson onside kick was recovered by Clemson with one second still on the clock.

Just before that, without his two-yard TD pass with 1-second left, the super-hero acclaim would have gone to the Alabama defense. The big guys from the Crimson Tide spent the night chasing

Watson, keeping the talented QB from overcoming Alabama's early lead.

But, not this time. Not this game. Clemson would not be denied and the Tigers had both the talent and the luck, and some might even say, even the officials on their side. Clemson's heralded QB, and the best QB in the nation per his coach Dabo Swinney calmly led his team to victory and to him goes the credit as game super-hero.

This QB, who is also a two-time Heisman Trophy finalist, performed flawlessly on this all-important drive down the field. Watson was the master on the field and the results have already made the history books. Clemson won by four. They are the National Champions.

DeShaun Watson, interviewed after the game told reporters that his message to his teammates on the drive was to stay calm; don't get nervous; and they would prevail. They did.

Watson guided the Clemson Tigers 68 yards in nine plays, completing a 24-yard pass to Mike Williams to Alabama's 39-yard line and a 17-yard pass to tight end Jordan Leggett that gave Clemson a first-and-goal at the 9. The Tigers got to the 2 when Alabama cornerback Anthony Averett was flagged for pass interference in the end zone.

"Everything was calm, and nobody panicked," Watson said. "I walked up to my offensive line and my receivers, and I said, 'Let's be legendary.' God put us here for a reason."

Coach Swinney offered: "He didn't lose out on the Heisman. The Heisman lost out on him."

From the two-yard line, with about 6 seconds left, Alabama was either going to be playing in OT with a field goal if Clemson's next play did not work; or time would run out by mistake; or of course option 3 was that the play would result in a touchdown.

Much to Alabama's chagrin, option 3 was operative. When Alabama double-teamed 6' 3" Mike Williams on the left side,

Clemson decided to go right against man to man coverage. They executed a clearly designed pick play, that even Watson admitted after the game was by design.

It was no accident and Alabama fans are still wondering where the pass-interference call v Clemson when on the prior play, Alabama had gotten flagged for a similar violation.

Regardless, the referees did not call it. On the play, Deshaun Watson's rolled right and threw a perfect 2-yard touchdown pass to Hunter Renfrow with just 1 second remaining.

This gave Clemson their wild 35-31 win over Alabama in the College Football Playoff national championship game. Clemson fans were ecstatic as they felt they should have won the marbles one year earlier. Alabama fans are not whiners or poor sports but came away in fact generally heartsick.

They know their star back Bo Scarbrough was out of the game after a half due to injury and they know there was the matter of those two picks, perhaps even legal picks but maybe not--that became touchdowns and there was no flag. Many fans that understand how a pick play works wonder how it could be used twice by Clemson with neither resulting in a penalty call. Bad luck?

It was not once in the fourth quarter, but twice that Clemson took the lead by completing passes at the goal line on what's best known as a pick play (although coaches call it a "rub"). The final pick play was on the winning throw from Deshaun Watson to Hunter Renfrow.

The play, which is clearly borrowed from the basketball court, is simple to execute and simple to spot. One receiver runs a route that might "accidentally" impede a defender from following a second receiver on his route. By "taking out" the defender, the receiver is sprung open for a quarterback to deliver what in most cases can develop into an easy toss to an un-defended receiver.

Often, officials will throw a flag for this is offensive pass interference when it happens and the official is inclined to find the flag. In 2014, Notre Dame lost in a game between top five teams due, in part, to a penalty on a play that was almost identical to the one that gave

Clemson its first national title since 1981. The Irish touchdown was taken off the board and they eventually lost the game.

So, where is the consistency? Ironically, on the play before the TD, Alabama was penalized for pass interference so we know the rationale for a no-call was not that there were no flags available in any of the officials' pockets.

Studying the rules, we know that it is a pure judgment call by the referees that is not reviewable, just like holding or defensive pass interference. One would think that at the worst, the referees would have gone one way one time and the other way the next time. In this game, both calls were given to Clemson. Just asking: Is that fair? Let's say I am asking both as an Alabama fan and a pundit. I am not whining. I am asking though!

Sure, Alabama could have played better. Sometimes it grated me that their offensive performance could not have been like the days when AJ McCarron was the Tide field general. Their offense was sluggish and they depended on their defense after Bo Scarbrough was no longer on the field. Derrick Henry made the difference in the 2016 game and he or a healthy Bo Scarbrough would have made a big difference on January 9 also.

Of course, when the stripe officials suit up in the same colors as the opponents, that often takes away a lot of great defensive actions, no matter how good the defensive unit may be playing. Making the game something that it was not however, cannot bring Alabama a W no matter their effort. Like all fans, the loss set me back and it took a few days to get the shock out of my system.

There were a lot of ups and downs in the game, especially at the end. Alabama quarterback Jalen Hurts had just given the Crimson Tide a 31-28 lead on his 30-yard scramble with 2:01 remaining. This had countered Wayne Gallman's 1-yard touchdown run with 4:38 remaining that had put the Tigers up 28-24. Two minutes is an awful long time and Watson engineered a drive that used it all up right to the last second before he passed for the score.

Last year Watson threw for almost 500 yards and this year, the Crimson Tide managed him better; but he still stole 420 yards on 36-of-56 passing and three touchdowns. Renfrow caught ten of his passes for 92 yards and two touchdowns and big 6'3" leaping Mike Williams adding eight receptions for 94 yards and one score.

Clemson packed in 511 total yards to 376 by Alabama and the Tigers posted a 31-16 edge in first downs. Alabama's bright side in the game was not its offensive production and because of that, its D had little time to rest.

Clemson ran 99 plays. All season long it was only Arkansas W (49-30) that hat had anything close to that (84 plays). Though in great shape, the D was not as well backed up as the 2016 team. Some say that this huge number of plays helped wear down the mighty Tide defense with tempo and consistent movement on offense.

Alabama did not get much rest as the offense ran just 66 plays. Its defensive depth was not at the same level as the 2015 team. The wear of those extra plays on the Alabama defense was evident in the second half. Clemson visited the red zone four times and they scored four times. Alabama had typically rejected opponents on two of every three red zone attempts. On the field, fatigue surely was a factor though there are no real excuses.

Nick Saban's Crimson Tide were clearly denied a fifth national championship in eight seasons under coach Nick Saban. The Tide managed just 131 passing yards, as Hurts had a tough night going 14-of-32.

Nick Saban saw it as it was. "They made the plays and we didn't," Saban said. "We could have done some things better, but I'm proud of the way our guys competed."

Without Bo Scarbrough's first down production, Alabama struggled for most of the second half offensively but the Tide did take a 24-14 lead on a 68-yard touchdown pass from Hurts to O.J. Howard with 1:53 remaining in the third quarter. Clemson fans quickly remembered Howard as the MVP of last year's title game with 208 yards on five receptions. Alabama had faked the look of a quick screen before Howard raced behind a confused Clemson secondary for the catch. And the TD.

It is significant that the Crimson Tide played almost the last 20 minutes without tailback Bo Scarbrough, who was injured after he had amassing 93 yards on 16 carries.

"Not to have him was probably a little bit of a disadvantage for us," Saban gave it a positive slant when he said. "I was pleased with our other backs who had an opportunity in this game, Josh Jacobs and Damien Harris, but we always miss a guy who's Bo Scarbrough 's size when we want to run the ball and take some time off the clock."

Alabama had to punt after a three-and-out on the night's opening possession. Clemson on its first drive then moved across midfield before they were stuffed by Tony Brown on a fourth down and 1 try on a pitch to Gallman. Alabama then took over on their own 41.

Bama got going on their second possession on a 20-yard scramble by Hurts down the right sideline to the Clemson 39-yard line and grabbed a 7-0 lead at the 9:23 mark of the first quarter on Bo Scarbrough's 25-yard scamper around left end.

Watson was a bit shaky at first but calmed down as the O-line settled down. He fumbled a low shotgun snap late in the first quarter. Alabama outside linebacker Ryan Anderson recovered the fumble at Clemson's 35-yard line, Mistakes stopped an Alabama advance. There was a false start on Cam Robinson and a 2-yard loss by Scarbrough and the Tide was forced to punt.

When they got the ball back, ArDarius Stewart started Alabama's second touchdown drive with a 25-yard run to Clemson's 49-yard line early in the second quarter. From here, Scarbrough broke loose moments later from 37 yards out to make it 14-0.

The Alabama fans and the Clemson fans had a feeling that Alabama was on the verge of breaking things open until Tigers receiver Deon Cain took a short Watson pass and weaved 43 yards to Alabama's 39. It was the juice Clemson needed to convince them they "could." It was a major momentum shift.

Watson was energized and calm by then. He completed a third-and-10 pass for Leggett for 26 yards to the Alabama 13 and ran in for an 8-yard score to pull the Tigers within 14-7 with 6:09 before halftime.

That would be the end of the first-half scoring, with the Tide held the seven-point lead at the break even though they had been somewhat outgained 203-183.

Alabama's Anderson struck again early in the second half, stripping Tigers tailback Gallman of the ball and returning the fumble to the Clemson 16. For whatever reason Alabama, just as it had done after Anderson's first fumble recovery, could not move the ball and had to settle for a 27-yard Adam Griffith field goal for a 17-7 lead.

Clemson was no longer intimidated to say the least. They reduced the lead to 17-14 with 7:10 left in the third quarter on a 24-yard touchdown pass from Watson to Renfrow. After a Tide, TD, The Tigers then pulled within 24-21 in the first minute of the fourth quarter on a 4-yard touchdown pass from Watson to Williams.

Clemson coach Dabo Swinney is one of Alabama's own. Swinney became just the second person to have won an Associated Press national championship as a player and coach. Swinney was a wide receiver on Gene Stallings' 1992 Alabama team that won the AP national championship and now he has coached Clemson to a national title over his alma mater Crimson Tide. Swinney still has a lot of love for Alabama and its supporters. He is a good guy

Coach Dabo Swinney was all emotion as he described the victory for Clemson: "This has been the most incredible team I've ever been around," Swinney said. "You saw their heart, and it's been there all year."

It was a big loss for Nick Saban. It was his first ever in a championship game. in six tries. Afterwards, speaking with ESPN's Tom Rinaldi, he was very gracious in defeat. Saban praised his team for all it accomplished in 2016, while also congratulating Dabo Swinney and Clemson on the victory.

Speaking for myself and millions of others, it was also a big loss for Alabama fans. There will be no brooding or whining, however, as there is next season and more as Alabama goes for its seventeenth National Championship. The fans, the team, the coach, and the University will al dust ourselves off and play strong again.

Watch out next year folks! It will be another great Alabama Crimson Tide football year. You can take that to the bank. Hope you enjoyed all the great Alabama coaches—both immortals and mortal.

Other books by Brian Kelly: (amazon.com, and Kindle)

Great Coaches in Penn State Football   Great coaches help make great PSU teams

Great Players in Penn State Football The best players in PSU's football program

Great Players in Notre Dame Football The best players in ND's football program

Great Coaches in Notre Dame Football The best coaches in any football program

President Donald J. Trump, Master Builder: Solving the Student Debt Crisis!

President Donald J. Trump, Master Builder: It's Time for Seniors to Get a Break!

President Donald J. Trump, Master Builder: Healthcare & Welfare Accountability

President Donald J. Trump, Master Builder: "Make America Great Again"

President Donald J. Trump, Master Builder: The Annual Guest Plan

Great Players in Alabama Football from Quarterbacks to offensive Linemen Greats!

Great Moments in Alabama Football AU Football from the start. This is the book.

Great Moments in Penn State Football PSU Football, start--games, coaches, players,

Great Moments in Notre Dame Football ND Football, start, games, coaches, players

Four Dollars & Sixty-Two Cents—A Christmas Story That Will Warm Your Heart!

My Red Hat Keeps Me on The Ground. Darraggh's Red Hat is really Magical

Seniors, Social Security & the Minimum Wage. Things seniors need to know.

How to Write Your First Book and Publish It with CreateSpace

The US Immigration Fix--It's all in here. Finally, an answer.

I had a Dream IBM Could be #1 Again _The title is self-explanatory

WineDiets.Com Presents The Wine Diet Learn how to lose weight while having fun.

Wilkes-Barre, PA; Return to Glory Wilkes-Barre City's return to glory

Geoffrey Parsons' Epoch... The Land of Fair Play Better than the original.

The Bill of Rights 4 Dummmies! This is the best book to learn about your rights.

Sol Bloom's Epoch …Story of the Constitution The best book to learn the Constitution

America 4 Dummmies! All Americans should read to learn about this great country.

The Electoral College 4 Dummmies! How does it really work?

The All-Everything Machine Story about IBM's finest computer server.

Brian has written 108 books. Others can be found at amazon.com/author/brianwkelly